Confronting Modernity in the Cinemas of Taiwan and Mainland China

TONGLIN LU
University of Iowa

CAMBRIDGE
UNIVERSITY PRESS

CAMBRIDGE UNIVERSITY PRESS
Cambridge, New York, Melbourne, Madrid, Cape Town, Singapore, São Paulo

Cambridge University Press
The Edinburgh Building, Cambridge CB2 8RU, UK

Published in the United States of America by Cambridge University Press, New York

www.cambridge.org
Information on this title: www.cambridge.org/9780521806770

First published 2002
This digitally printed version 2007

A catalogue record for this publication is available from the British Library

Library of Congress Cataloguing in Publication data
Lu, Tonglin
    Confronting modernity in the cinemas of Taiwan and Mainland China / Tonglin Lu.
        p.   cm.
    Includes bibliographical references and index.
    ISBN 0-521-80677-1
    1. Motion pictures – Taiwan – History.   2. Motion pictures – China – History.   I. Title.
PN1993.5.T28 L828 2002
791.43´095124´9 – dc21

                                                                            2001025411

ISBN 978-0-521-80677-0 hardback
ISBN 978-0-521-03727-3 paperback

CONFRONTING MODERNITY IN THE CINEMAS OF TAIWAN AND MAINLAND CHINA

This book is a cultural study of New Wave cinema that considers the experience of modernity and modernization in Taiwan and mainland China. Following separate paths, Taiwan and China have both rapidly modernized, economically and culturally, since 1949. Despite differences in the political, social, and economic systems of the two regions, the process of modernization has challenged traditional cultural norms in both. At the same time, the significant differences in this process respectively shape perceptions of tradition in the two regions to the extent that the notion of Chinese tradition also differs in Taiwan and on the mainland. In fact, tradition itself is often reconstructed retrospectively for the sake of modernization.

Tonglin Lu examines how differences in cultural formation between Taiwan and China have influenced reactions to modernity and how cultural identity has taken different forms on both sides of the Taiwan Strait. She illustrates the expression of these differences in the experience of modernity through her analysis of paradigmatic films produced in both countries, with a particular emphasis on their formal experiments.

Tonglin Lu is Associate Professor of Asian Languages and Literatures at the University of Iowa. She is the author of *Rose and Lotus: Narrative of Desire in France and China* and *Misogyny, Cultural Nihilism, and Oppositional Politics: Contemporary Chinese Experimental Fiction.*

*To my friend James
and my sister and friend Tongyan,
with love.*

CONTENTS

ILLUSTRATIONS

ACKNOWLEDGMENTS

My fascination with Fifth Generation films began in the mid-1980s. In 1991, the Chinese Cinema Festival at Montreal made me also aware of some wonderful Taiwan New Cinema works. Although each of these two contemporary cinemas in the Chinese language contained a wide range of heterogenous works, some directors on both sides of the Taiwan Strait, at least at the early stages of their careers, have had one desire in common: to subvert their respective cinematic traditions through formal experiments. Since the early 1990s, while working on my book on contemporary mainland fiction, I started thinking about a cultural-studies project focusing on contemporary Taiwan and mainland cinemas, partly because I was also interested in sorting out some commonalities and differences between the cultures on the two sides of the strait after decades of geopolitical segregation. From the very beginning, this project has received various institutional supports: a generous travel grant from Asian Art Council for a research trip to Taiwan in Summer 1993, a one-year senior research grant at the Center for Chinese Studies at UC Berkeley (1993–4), as well as a developmental leave in Fall 1996 and several international travel grants from the University of Iowa.

First, I would like to thank my students at the University of Iowa, Mitsuyo Wada-Marciano, Elissa Rashkin, Michael Ray, Stephanie Savage, Zhang Zhen, and many others, whose discussions in my several Chinese (Asian) cinema classes in the early 1990s inspired me to write this book. At the same time, I would like to express my gratitude for the support of my friends and colleagues at the University of Iowa: South Coblin, Cheryl Herr, Philip Lutgendorf, Maureen Robertson, and David Stern. Maureen read most of the draft version of my manuscript carefully and gave me many insightful suggestions. I would also like to thank Chris Berry, Rey Chow, Yi-tsi Feuerwerker, Poshek Fu, Marie-Claire Huot, Kao Yung-kung, Wendy Larson, Gregory Lee, Tim Reiss, David Der-wei Wang, and Zhang Yiwu for their help at various stages of my writings, as well as the two anonymous readers from Cambridge University Press for their constructive suggestions. I am particularly indebted to Wu Nien-chen, who provided me with most of the videotapes of Taiwan films. My interviews with filmmakers

Chen Kaige, Hou Xiaoxian, Li Shaohong, and Tian Zhuangzhuang also helped me better understand their works. My gratitude also goes to Beatrice Rehl, my editor at Cambridge University Press, for her remarkable understanding, intelligence, efficiency, and sense of humor, which make the publication process a pleasant experience. I would like to acknowledge Ann Klefsted's careful and highly competent presubmission copy-editing of the manuscript, which has improved not only the quality of this book but also my English writing in general. I would also like to thank Zhou Minyu for her methodical indexing and Peggy Timm, the departmental secretary, for her assistance. Finally, I would like to express my infinite gratitude to Michael Gnat, my production editor, for his effectiveness, professional rigor, and perfectionism. Without his persistent e-mail messages, I must confess, the book would have turned out very different from its current form.

I have dedicated this book to James Sing and Lu Tongyan. Over the years, their friendship and love have provided me with great support in various aspects of my life.

INTRODUCTION

THE DISCOURSE OF MODERNITY IN CHINESE CULTURE

In traditional China, Confucian scholars repeatedly stated, "Wen yi zaidao" or "Writing must carry the Tao" (*Tao* here means principle, moral, ethics).[1] During the twentieth century, many of their descendants, modern Chinese intellectuals, have explicitly rejected this concept in the process of modernization (or westernization). For better or worse, however, they still remain committed to the Tao – even in their "pure" and "apolitical" cultural productions. In most of these cases, the "purity" is mainly resistance to the dominant ideology, as in the school of "art for art's sake" (*wei yishu de yishu*) in the May Fourth movement near the beginning of the twentieth century[2] and the Fifth Generation cinema, with their formal experiments, at the century's end. Through the imperial examination system, which translated scholarly excellence into political success, members of the elite class in traditional China assumed high office, which ideally carried with it heavy moral responsibilities. Partly thanks to this tradition, Chinese intellectuals have always been particularly self-conscious about their moral roles. Traditional scholars of the past dynasties in general used the expression "Tao" in this specific context to refer to Confucian ethics. Since the May Fourth movement, although the phrase sounds outmoded, if not downright reactionary, modern intellectuals still implicitly but self-consciously carry their Tao(s) in their own ways. Carrying the Tao in a modern context often means to spread the discourse of modernity in order to contribute to the modernization process in China.[3] In its ambiguity, this discourse can be articulated from different or even opposite perspectives, from communism to liberal humanism.

In his "Beyond Eurocentrism," Enrique Dussel attributes the origin of modernity, which established the central position of Europe in relation to the rest of the world, to European expansion in Amerindia at the end of the fifteenth century. In other words, the conquest of the new continent stimulated the industrial revolution, not the other way around, as is commonly assumed, since it demanded "*efficacy,* technological 'factibility' or governmentalism of the management of an enormous world system in expansion." As a result, the "new philosophical paradigm" of the Enlightenment is "the expression of a necessary process of *sim-*

1

plification through 'rationalization' of the life-world, of the subsystems (economic, political, cultural, religious, etc.)."[4] Despite its often ambiguous nature and emphasis on changes, the centrality of the Western world in the discourse of modernity has essentially remained unchanged – albeit it has been challenged. Throughout the centuries, the West has represented itself as the only "modern civilization," according to whose standard the rest of the world needs to be "modernized" or "civilized."[5] Embedded in the discourse of modernity, this "invisible center"[6] has penetrated educational systems in various countries, which have been to different degrees "modernized." This modernization process has often originated in violence, as in the case of European expansion into Amerindia.

In the same vein, the origin of Chinese modernity can be traced to the First Opium War in 1839–42. Because this war radically disrupted the traditional economic and social structure, it was the catalyst for a sea change on the cultural and the ideological front in China.

On August 29, 1842, at the end of this war, the Qing government and Great Britain signed the Treaty of Nanjing. In this first of a series of unequal treaties, China was forced to cede Hong Kong to Britain, to open five ports to British trade and residents (Guandong, Xiamen, Fuzhou, Ningbo, and Shanghai), and to pay twenty-one million Mexican dollars to cover the cost of war for the British Indian government as well as for the loss of opium by British merchants.[7] Since then, Britain, other Western powers (America, France, Germany, Russia), and Japan, following the same lucrative model, repeatedly engaged in wars against China, through which they imposed similar treaties upon their weaker and weakened opponent.[8] Not surprisingly, this practice had devastating effects on the Chinese economy and directly and indirectly triggered civil unrest in the heart of the ancient continent.

For historians trained on the mainland, the principal motivation for Britain to start this war was deceptively simple. In order to eliminate their trade deficits, the British empire forced the Qing rulers to accept their opium trade from India, since it was the single most profitable trade available to their merchants in China, whose confinement policy made any other British trade difficult.[9] Some sinologists in the West offered different interpretations. John Fairbank, for example, attributed the cause of this war mainly to the "tributary system," a "sinocentric world order," and the Qing government's "inertia."[10] James Polachek named this the "inner Opium War" (his book title), since he believed that "sinocentric ideological arrogance" among various factions of radically "xenophobic" Qing officials provoked this war. [11] Apparently, these historians were oblivious to the fact that the British government fought this war on China's territory mainly for its trading privileges, including the privilege of selling opium to the Chinese. Regardless of how ignorant the Qing government might have been regarding the great Western civilization, did British officials in China show any willingness to understand their host country? Like Friday in Defoe's *Robinson Crusoe*, the slave must learn his master's language to qualify as a potential human being, whereas the master justifiably ignores his slave's language and culture, which are beneath his noble attention.[12] Fairbank compared China's situation with Japan's successful modernization in order to make it bear more responsibility for its failure in this East–West encounter.

Taiwan's economic miracle during the 1970s and 1980s, along with similar developments in several other Asian countries, can be considered an extension and reoccurrence of the Japanese model in twentieth-century Asia. This success model, however, which has indeed improved "people's livelihood" (*minsheng*) in Taiwan – as Sun Zhongshan put it at the beginning of the twentieth century[13] – has also brought about complicated social and cultural problems in the rapidly "modernized" Taiwan society. Since the dependence on Western investments for economic development has further reinforced the cultural hierarchy between the East and West, modernization of the national economy has been accompanied by the westernization of cultural values. The crisis caused by cultural and axiological clashes is one of the favorite topics for Taiwan New Cinema directors.

Although Chinese and Western historians largely differ in their interpretations of the Opium War (some younger-generation historians in this country have adopted a "China-centered approach"),[14] they do share much common ground. Partly based on Marx's interpretation of this part of history, Chinese historians often emphasized popular resistance to British invaders as an expression of nationalist awareness. Prasenjit Duara rightly points out that, at an early stage of Chinese modernity, the history of modern China has already been "narrativized in the Enlightenment model," "the linear, teleological model," under the influence of the global discourse of social Darwinism.[15] Either defending the anti-imperialist history of Chinese people or blaming the Qing government for provoking the Opium War, both Chinese and Western historians have in fact attributed a negative role to Chinese cultural tradition. "The preoccupation with the utopia of modernity in the Chinese narrative of History, its role as the only standard of value, closed off much that its older histories, narratives, and popular cultures had to offer."[16] For Fairbank or Polachek, "the generally conservative drifts of central-government leadership,"[17] namely, the Qing government, personified China's past; whereas for most historians in China, people's struggles against Western imperialists showed a great progress toward modernity, and their awakening nationalism marked a radical break from their feudal past. In short, for both Western and Chinese historians, Chinese tradition was the designated villain in the Opium War. In addition, historical interpretations of this period in China have been shaped by Karl Marx's writings on this subject.[18] Despite his anti-imperialist stance, Marx often uses racist expressions, such as "barbarous" and "hereditary stupidity," to describe Chinese culture and people.[19]

According to a social Darwinist logic embedded in historical records of modern China on both sides of the ideological arena, China has its cultural tradition, which may be either glorified or nullified, but westernization represents its only future in the modern world. Following this implicit logic, if Chinese want to survive in the modern world, they must identify with the Western value system in the modernization process. At the same time, the differentiation of various stages of progress in human societies also allowed modern Chinese intellectuals to establish a racial hierarchy within their own culture, based on a division of relatively modernized, progressive, mainstream Han Chinese majorities and allegedly primitive, backward, marginalized ethnic minorities. Therefore, although modern Chinese intellectuals occupied peripheral positions vis-à-vis their Western counterparts internationally, the same racial hierarchy helped them preserve their central positions within their own nation facing the ethnic Other. Duara demonstrated how Chinese revolutionaries and reformers at an early stage "absorbed the international discourse of racist evolutionism."[20] The influence of this discourse still is visible in contemporary China, as in Tian Zhuangzhuang's two minority films in the mid-1980s.[21] According to this linear model of "universal" history, the Chinese premodern past, which includes complicated layers of various traditions, has been reduced to a vague notion of Chineseness. This Chineseness, often simplistically identified with Confucianism, has been implicitly or explicitly perceived as an obstacle to progress in the modernization process by various generations of reform-minded Chinese intellectuals. In this book I focus on how the racist evolutionist discourse has influenced modern Chinese intellectuals' self-perceptions vis-à-vis the Western world. Globally, this self-perception is often implicitly and explicitly associated with an endorsement of the racial hierarchy in the West, namely, admiration for Western power and contempt for the other third-world nonwhite populations, despite a camaraderie supposedly established among the oppressed nations. This general embrace of the cultural and racial hierarchy by Chinese intellectuals does not help them discard their past as a "mummy," which was further dissolved by its contact with the West.[22] In a vicious circle, the more they position themselves as superior in the face of other races, the more they reinforce an inferiority complex regarding the supposed master race of the modern world, despite their resistance to the racial oppression from their own stance. As an epitome of modern technology and culture, contemporary new-wave Chinese cinemas on the mainland and in Taiwan exemplify at different levels the complex and complicated relationship between China and the West. The films I have chosen for the present work are both symptomatic of this cultural complex among Chinese intellectuals and representative of their resistance to Western cultural domination.

In the course of modern history, Chinese intellectuals have gradually embraced various discourses of modernity, hoping to modernize and thus empower their nation.[23] Early in the twentieth century, the May Fourth movement, considered the turning point of Chinese modernity and the Chinese equivalent of the European Enlightenment, used "complete westernization" (*quanmian xihua*) as one of its slogans. Initially promoted by Hu Shi, a May Fourth liberal intellectual, the slogan aptly summarizes the intellectual trend of this era.[24] At the same time, Lu Xun, the well-known May Fourth radical writer, created as a metaphor for China the image of an immense iron house.[25] In this windowless prison, almost everyone is in a deep sleep. An enlightened few who remain awake debate as to whether they should awaken their compatriots. They are not sure whether awakening them would lead to the desired destruction of this iron house, as a result of the collective effort of all the Chinese, or whether, more likely, this would merely force their countrymen to face their tragic end clearheadedly. Lu Xun's metaphor has had an everlasting influence on the educated class of the twentieth century, Despite his ideological differences, Hu Shi made a statement from a similar perspective: "China has five enemies: poverty, physical sickness, ignorance, corruption, and civil war. . . . Imperialism is not one of them, since an imperialist country cannot invade a nation free of these five evils. Why can't an imperialist country invade America or Japan?"[26] Ironically, the American continent had already been colonized, and Japan was the imperialist country in Asia. Like Lu Xun, modern intellectuals often perceive themselves both as insiders in China, victimized by the suffocating social environment, and as outsiders, due to their awareness of open space beyond their cultural horizon – namely, the West. Intellectuals of different generations have chosen this position partly because they attributed China's repeated military and political defeats in the international arena to cultural inferiority.

Despite the statements of these prominent intellectuals, this reasoning does not sound logical. How could the West's capacity to impose opium or unequal treaties upon China prove its cultural superiority? In fact, this argument is not too difficult to understand. Overwhelmed by the West's technological power, disoriented and humiliated by China's repeated defeats, Chinese intellectuals who asked themselves the reason for these defeats could no longer find an answer to this question in the value system of the "Middle Kingdom." Therefore, they looked beyond their cultural boundary – to the West – and found an answer in social Darwinism, the predominant global discourse at that historical moment. As a matter of fact, social Darwinism did not bring anything new to this world. Instead, it merely justified an old logic of "might makes right" in the name of natural law, which provided this logic with a scientific outlook.

James Pusey comments:

After the Opium War, Chinese had very slowly come to feel that China's armaments were inferior. Later, many had come to feel that China's political institutions were inferior. But now Liang Ch'i-ch'ao and Yen Fu said that China's historians, philosophers, and scholars were inferior, seemingly that China's whole civilization was inferior – because China's "ancestors" were inferior. This was a loss of "faith in our fathers" probably more traumatic for Chinese than the post-Darwinian loss of "faith of our fathers" was for so many nineteenth-century Westerners.[27]

Interestingly, Pusey uses only the word "fathers" to describe either Chinese or Western ancestors – as if chidren (all of them male) could come into this world without mothers. Although this sounds absurd, Pusey's expressions accurately reveal the patriarchal nature of the modernization process in China. During the May Fourth period, for example, although women paid high prices for their connections to the modernization movement, their positions within this movement remained marginalized. Whenever there was an ideological or political backlash, as in the case of Jiang Jieshi's New Life movement, women were among the first to be punished for their suspected participation in the movement.[28] On the one hand, their suffering was a favorite subject for May Fourth male writers; on the other, women were rarely granted independent spaces within this movement. Moreover, feminist positions articulated by women writers were criticized by their male counterparts for lacking social commitment to the "universal standard" of national salvation.[29] In other words, women could function as *objects* of salvation in the new patriarchal order, but they could not face their (male) saviors as *subjects* on an equal footing. Despite its patriarchal undertone, Pusey's statement identifies an important difference between Western "original" and Chinese belated modernity. If social Darwinism secularized the Western world by undermining the Christian faith of its modern inhabitants, it forced Chinese intellectuals at the early stage of modernization to adopt a much more iconoclastic attitude toward their cultural heritage. Considering their cultural tradition as "unsuited" to the modern world, these intellectuals tried their best to reject it radically, despite, or because of, their close ties to this tradition.

At the turn of the century, especially after Yan Fu's translation of Thomas Huxley's *Evolution and Ethics* in 1898,[30] social Darwinism was in vogue among intellectuals of various ideological backgrounds, such as Sun Zhongshan, perceived by the Nationalist government as the father of the Republic of China,[31] and Chen Duxiu, founder of the Communist Party.[32] As part of the package of the discourse of modernity, the explanation of China's troubles according to social Darwinism follows the fetishistic logic of the capitalist market economy.[33]

According to this logic, military, economic, and technological power are an expression of cultural excellence. As a result, Western imperialism is implicitly not only justified but also to a degree glorified in the name of a law of nature, the "survival of the fittest." Since this logic equates military power with cultural excellence, the Chinese elite felt that, despite their deep resentment toward Western imperialism, they needed first of all to undergo a radical cultural change, to become westerners, or at least westernized, to overcome their (acknowledged or implied) cultural inferiority. Only then would they be able to play leading roles in modernizing China, which would empower their nation in the international arena. Partly for this reason, reformers and revolutionaries in modern Chinese history often describe their political and ideological movements as "cultural." The May Fourth movement is also called the New Culture movement (*xin wenhua yundong*); Mao Zedong named his last grandiose political gesture the Cultural Revolution. In the same vein, torn between attachment to their cultural roots and eagerness to modernize their nation, Chinese intellectuals have examined their own cultural tradition from modernized or westernized perspectives. Despite their changing perspectives, one factor has remained constant: The perspective of a modern Chinese intellectual is often inherently self-contradictory, since he[34] occupies the position of both the viewing subject, as enlightened by Western culture, and the viewed object, as partially a product of the Chinese cultural tradition. Caught between his imaginary identification with the progressive West and his position as a citizen of an oppressed nation, the modern Chinese intellectual often vacillates between nationalism and rejection of his own cultural tradition.

Strictly speaking, there is no open space outside the Chinese iron house. To a greater or lesser degree, each culture (including America) has its own iron house, unless it is willing to give up its centrality based on a distinction between the "civilized us" and the "barbarian other," because this imaginary centrality hinders a culture from adopting a genuinely open attitude toward its peers. As a matter of fact, one of the positive effects of the modernization process in China was to shake the Chinese conviction of their own centrality – as suggested by the name Middle Kingdom (*Zhongguo*). This process has replaced it with an invisible center, Eurocentrism, and substituted the discourse of modernity for the Tao of Confucianism. After having forced various cultures in the world to open their doors in the course of European economic and cultural expansion, the Eurocentrism embedded in the discourse of modernity has become one of the last iron houses, since it imprisons our ways of thinking by subsuming various value systems from diverse cultures under one ultimate reference. As in the case of China, however, this iron house is not as hopelessly claustrophobic as described by Lu Xun. Because of its ambiguous nature and open-endedness, the discourse of modernity has always been a double-edged weapon, even toward its own closure. Equality, one of the significant components of Enlightenment ideology, cannot help undermining and, in the final analysis, disrupting the centrality of the West, as marginalized cultural groups have begun to claim their rights following the same logic in a gradually shrinking world with a global economy.

The discourse of modernity has been able to maintain its dominant position in the world because it is backed by Western military, technological, and economic power; its disruptive function in regard to closures in other cultures also to an extent justifies its dominance in the eyes of reformers in these cultures. Since it has been able to initiate some much-needed changes, the discourse of modernity has made it easier for intellectuals in peripheral societies to embrace its logic. At the same time, because the modernization process always tends to replace the traditional native center (Confucianism, in the case of China) with its apparently more flexible invisible center, the modernization process in a third-world country often functions as "supplement"[35] or "pharmacon"[36] – to borrow Derridean expressions – which generates new problems by claiming to cure old sickness, as in the case of the Chinese socialist revolution and Taiwan's recent rapid economic growth. One of the limitations of the discourse of modernity orig-

inates precisely from its fetishistic equation of military and economic power with
cultural excellence. On the one hand, this equation enables the modernization
process to devalue and dismiss any differences existing in indigenous cultural
tradition as not universal. Therefore, the process of modernization (or westernization) often has created a partially uprooted community as its by-product. On
the other hand, this logic hinders normal communication between the supposed
center and its periphery. Today, this fetishism still prevails in the nationalist expressions of third-world countries as well as other instances. For example, after
the bombing of the Chinese embassy in Belgrade, I returned to China. Most of
the Chinese friends to whom I spoke could not believe that the bombing might
be a mistake. They repeatedly asked the same rhetorical question: "How could
Americans, citizens of the most technologically powerful country, make such a
stupid mistake?" Although my friends were neither blind believers of the party's
nationalist propaganda nor unexposed to the global economy, they still believed
in American infallibility.

To different degrees, consciously or unconsciously, as third-world intellectuals we also bought into this fetishistic logic embedded in the discourse of modernity. Writing in English, the "universal" language of modernity (although my
mother tongue is spoken by the greatest number of people in the world) and from
the perspectives of American academicians, how can we, instead of continuing
to spread Eurocentrism embedded in the discourse of modernity, contribute to
its deconstruction? Enrique Dussel suggests "transmodernity" as an alternative
to modernity or even postmodernity.[37] Transmodernity emphasizes cross-cultural
exchanges instead of one-way changes imposed by the center upon its periphery. In order to become transmodern ourselves, however, we need first of all to
decolonize our own ways of thinking. That's partly why I have chosen contemporary Chinese (and Taiwanese) new-wave films to study here, since I feel
certain affinities with their positions in my native culture, despite gender and geopolitical differences. After all, we are using "languages" (English or visual language) that are to varying extents considered "imported" in our native land and
"universal" in global culture. Criticism of their works on my part is also an attempt to overcome my own limits. It is an attempt at self-decolonization.

CULTURAL TRADITION AND THE MODERNIZATION PROCESS

Although intellectuals have played a crucial role in spreading the discourse of
modernity in China during the twentieth century, their relationship with this discourse has always been ambiguous. At the end of the century, because their societies have been considerably modernized, Chinese intellectuals on both sides
of the Taiwan Strait must rethink their own relationships with the local versions
of the discourse of modernity, while facing the consequences of modernization.
Modernity, which is no longer an abstract idea, has become for them part of daily
reality in the era of globalization. In different ways, modernization processes

have deeply shaped the concept of Chinese culture on both sides of the Taiwan Strait to the point that the same concept may refer to entirely different value systems.

Due to its youth, imported nature, and dependence on technology, cinematic representation has been closely associated with the discourse of modernity. In the course of modern Chinese history, filmmakers have generally been perceived as "modern," somewhat "avant-garde," and often "westernized."[38] Furthermore, they use an arguably international language – visual language – as their means of expression. They speak, then, an international language that bears certain foreign characteristics. These qualifications are particularly applicable to the mainland Fifth Generation and the Taiwan New Cinema directors of the 1980s and 1990s, because both won international recognition while encountering box-office failures at home. Despite this prima facie resemblance, the two schools remain fundamentally different at both the formal and the ideological levels, shaped by their respective cultures, which are modernized in different ways. Given several decades of geopolitical segregation between mainland China and Taiwan, these differences are to be expected.

Mainland Fifth Generation and Taiwan New Cinema filmmakers occupy other similar territories in their respective societies as well. Coincidentally, the two schools obtained international recognition in the early 1980s. At least at the beginning of their careers, both mainland Fifth Generation and Taiwan New Cinema directors shared one piece of common ground: They were driven by their desires to transgress conventional filmic forms in their respective cultures. Chen Kaige and Tian Zhuangzhuang on the mainland, and Hou Xiaoxian and Edward Yang (Yang Dechang) in Taiwan, went much further in this respect than most of their colleagues. To different degrees, one can say that they succeeded in creating their own cinematic "languages," often defined against previous mainstream genres, namely, mainland socialist-realist and Taiwan escapist-melodramatic cinemas. This emphasis on formal innovation, partly inspired by postwar European cinemas, distinguishes them in the history of Chinese cinema, although in their later works they tend to pay less attention to formal experiment mainly due to commercial pressure, especially for the mainlanders. (Hou Xiaoxian, the well-known Taiwan director, however, has become more daring in some of his late films: *Puppetmaster,* for example.) In Parts I and II of this book, I have chosen to discuss the films of these four directors largely because of their success in subverting their respective filmic traditions. Part III is tied less to the notion of formal innovation than to that of globalization: Chapter 5, on the Zhang Yimou model, actually points out the end of formal innovation among Fifth Generation directors, for whom commercial concerns have become predominant in the era of globalization. Chapters 6 and 7 deal with the impact of globalization on their respective societies.

I have chosen the works of these directors for another reason – their ages. The New Cinema and Fifth Generation filmmakers were born either right before or right after the victory of the Communist Party over the Nationalist government in 1949. This dramatic event has directly or indirectly caused great social changes on both sides of the Taiwan Strait. In various forms, these changes have left strong imprints on the lives and works of these directors. Although some directors of the next generation have also paid special attention to formal innovation (Cai Mingliang, for example), this radical transition has less impact on their works, whereas the works chosen in this book in a sense exemplify the transitional era at the social, ideological, and economic levels.

Born immediately after the advent of the People's Republic of China, the Fifth Generation directors grew up during the Cultural Revolution. Instead of continuing their high-school educations, most of these former Red Guards spent their formative years in the countryside as "educated youth" (*zhishi qingnian*).[39] In 1978, through a highly competitively national entrance examination, most Fifth Generation filmmakers entered the Film Academy as members of the first directing class in post–Cultural Revolution China. They made their first works in the midst of the post–Cultural Revolution ideological vacuum of the 1980s, during the collapse of communist ideology in China. On the one hand, these filmmakers are the descendants of the May Fourth movement at the beginning of the century. One of the important ideological components of the May Fourth movement was its radically antitraditional stance, exemplified by its famous slogan: "Smash the Confucian Temple" (*zalan kongjiadian*). The Chinese Communist Party, which had grown from the May Fourth movement, inherited its antitraditionalist agenda. Most Fifth Generation directors then inadvertently followed in the party's footsteps in this respect.[40] On the other hand, as disillusioned offspring of socialist revolution, in their early works they constantly question and subvert communist ideology. Often, in order to reconcile their antitraditional stance and their subversive positions against the party, these directors associate the Communist Party with China's past, and reject both communist and Confucian value systems as two sides of the same traditional coin. Consequently, their subversive acts take on much broader and more complex cultural dimensions than the mere criticism of communist ideology.

Following the defeat of the Nationalist government, which led to the exodus of its adherents from mainland China to Taiwan, New Cinema directors were born either in mainland families in exile, or in Taiwanese families under the leadership of a minority government.[41] At first glance, the distinction between the Taiwanese (*bensheng ren*) and the mainlanders (*waisheng ren*) seems arbitrary. The line of demarcation is drawn on the basis of date of arrival in Taiwan, namely, whether a family, who had in most cases come from mainland China anyway, settled in Taiwan before or after the end of the half-century Japanese occupation in 1945.[42] Despite its arbitrariness, this distinction has deeply affected Taiwan society at different levels, due in part to the political interests of the governing party. Unlike the mainland Communist government, the Nationalist government categorically rejected the May Fourth antitraditional agenda, which it perceived as partly responsible for the emergence of communist culture.[43] Instead, the government has embraced a romanticized version of Chinese tradition and anchored itself to an idealized China, since the actual mainland had become a temporally and spatially distant entity.

From a different perspective, this romantic vision of Chinese tradition has also embraced the notion of cultural hierarchy implied in the discourse of modernity: The West represents the present and future, whereas a non-Western culture can in most cases safely enjoy its past glory, which has disappeared in the modern era anyway. At the same time, the Nationalist Party has been using as a major component of its state ideology the Three People's Principles (*sanmin zhuyi*): nationalism (*minzu zhuyi*), democracy (*minquan zhuyi*), and people's livelihood (*minsheng zhuyi*). These principles were advocated by Sun Zhongshan during the National Revolution in 1911. At the beginning of the century, Sun also promoted the "ideology of enrichment" (*facai zhuyi*), in order to resolve the problem of people's livelihood in China, thus emphasizing one particular aspect of the modernization process, economic development.[44] From the outset of their exodus to Taiwan, the Nationalists seemed to follow this ideology faithfully, emphasizing land reform and rapid industrialization while relying heavily on American economic and political support as well as multinational investments. During the 1970s and 1980s, Taiwan enjoyed the fastest economic growth in the world, which brought about radical changes in life-styles, social relations, and value systems. Often, these changes were at odds with the government's own official traditionalist stances – at least superficially. Chinese tradition has become a museum object in the midst of rapid social, cultural, and axiological changes.

This mixture of elevation of traditional Chinese culture (implicitly against the local one), nationalist ideology, and American colonial presence without official colonial institution has created a cultural complex captured in the works of Taiwan New Cinema studied in this book. Following in the footsteps of Native Soil literature in the 1970s, these directors in the 1980s have shifted from escapist portrayals of the upper class in their predecessors' films, which were often situated on the mainland and bathed in a nostalgic light, to the everyday life of common people in Taiwan. Amid cultural and axiological clashes at various levels, their works focus on confused cultural identities, conflicting value systems, and alienation in a rapidly changing world of modernity.

One can say that the communists on the mainland and the Nationalists in Taiwan followed two radically different paths toward modernization during the second half of the twentieth century. One factor they hold in common, however: Both the ideological revolution under the guidance of Western thought and the economic miracle created with the aid of Western investments and technology have brought about radical changes in their respective societies. Mainland Fifth Generation films and Taiwan New Cinema have both been shaped by these changes. In the former, residual influences of communist ideology, often exemplified by the Cultural Revolution, prevail; in the latter, a clash between the westernization of cultural values brought about by rapid modernization on the economic and the technological front and an officially and artificially maintained traditional value system takes precedence over direct political conflicts. The conflict between the "mainlanders" and "Taiwanese," however, has been highly politicized as well. Furthermore, due to the Japanese half-century of occupation prior to the end of the Second World War and the dependence of the Nationalist government on American military and economic power, particularly at the beginning of its political exile from the mainland, Taiwan bears many characteristics of a postcolonial society, whereas mainland China has never been directly colonized. Especially from the 1950s to 1970s China was almost completely isolated from the rest of the world for ideological and political reasons. Although in the United States we still teach mainland and Taiwan films under the same course title – Chinese cinema – the "Chinese" in "Chinese cinema" refers to several distantly related cultural identities. (Hong Kong cinema is another case in point.) Abdul R. JanMohamed and David Lloyd state:

To date, integration and assimilation have never taken place on equal terms, but always as assimilation by the dominant culture. In relations with the dominant culture, the syncretic movement is always asymmetrical: although members of the dominant culture rarely feel obliged to comprehend various ethnic cultures, minorities are always obliged, in order to survive, to master the hegemonic culture (without thereby necessarily gaining access to the power that circulates within the dominant sector).[45]

Regardless of how successful the Fifth Generation and New Taiwan cinemas have been in the international film milieu, this (limited) recognition usually is based on two aspects: the formal or the exotic. Their works are praised either as highly formally innovative (in other words, how well they have mastered the new-wave visual language of the West – thus, our modernist language) or exotic (as revealing the mystery of an inscrutable Other). This may explain why, in the United States, mainland, Hong Kong, and Taiwan cinemas are still perceived as a homogeneous entity called Chinese cinema, though they are products of the vastly different cultures of three geopolitically segregated regions. Not surprisingly, cultural aspects are the least important agenda in the West's assessment of this minor cinema.

Nevertheless, as the last generation of artists of the transitional stages from a traditional agricultural society to a global market economy, these filmmakers on both sides of the Taiwan Strait exemplify their cultures in transition. In this sense, their works are cultural texts par excellence. Furthermore, as intellectuals in their own right, they play important roles in reformulating the current versions of discourses of modernity in their respective societies. In most cases, their attitudes toward their previous local versions are often critical. On the one hand, they are eager to "carry the Tao" – namely, to use their texts to empower their societies through modernization – by trying to create an internationally recognized national cinema. On the other hand, they also realize that modernization itself is a double-edged weapon, since both societies have to different degrees undergone this process in violence. Furthermore, they themselves have both benefited from and suffered the consequences of this process. Although the interplay between tradition and modernity occupies a prominent place in the works of both mainland and Taiwan experimental filmmakers, Chinese tradition takes on different features on the two sides of the Taiwan Strait because their notions of tradition include various elements of their respective modernization processes. For example, the Fifth Generation directors define communism as part of Chinese tradition, whereas their Taiwan New Cinema counterparts treat the colonial past and the consequences of rapid industrialization as important cultural components. What is particularly interesting is that they often try not only to carry the Tao, but also to question the Tao, by problematizing their own relationships to the local version of the discourse of modernity. This deeply rooted skepticism, shared by both Fifth Generation and New Cinema directors, contributes to the experimental quality of their works through its open-endedness.

STRUCTURE OF THE BOOK

This book is divided into three parts: The first focuses on two mainland directors, the second on two filmmakers from Taiwan, and the third on the impact of globalization on both sides of the Taiwan Strait.

PART I: ON THE CULTURAL AND IDEOLOGICAL MARGINS

The Fifth Generation cinema is relatively well-known in the West. In 1987, Paul Clark introduced the Fifth Generation in his *Chinese Cinema: Culture and Politics since 1949*.[46] In 1989, several American film journals devoted special issues to Chinese cinema.[47] In addition to numerous journal articles during the late 1980s and the 1990s, several anthologies also contributed to the study of the new-wave mainland cinema.[48] In 1995, Rey Chow concentrated on the works of Fifth Generation directors in her book *Primitive Passions*.[49]

As Chow's title suggests, the Fifth Generation directors are interested in portraying "primitive" aspects of culture – portraying them, in a sense, passionately. In Part I, I examine their passion for "primitive" or marginalized cultures by analyzing the works of two Fifth Generation directors, Chen Kaige and Tian Zhuangzhuang.

The Communist Revolution can be perceived as a radical modernization process for China. It has deeply subverted the foundation of traditional society by introducing various modern agendas such as women's emancipation, economic equality, and the welfare state, at least on the surface. These agendas radically disrupted a traditional Confucian hierarchy, replacing it with a new communist one that is totalitarian in nature.

Hannah Arendt distinguishes totalitarianism from traditional tyranny:

The decisive difference between totalitarian domination, based on terror, and tyrannies and dictatorships, established by violence, is that the former turns not only against its enemies but against its friends and supporters as well, being afraid of all power, even the power of its friends. The climax of terror is reached when the police state begins to devour its own children, when yesterday's executioner becomes today's victim.[50]

During the Cultural Revolution, totalitarian terror reached its climax. Chinese society from 1966 to 1976 underwent a social atomization through which "every kind of organized opposition disappeared" – to use Arendt's expression. As the children of the Cultural Revolution, the Fifth Generation filmmakers have been greatly affected by the traumatic experiences of their formative years. After having participated in the movement as Red Guards in high school, these former supporters of the Cultural Revolution were sent to the remote countryside to obtain "reeducation" (*zai jiaoyu*) from the laboring class, which they stood in need of because of their own petit-bourgeois background. (By the Maoist definition, intellectuals, which included anyone who had part of a high-school education, belong to the petite bourgeoisie.) Most peasants did not welcome these city kids, who competed with them for limited resources despite their lack of basic farming skills. As marginalized individuals in marginalized regions, educated youth in exile were forced to reexamine their cultural center, which had been their home up to this point, as well as their former beliefs, implanted by the official educational system led by the Communist Party. At many levels, the works of the Fifth Generation filmmakers, especially the early ones, are fruits of this long period of reflection and reexamination.

Their relationships with the dominant ideology are often ambiguous. They were initially supporters and finally victims of totalitarian terror. From which perspective can they criticize the origin of this terror effectively? Furthermore, since communist ideology has already subverted traditional culture through its radical revolution, and the party has played an important role in the modernization process by positioning itself against the Confucian tradition, does a subversion of this already subversive ideology need to return to the past, take recourse to traditional culture, in order to redefine itself against the current mainstream?

Partly to address these questions, both Chen Kaige and Tian Zhuangzhuang in their early works chose to portray "primitive" cultures or marginalized societies, namely, remote countryside or minority communities. Many of their former classmates made a similar choice. This choice symbolically reflected their own positions: They were situated neither outside nor inside the mainstream culture and ideology, but at their borders. Vis-à-vis the marginalized communities, they also occupied borderline positions. In other words, the marginalized communities offered them spaces to distance themselves from the mainstream, to which they would return in the end despite their ideological and cultural discontent. In the final analysis, the margins are used as the Other of the center, through which its ideological and cultural values are problematized. These filmmakers then did not need to take a regressive step toward the past in order to step out from the current mainstream ideology, which had originated in subversion of the past. While associating the communist ideology with a Confucian past, they moved toward an Other spatially situated outside the mainstream culture. As a result, they transformed a temporal movement into a spatial one. In other words, they subverted this already subversive ideology from a geographical distance instead of from a historical past, which had already been used as the object of the previous subversion. For this reason, they still held a modern position vis-à-vis the communist version of the discourse of modernity. This spatial movement was ultimately temporal as well, since a marginalized community is supposed to be primitive – relatively free of modern influence. According to the linear logic embedded in the discourse of modernity, these spatial margins still represent a past, which is even more remote from the modern era than the Confucian past. From these margins, both Chen Kaige and Tian Zhuangzhuang articulate powerful criticisms of communist ideology as part of Chinese cultural tradition – a gesture that associates them with the May Fourth intellectuals and thus, indirectly, with the target of their criticism, their communist forefathers, while dissociating them from a Confucian past.

Chen Kaige's first film, *Yellow Earth* (*Huang tudi*, 1984), is a milestone for the Fifth Generation, through which he also established his personal signature. This film debunks the communist ideology of peasants' salvation granted by the party by associating it with the dragon king, symbol of traditional superstition. The failures of promised salvation by both the dragon king and the party leave peasants, the overwhelming majority of the Chinese population, in their ageless suffering. *Big Parade* (*Da yuebing*, 1986) serves as an allegory for the tight political control the party machine has over the Chinese people, while studying the effect of the people's voluntary or involuntary participation in the constitution and maintenance of this political machine. *King of the Children* (*Haizi wang*, 1987) traces the origin of the Cultural Revolution not only to communist ideology but also to traditional Chinese culture, since both, according to Chen, oppress individual initiative through the cultural practice of copying. By ceaselessly forcing people to copy texts from childhood on, traditional and communist cultures mirror each other and repeat themselves in an endless vicious circle. The film ends in a radical gesture that symbolically breaks this circle, by throwing almost everything, including this cultural practice, into a blazing mountain fire. This hopeless gesture reminds us of the May Fourth movement and the Cultural Revolution, which the film tries to portray in a negative light, partly because it is based on the same social Darwinist notion of linear historical progress. In order to achieve this progress, one needs to reject the past as completely as possible. As Mao stated: "On a piece of white paper, one can draw the newest and most beautiful picture."

In his two minority feature films, *On the Hunting Ground* (*Liechang zasa*, 1985) and *Horse Thief* (*Daoma zei*, 1986), Tian Zhuangzhuang created a new cinematic model through his documentary approach, which subverted the melodramatic pattern of his predecessors in socialist-realist cinema. Both films emphasize the relationship between individuals and their communities. On the one hand, these communities reject any transgressor of their rules. On the other, the arbitrariness of the rules seem to invite transgression and make conformity to the rules difficult, if not impossible. Using minority cultures as allegories of the dominant Han culture, Tian's films revive the nightmarish situation of the Cultural Revolution indirectly. In his later film *Blue Kite* (*Lan fengzheng*, 1993), Tian approached the subject of political movements directly. Contrary to the documentary style in his earlier minority movies, the world of *Blue Kite* is mostly presented through a boy's subjective perspective. The subjective point of view in Tian's later film underscores the objectification of the ethnic Other in his two minority films, be this Other represented by Mongolian hunters or Tibetan horse thieves. This objectification is implicitly based on a division inherent in the discourse of modernity, namely, primitive ethnic minorities versus the modern Han Chinese majority, which can be traced back to the beginning of the twentieth century. Through a negative path, Tian uses minorities as an Other to create a new Chinese identity, an identity different from the official one. This negative cultural identity serves as a firm ground from which to critique the dominant ideology. At the same time, the treatment of minority culture as an empty signifier inadvertently reinforces the cultural and ethnic hierarchy inherent in the official discourse.

PART II: IN SEARCH OF TRADITION IN THE MIDST OF MODERNIZATION

It is difficult to perceive the Fifth Generation filmmakers as nostalgic, since the past, be it communist or traditional, is an object of their subversion. However, their obsession with primitive and marginal cultures reveals a deep-rooted nostalgia, "nostalgia for the present," to borrow Fredric Jameson's expression.[51] This nostalgia re-creates an object that has never been lost, a utopian past free of cultural and ideological influences, which is exemplified by Chen Kaige's cowherd and Tian Zhuangzhuang's minority culture. Sometimes, the reconstructed object of this nostalgia may take on purely negative features, which are used to criticize traditional China, as in many films made by Zhang Yimou and other Fifth Generation directors. This negative attitude toward their own cultural tradition, which they have inherited from their May Fourth and communist forefathers despite their subversive intent toward them, marks one of the major differences of the mainland experimental filmmakers from their Taiwan counterparts.

In comparison with mainland filmmakers, Taiwan New Cinema directors are less known among Western film critics, although they have also obtained several important international film awards. They are unsuccessful in terms of domestic box office, similar to most of their Fifth Generation colleagues on the mainland. Fewer Western-language film journals study their works:[52] Scholarly articles on Taiwan cinema, most in English, are published in journals specializing in Asian cinema.[53] During the 1990s there were several anthologies published that included articles on Taiwan cinema.[54] The relatively subdued reaction of Western film critics to Taiwan New Cinema can be explained, paradoxically, by the similarities of the life-styles pictured to those of Western audiences. In comparison with mainland films, Taiwan films are much more closely related to the daily reality of consumer society in the West. In this sense, they are too familiar to provide images of an exotic Other.

If both Chen Kaige and Tian Zhuangzhuang are the children of the Cultural Revolution, Hou Xiaoxian (Hou Hsiao-hsien) and Edward Yang (Yang Dechang) are the children of the massive migration of civilian and military personnel with the Nationalist government from the mainland to Taiwan at the end of the 1940s. In the case of the Fifth Generation directors, Chinese tradition has been negated by the Communist Revolution; consequently, the past must be re-created from ground zero in their films. By contrast, the New Cinema directors indeed have a past, which is spatially lost on the mainland and temporally lost in the precommunist era. Furthermore, this past, which is mainly fictional as well, had been sanctified as the golden age of Chinese culture by the Nationalist government at the beginning of their power. By elevating traditional Chinese culture, which originated on the mainland, to the altar of the ultimate reference, and by strongly identifying with this imaginary center, the Nationalist government justified its dominant position in the land of its political exile. The official ideology thus considered local Taiwanese culture peripheral to mainstream Chinese culture, and the Taiwanese ideologically inferior, because they had been "enslaved" (nuhua)[55] by the half-century of Japanese occupation.

For political reasons, the official ideology deepened the division between the local Taiwanese and the mainland immigrants in the late 1940s by re-creating ethnic differences based on the date of the arrival of a family in Taiwan. This ethnic difference did help maintain minority rule for several decades. At the same time, this division also reinforced the sense of homelessness of mainland immigrants, because as "outsiders to the province" (waisheng ren), theoretically speaking they could never truly consider Taiwan their homeland. Since the state of homelessness coincides with modernity,[56] homelessness experienced by mainland immigrants was further reinforced by rapid industrialization and modernization during the 1970s and 1980s. Because of the Japanese occupation and the initial dependence of the Nationalist Government on Western (especially American) support, the centrality of traditional Chinese culture, which the government tried to establish against the local culture, has always been severely disrupted by the powerful influence of Western (or westernized, i.e., Japanese) culture, backed up by its economic power. As a result, detached from the native land and submerged by alien culture, this centrality is doubly fictional. Following the "ideol-ogy of enrichment" (*facai zhuyi*), a version of discourse of modernity promoted by Sun Zhongshan at the beginning of the century, the Nationalist government transformed Taiwan from an agricultural society in the early 1960s to a labor-intensive, export-oriented industrial society in the 1970s, and then to a high-tech-based, capital- and knowledge-intensive consumer society in the 1980s.

Born in mainland China, growing up in Taiwan, surrounded by the nostalgic feelings of their family members of the older generation, and facing a rapidly modernized postcolonial society, both Hou Xiaoxian and Edward Yang are fa-miliar with the same sense of homelessness amid the unstable world of shifting (and alienating) identities. Although they are defined by the official culture as mainlanders (*waisheng ren*), or "outsiders to the province," they are in fact Tai-wanese: They have been living there since they were toddlers, and their mem-ory of their "origin" is at best fuzzy. Nourished by the official ideology and fam-ily memory, any mainland origin for the two Taiwan directors is by definition fictional.

Arjun Appadurai comments on the state of immigration in the global era:

What is new is that this is a world in which both points of departure and points of arrival are in cultural flux, and thus the search for steady points of reference, as crit-ical life choices are made, can be very difficult. It is in this atmosphere that the in-vention of tradition (and of ethnicity, kinship, and other identity markers) can become slippery, as the search for certainties is regularly frustrated by the fluidities of trans-national communication.[57]

In postindustrial Taiwan, ethnic identity, which has been created and main-tained for the needs of the dominant group, has become a political choice – as reflected by Hou's search for a native father figure in his works, and to a lesser degree by Yang's modernist approach. In Yang's films, tradition, which often functions as an empty signifier, has become the symbol of homeless modernity.

Hou Xiaoxian has been interested in searching for a Taiwan identity in his films. His works, usually set in either a rural area or a small town in the less in-dustrialized South, focus on personal histories in which family ties play an im-portant role. As a result, his films seem closely related to traditional culture, which is broadly defined as Chinese. At the same time, various groups in his films often use different languages: Minnan dialect, Mandarin, Cantonese, and occa-sionally Japanese. All these diverse cultural components contribute to forming a concept of a hybrid identity, suitable to the current population in postcolonial Taiwan. Furthermore, Hou's search for a new identity coincides with a desire to reinvent a powerful father figure, which his mainlander biological father in *A Time to Live and a Time to Die* (*Tongnian wangshi*, 1985), weakened by his physical sickness and cultural alienation, failed to be. Hou seemed to find this powerful image in Li Tianlu, the protagonist of his later film *The Puppetmaster* (*Ximeng rensheng*, 1993), who is deeply rooted in both traditional Chinese patriarchy and the Taiwan native soil. In this context, his search for a new cultural identity through the reconstruction of a father figure reveals to what extent a stable cultural identity is patriarchal, regardless of its subversive potentials. From two completely different perspectives, both Tian Zhuangzhuang and Hou Xiaoxian have to use an Other, defined by either minority or gender, to construct cultural identities as the last anchorage in the changing world of globalization.

Unlike Hou, whose films focus on traces of bygone traditional culture(s), mostly located in rural areas, Edward Yang's works are always about Taipei, the modern city. In his films, the city often appears detached from its past, and its human inhabitants are submerged in an ocean of gigantic machinery, impersonal high-rises, and indistinguishable streets. Traditional family ties are subverted by the worship of money, which has created an increasingly alienating atmosphere. In *Taipei Story* (*Qingmei zhuma,* 1985), for example, a young couple, who have known each other since childhood, are gradually drifting apart, partly because the male protagonist has alienated himself from the modern city by stubbornly sticking to traditional family ties. The absence of human ties engenders terror, as it may make an ordinary citizen a potential terrorizer, as shown in *The Terrorizers* (*Kongbu fenzi,* 1986). Due to its purely performative nature in a highly commercialized society like Taipei, the concept of affection (*qing*), which Yang in his *Confucius's Confusion* (*Duli shidai,* 1994) portrayed as a central value in traditional Chinese society, has become an absurdly comic spectacle. Despite his ironic approach to the modernization process, Yang's portrayals of its negative consequences are still based on a dichotomy inherent in the discourse of modernity, which was imported to China at the beginning of the twentieth century: the dichotomy between traditional China and the modern West. Following its implicit logic, whatever is perceived as traditional belongs to China, and whatever is perceived as modern must be a derivative of Western culture. Interestingly, women, usually portrayed by Yang as more adaptable to new environments, often represent the threatening, dark side of modernity in his films.

PART III: THE THIRD-WORLD INTELLECTUAL IN THE ERA OF GLOBALIZATION

In the midst of globalization, cultural boundaries have become increasingly blurred, and the value system of the global market economy has become increasingly dominant. Uncomfortably modernized or westernized, a third-world intellectual often feels doubly marginalized by the "invisible center,"[58] with which he or she consciously or unconsciously identifies, and by the community, to which he or she physically belongs. First, a third-world intellectual can never truly belong to the (Western) center, despite his or her modernized value system. Second, the westernized system alienates him or her from a native land, which is also strongly affected by the process of globalization, but in different ways. This type of alienation has been a recurrent theme in new-wave films on both sides of the Taiwan Strait. If ethnic identity has become a matter of choice in the global culture, however, as in the case of the two Taiwan directors discussed in the previous section, one can certainly choose different perspectives from which to deal with one's own alienation. In this third part of the book, I have selected three filmmakers in order to examine, through their works, how they approach the problem of their own marginalization.

Zhang Yimou is no doubt the best-known Chinese director in the West. In his three early films, two of which were sponsored by multinational corporations, China occupies a feminized space of the Other. Thanks to his unusual visual sensibility, he stages this Other for the gaze of those outside Lu Xun's iron house – China – by appealing to the Western imaginary of an exotic and eroticized Orient. In the process of self-Othering, Zhang successfully commodifies the marginalized position of his own culture. Partly due to his marketing skills, his films have won several prestigious awards in the West and enjoy relative box-office success even in America. In this case, market power has also become justification for the cultural centrality of the West. A number of Chinese filmmakers, including Chen Kaige and Li Shaohong, imitated Zhang's visual style in the early 1990s by multiplying various erotic images of the oriental Other for global consumption. Consequently, these films, usually sponsored by multinational corporations and catering to the tastes of global audiences, can be perceived as following the same model – the Zhang Yimou model. To a great degree, this model also marks the end of formal experiment for the Fifth Generation directors because they must adopt a much more conventional way of filmmaking in order to meet the demand of the global market.

Fifth Generation director Li Shaohong deals with the problem of alienation of an intellectual in his own community in the midst of globalization. Her film *Bloody Dawn (Xuese qingchen,* 1990) is loosely based on *Chronicle of a Death Foretold,* a magic-realist novel by the Colombian writer Gabriel García Márquez. The murder in the film happens in a remote Chinese village instead of in a South American small town. Through this seamless insertion of the Colombian story into the Chinese village, *Bloody Dawn* deconstructs a clearly defined cultural boundary. In her film, Li focuses on a problem (lack of education) that currently exists in postsocialist China amid rapid commodification of social values. She shows the murder of the only available teacher in the village and the collective reaction to his death. At the same time, the film deals with gender issues visually but not discursively, emphasizing through images the importance of female virginity, the traffic in women, and domestic violence. Thus she avoids duplicating the party's minority discourse on women's emancipation, one of the major components of the communist discourse of modernity. Although Li's film is an adaption of a non-Chinese fiction, it directly addresses problems currently existing in postcommunist China, unlike films following the Zhang Yimou model, and does so from the perspective of a woman intellectual caught between global culture and her own community. On the one hand, the film questions the party's minority discourse; on the other, it implicitly looks down upon the indigenous culture as backward, thus inadvertently following the logic of the same discourse.

Wu Nianzhen, formerly a Taiwan Native Soil fiction writer and one of the most prolific New Cinema screenwriters, questions the role of the local intellectual in the process of globalization in his *Buddha Bless America* (*Taiping tianguo,* 1996). Instead of portraying the native intellectual's alienation within his community, as in Li's film, Wu's work ironically shows how this intellectual alienates himself from the entire community by blindly subscribing to the orientalist component of the discourse of modernity. With a twist of self-mockery, the film ridicules the fetishistic logic in this discourse – that is, the equivalence of technological development with cultural excellence – by portraying the encounter and confrontation between American soldiers and Taiwanese farmers in an American temporary military base in Taiwan. Among all the films studied in this book, *Buddha Bless America* is the only one that directly problematizes the relationship between the third-world intellectual and the discourse of modernity. In this sense, it reflects an emerging critical awareness of this relationship among Taiwan intellectuals. Although Native Soil writers had started examining the postcolonial situation in Taiwan as early as the 1970s,[59] Wu's film represents a much more conscious effort to deconstruct the fetishist component of the cultural hierarchy inherent in the discourse of modernity.

Part I

ON THE CULTURAL AND
IDEOLOGICAL MARGINS

1

CONTINUITY AND SUBVERSION

CHEN KAIGE: *YELLOW EARTH; BIG PARADE; KING OF THE CHILDREN*

In an interview, Chen Kaige explains his view on the relationship between the Cultural Revolution and Chinese tradition:

If you insist that my films have a critical edge, I prefer to perceive them as cultural critique, critique of Chinese culture. Take the Cultural Revolution as an example: I have always believed that it was closely linked to traditional Chinese culture. . . . On the surface, the Cultural Revolution was to eliminate culture. In reality, what it eliminated was only artistic objects from the past. At an ideological level, the Cultural Revolution can be perceived as a repetition, continuation, and development of traditional culture. . . . In the final analysis, what has our cultural system offered us? In my opinion, pretending that we are a great nation with five thousand years of civilization has simply become a joke. Every Chinese must look back, examining our way of thinking thoroughly. Furthermore, some of us must do this for the Chinese nation.[1]

Although Chen associates his critical attitude toward traditional Chinese culture with that of unspecified Taiwan scholars,[2] his notion of Chinese culture is certainly distant from that in Taiwan New Cinema works roughly contemporary with his own. In Hou Xiaoxian's films, for example, traditional Chinese culture is often idealized as a bygone patriarchal structure to which the filmmaker reveals a nostalgic attachment. This patriarchal structure is portrayed as disrupted and threatened by Taiwan's repeated experiences of colonization and massive industrialization. In Edward Yang's films, values of traditional Chinese culture in Taiwan's initially agricultural society are portrayed as suffering and fading, overwhelmed by rapid industrialization and commercialization. Despite Yang's much less sentimental approach, his portrayal of this past is nostalgic in his own way. Most New Cinema filmmakers in Taiwan reveal a special fondness for their childhoods or the historical period of their childhoods. A great number of Hou's films are devoted to this subject.[3] Yang's film *A Brighter Summer Day* is also related to his own memory of the same period – like many examples from other filmmakers (e.g., Wu Nianzhen's *A Borrowed Life* [*Duosang*]). In these (auto)-

biographical films, childhood serves as a metaphor for lost innocence in traditional preindustrial society.

By contrast, the Fifth Generation directors on the mainland did not share the same sense of lost innocence vis-à-vis traditional society. Instead, in line with May Fourth and communist ideology, they view the past as an object of constant subversion. As Chen demonstrates in *King of the Children,* innocence for him can only exist in human nature, uncontaminated by any culture. Similarly, Chen defines Chinese communist culture as a continuation of its target of subversion – traditional Chinese culture. Following the same logic, communism is no longer a subversive force against the tradition but rather its successor. As a result, in Chen's view, not only is traditional Chinese culture responsible for what happened during the Cultural Revolution, but also Maoist ideology is the logical extension of traditional culture. At the same time, like their Taiwan colleagues, Chen and other graduates from China's Film Institute search for relatively innocent human relationships – not in their own cultural tradition, which has already been thoroughly subverted by their fathers' generation, but in marginal communities within China, either among minorities (as in Tian Zhuangzhuang's case) or in border or agricultural regions relatively distant from the current political and cultural center (as in the early films made by Chen Kaige and Zhang Yimou).

Ironically, the portrayals of traditional Chinese culture by mainland and Taiwan New Cinema filmmakers, despite their differences, resemble each other on one point. Their subversive intent notwithstanding, they are implicitly consistent with the dominant ideologies in their respective societies. Since the Nationalist government arrived in Taiwan in the late 1940s as the politically dominant minority, it has attempted to legitimize its power by projecting the cultural center onto mainland China, which it portrayed as the dreamed-of but temporarily unreachable motherland. Because of the Nationalists' political exile, for them this center can be situated only in the past, in traditional culture, not in the present, since China is occupied by their enemy. As a result, this subtle romanticization of the filmmakers' childhood situated in a warmer and more humanized past smacks of the government's nostalgic projection of power on a distant cultural center, which can be reconstituted only romantically, in memory. In the same vein, the almost intransigently negative attitude of the Fifth Generation on the mainland toward their cultural past is coherent with the May Fourth tradition, in which the Communist Party originated. In *Yellow Earth,* for example, the communist regime in Yan'an is criticized not for breaking away from traditional Chinese culture but for its inability truly to dissociate itself from tradition despite its apparently revolutionary stance. Chen Kaige's gesture of burning the past in the fire at the end of *King of the Children* is not substantially different from the May Fourth slogan: "Smash the Confucian temple" (*zalan kongjiadian*). If Chen believes that the Cultural Revolution is a continuation of traditional culture, his own statement can be perceived as a continuation of the Cultural Revolution.

1. The soldier describes life in Yan'an to Cuiqiao's family in *Yellow Earth,* directed by Chen Kaige (1984). COURTESY OF THE MUSEUM OF MODERN ART.

In this chapter, I study Chen's three early movies, *Yellow Earth* (*Huang tudi,* 1984), *Big Parade* (*Da yuebing,* 1986), and *King of the Children* (*Haizi wang,* 1987), since all three of them focus on cultural criticism from different perspectives and at various levels.

YELLOW EARTH

The story line of this film is extremely simple: In 1939, an Eighth Route Army soldier, Gu Qing, is sent by the party to a remote village in Shaanbei to collect folk songs because the party leaders want to use the music, with new revolutionary lyrics, for propaganda. Gu lives in one of the poorest peasant households – as dictated by communist ideology. Gradually, he becomes well-acquainted with all three members of the family: the widower father (who is nameless), his adolescent daughter, Cuiqiao, and her kid brother, Hanhan. Cuiqiao is soon going to marry a man whom she has never met, for the money her father received from him as bridal gifts to pay off his debts. Without any clear knowledge of Cuiqiao's situation, Gu Qing describes to her family the new life on the revolutionary basis in Yan'an, especially that of emancipated female soldiers [Fig. 1]. The two members of the younger generation of this family show a great interest in the new world. At Gu's departure, Cuiqiao wants to follow him to join the Eighth Route Army in Yan'an – partly in order to avoid the arranged marriage. Gu refuses to bring her to Yan'an without the party's permission, whose rules he has to obey. At the same time, he promises to return to rescue her from the dreadful prospect of marriage after obtaining the party's permission. After Gu's departure, Cuiqiao is forced into marriage and soon after escapes from her husband's family. Apparently, she is drowned in the Yellow River. When Gu returns, he sees the peasants' ritual of praying for rain. The film ends in a shot of Hanhan running toward Gu against the crowd. However, my simplistic description of the story line misses an important character – the yellow earth of the title – which is, despite its silence, the most important persona, according to Chen's own explanation in his speech at the University of Minnesota.[4]

The film starts with an impressive extremely long shot of this protagonist, yellow earth, associated with powerful wind in the sound track. The land itself cannot move, but the background sound of the wind creates the illusion of its mobility, as if the sound resulted from the land's vibration. Moreover, a tracking shot of the land superimposed with a still image of another portion of the same land powerfully reinforces this illusion. During the first sequence, the image of the upper part of moving land combined with its static lower part repeatedly appears on the screen. When Gu Qing walks in the middle of this unlimited loess plain at the beginning and the end of the film, he appears so small that he often becomes invisible, as if he were a mere decoration of the yellow earth rather than the protagonist of the film. He is often situated in offscreen spaces, whereas the image of the earth is overwhelmingly dominant onscreen during his trips. If he appears on the screen, Gu often positions himself in the center of the frame. Due to this relatively unchanging position, his walking appears more static than the tracking shots of the upper level of the land. Motion and stability become relativized, if not reversed, in comparison with commonsensical perception. Furthermore, this dynamic image of the loess plain is associated with the sound of a folk song, one that does not originate from any visible individual but seemingly resounds over the entire plain, as if the limitless yellow earth itself were singing.

Except for the two well-known crowd scenes – the peasants waist-drum dancing in Yan'an and, at the end of the film, praying for rain – the camera in this film remains almost motionless, to the point of creating a photographic effect in many shots. The lack of camera movement, which appeared so completely at odds with cinematic conventions in China at this moment, caused animated debates between supporters and opponents of Yellow Earth at a conference devoted to the film.[5] The photographic quality of its shots symbolically represents a stabilizing mental frame for most peasants, such as the father, suggesting that changes, whether social or psychological, were extremely difficult if not impossible in this stagnant world. In both collective sequences, the apparent dynamism and energy of the masses are perceived in the film as a manifestation of a great but passive (or "blind,"[6] to use Chen's own word) force. In this sense, the series of shots of the yellow earth itself can be taken as an equivalent of a third crowd scene at a symbolic level. If the yellow earth is indeed an important character, as the director repeatedly stated, this protagonist is assuredly a collective one. Despite its lifeless nature, the prehistoric loess plain is the cradle of Chinese civilization and the historical location of the capitals of eleven dynasties, as well as the revolutionary basis of Mao's army. At the same time, it is also the land of poverty and backwardness. It personifies the Chinese nation in its complicated and often self-contradictory nature.

In the first place, the yellow earth in the film is a symbol of Chinese culture, which is conceptualized through the subjective point of view of Gu Qing. As a relatively educated outsider, the soldier attentively records his impressions of the primitive land.[7] To a large extent, his perception indirectly represents the directorial point of view of China as an agricultural nation. Chen describes his two dynamic crowd scenes thus: "I use these two scenes in order to make an obvious contrast: People of the same nation can beat waist drums passionately and enthusiastically or pray to the heavens and earth with ignorance. This is the dual nature of the Chinese nation."[8] The combination of the dynamic and motionless parts of the loess plain symbolizes the same dual nature of the Chinese nation. As in the case of the peasants' energy, the earth's tremendous power is mainly portrayed as "blind," that is, free of any ethical or conscious guidance.[9]

TRADITION AND REVOLUTION

At the end of Gu Qing's lonely journey, a group of people finally emerges in the soldier's field of vision. Gradually, they reveal themselves to be members of a traditional wedding party. Then, a series of close-ups focus on fragmentary bodies of various individuals, such as the musician's hands with his *suona* horn, the bride's feet, and the shoulders of carriers of the bridal chair. (In a later sequence on Cuiqiao's wedding, the film uses exactly the same shots to emphasize the repetition of the same ritual, objectifying and meaningless.[10]) The wedding party arrives in the village, watched by a group of peasants. In the crowd, a close-up shows Cuiqiao standing under a line of Chinese characters: "Three Obediences and Four Virtues" (*sancong side*) – the oppressive rules governing women in traditional Confucian society. Cuiqiao is illiterate – as she later indicates in her response to Gu Qing's proposition to write a couplet for her family: "I cannot recognize characters, so they can't recognize me." But the second half of her statement is not necessarily true: The rules seem to have no trouble identifying each of the women, despite the illiteracy of almost all the peasants. The association between her image and these characters summarizes the fate of women on the loess plain. Although they do not understand these oppressive rules in their written forms, women cannot avoid living under their tight control – like the current young bride and her vicariously concerned observer, Cuiqiao.

Later on, Gu Qing promises Cuiqiao to write a couplet for her to replace the fake couplet with meaningless circles on the door frame of their cave. As in the case of his promise to return before April (Cuiqiao's wedding date), Gu fails to keep his word. After his departure, the so-called couplet remains unchanged on the door frame – colorless and shapeless. Ironically, Gu's promise will be fulfilled by an invisible hand, which contradicts his belief by restating the same kind of traditional ethics as in the first shot of Cuiqiao under another woman's wedding couplet. After Cuiqiao leaves her father's cave, a new couplet appears on the door frame: "Since ancient times marriages have been decided by the heavens; nowadays wealth is bestowed by fate" (*zigu hunjia you tianding, erjin fugui zai mingzhong*). Despite his promise and good intentions, Gu Qing fails to liberate Cuiqiao from oppressive traditional ethics despite his revolutionary intent. In this sense, he also sustains traditional ethics. When Cuiqiao expresses her desire to join the Eighth Route Army in Yan'an, Gu Qing explains that he cannot take her because of the party's rules. She asks: "Why not change the rules?" Gu Qing answers: "It's impossible, because we rely on these rules to fight for central power" (*zan gongjiaren jiukao zhe guiju da tianxia de*). Cuiqiao's father gives his daughter to a man who pays him money, because nobody can change rules – as he tells his daughter. For the soldier, a woman's fate is subservient to the political struggle by means of which the party grasps power. In both cases, it is less important to prevent a woman from suffering than to respect rules, be they defined by the traditional patriarchy or by a modern political party. As a result, one can say that both traditional and revolutionary rules are indifferent to women's fate.

After the sequence where Cuiqiao happily watches Gu Qing teaching Hanhan a revolutionary song, she returns home and encounters the matchmaker sent by her fiancée's family. Stunned, she stays in the doorway even after the matchmaker's departure. A close-up focuses on Cuiqiao's face, speechlessly listening to her father's offscreen voice. The voice seems unnaturally slow and tiresome, as if it were a broken record. The audience can watch how these sentences, pronounced by this somehow depersonalized voice, change the facial expression of the silent daughter, yet cannot see the expression of the speaking father. His invisibility gives his words an abstract quality, as if they were articulating impersonal rules. Like the characters written on the door in the first wedding scene, where the daughter was only a spectator, the father's words are the rules that a daughter must obey – following examples of numberless women before her. Any dialogue becomes impossible between them because the daughter's face is presented as an objectified spectacle and the father's voice as a faceless authority. He pronounces, "Every girl must follow this road" (*shuijia de nüzi buzou zhege lu*). The father speaks from the standpoint of a timeless tradition.

Later in another sequence, Cuiqiao faces a different disembodied male voice. Her conversation with Gu Qing before his departure reminds us of that with her father. Gu is inside the cave after briefly facing her. Cuiqiao sits beside the door, facing the camera. Gu's offscreen voice has a strange effect on Cuiqiao's face. Shaken by the news of his immediate departure, Cuiqiao asks him: "Won't you collect folk songs? Won't you help my father to plow the land? Won't you teach my brother to sing songs of the Red Army?" All these questions remain unanswered, partly because Gu fails to address her urgent need, which these questions indirectly reveal: the need for his help. Instead, Gu only suggests that she buy clothes for herself with the money that he leaves for his room and board. With tears in her eyes Cuiqiao responds, "I have already got them [new clothes]." Despite the exciting description of Yan'an's new life for women, all this soldier is able to offer to Cuiqiao before his departure has already been offered by her arranged marriage, and in much greater quantity: new clothes. Once again, traditional patriarchal society and the soldier's revolutionary community play the same role vis-à-vis the oppressed young woman Cuiqiao. What they offer to her has nothing to do with what she truly needs. It cannot compensate for her suffering, imposed on her by their patriarchal rules. The soldier's arrival has raised the girl's hopes for change, but he cannot fulfill the party's promise to change her fate fundamentally – a promise made to all Chinese women.

SOUND AND IMAGES

At first glance, in both scenes where Cuiqiao onscreen confronts a disembodied male voice, either her father's or the soldier's, this association (or rather dissociation) of image and voice[11] appears to reconfirm an image of traditional gender hierarchy that prevails in classical Hollywood cinema. According to some film critics, the more disembodied a voice is, the more authoritarian it becomes, because of its greater identification with the cinematic apparatus.[12] Kaja Silverman states:

Hollywood dictates that the closer a voice is to the "inside" of the narrative, the more remote it is from the "outside," i.e., from that space fictionally inscribed by the disembodied voice-over, but which is in fact synonymous with the cinematic apparatus. In other words, it equates diegetic interiority with discursive impotence and lack of control, thereby rendering that situation culturally unacceptable for the "normal" male subject.[13]

As if to prove this logic, Chen's use of embodied or disembodied voices is strictly organized on gender lines. On both occasions, it is on Cuiqiao's face that the dramatic impact of fatherly authorities are staged, whether they represent the ancient tradition or the newly established communist power. In comparison with the male characters' lack of any facial expression, Cuiqiao's relatively more expressive face is also almost the only image that registers human emotions – it reveals shocks caused by male authoritative voices. At the same time, the lack of male facial expressions can be interpreted as symptomatic of their refusal of change. Almost all male characters, except for Hanhan, Cuiqiao's young brother, do have a hard time accepting changes. Although on the surface the soldier himself almost personifies cultural and political change, he refuses to change his "rules" (*guiju*) to help Cuiqiao realize her hope. Like Cuiqiao, almost all the male characters sing, albeit less often than she does. However, the lyrics of their songs are centered on external objects – on other people's marital happiness or pain, on hardship in general, and on the fates of unknown people, but not on their own subjective world. By contrast, Cuiqiao's songs always reveal her most intimate emotions: sadness, fear, hope, and passion. In this respect, *Yellow Earth* indeed "equates diegetic interiority with discursive impotence and lack of control, thereby rendering that situation culturally unacceptable for the 'normal' male subject"[14] – as in classical Hollywood films. Silverman writes: "By confining the female voice to a recessed area of the diegesis, obliging it to speak a particular psychic 'reality' on command, and imparting to it the texture of the female body, Hollywood places woman definitively 'on stage,' at a dramatic remove from the cinematic apparatus."[15] The comparison between Cuiqiao's expressive body language and the disembodied male voices indeed makes the latter appear less vulnerable and less exposed.[16] At the same time, in Chen's film, Cuiqiao's emotions also reveal the impotence of the men, since the male characters themselves are to a large degree slaves of the imperial rules that they impose upon themselves and for which Cuiqiao sacrifices her life. The clear-cut gender hierarchy becomes a double-edged weapon: It deconstructs its own basis by making the daughter a beautiful sacrifice to the (biological or figurative) father's impotence, in both the traditional and communist patriarchal systems.

Prior to their final separation, Cuiqiao enthusiastically sings a song for Gu Qing. Instead of taking out his notebook, as she suggests, Gu listens to the song, expressionlessly. Shortly after, he turns his back on Cuiqiao and disappears into the immense loess plain. Meanwhile, Cuiqiao sadly continues her song: "Neither can folk songs save me" (*shange ye jiubuliao Cuiqiao wo*). The last syllable trails and vibrates until it gradually becomes lost in the empty plain. This scene is even more interesting if we remember that collecting folk songs was the whole purpose of Gu Qing's trip. On the one hand, the party wants to represent itself in a new form of folk song, a form that symbolizes the people's awakening consciousness. On the other hand, both the party and its representative, the collector of songs, fail to respond to the desperate voices of people, articulated by Cuiqiao exactly in the form of folk songs. Instead of being incorporated in the system of male desire as its object, the woman in Chen's film is shown as an isolated stage of emotions, which largely fails to receive any response from men, who are often situated outside the visual field. The short circuit between the woman's body and any possible response from her male interlocutor, be it her biological father or an icon of hope for a new mode of life, makes the suture for the (male) subject that occurs in a traditional Hollywood context impossible here, despite the clearly drawn gender line. As Rey Chow points out:

The status of Cuiqiao's singing must therefore be understood as much through its pitch, its rhythm, its lyrical elusiveness, and its referentless resonances as through its verbal content. Its significance is to be found between exteriority and interiority, in an interplay between the "subjective, immediate realm"and its "external representation."[17]

This indeterminacy results from the ambiguity of Cuiqiao's status in relation to the opposite sex. She is a victim of their indifference toward her need and fate, sometimes despite their good intentions. At the same time, she also acts out their own victimization imposed by tradition, politics, and culture. Her songs are post-dubbed without any association of lip movements. This dissociation between image and sound can be interpreted in both ways: Her voice is interior; and it also has an exterior aspect because it looks as if these songs "[broke] away from the humanly specific and emanate[d] from nowhere and everywhere."[18] These two aspects are not contradictory; both present Cuiqiao's interiority as a reified stage. At the same time, her interiority symbolizes the fate of a much larger community. The same community is also represented by another image: the yellow earth. As the female lead, Cuiqiao is both the most expressive and the emptiest signifier in the film: expressive because not only does she offer a timeless image of the Chinese woman but she also symbolizes a predominately male community; empty because she has to forgo her subjective position to represent this community.

NEGATIVE UTOPIANISM

In *The Geopolitical Aesthetic,* Fredric Jameson recognizes the significant differences of cinematic spaces in the films of the Chinese Fifth Generation and Taiwan or Hong Kong New Cinema.[19] In his more recent book *Seeds of Time,* he also modifies his previous division of the three worlds while discussing a Russian novel.

We will begin to discover, indeed we are already doing so, that people formed in a nonmarket non-consumer-consumptive society do not think like we do. Indeed, if we resist the temptation (now everywhere resurgent) to attribute such differences to the old stereotypes of nationalism and ethnic peculiarity – here the differences in some properly Slavic *Weltanschauung* – we may well even discover the rudiments and the nascent forms of a new form of socialist culture that is utterly unlike "socialist realism" and intimates some far future of human history the rest of us are not in a position to anticipate.[20]

Jameson defines this socialist culture in terms of negative-utopian or anti-utopian elements. According to his analysis of a Russian novel on a peasant utopia, *Chevengur,* written by Andrei Platonov in 1927–8, these elements are manifested by a rhetorical feature that is highly indeterminate – irony.[21] To a large extent, Chen Kaige's early films, especially *Yellow Earth* and *Big Parade,* present certain similarities to this Russian novel. The ambiguity toward utopia results from the conflicts between Chen's residual idealism, on the one hand, and his deep disillusion with collective belief caused by the destructive power of the Cultural Revolution on the other. However, the preoccupation with utopianism not simply as a fantasy space but as part of daily reality is not necessarily an exclusive property of intellectuals from various socialist cultures. During wartime, the scarcity of consumer goods temporarily put industrialized countries in proximity to the so-called third world. The need to confront common enemies in everyday life also contributed to the formation of a collective entity among radical intellectuals in postwar Europe. This similarity may partly explain the impact of postwar European filmmakers on Chen, who claims that Chinese filmmakers of his generation share common ground with postwar European directors.

Millicent Marcus comments on *The Bicycle Thief,* Vittorio De Sica's Italian neorealist masterpiece:

The demise of postwar idealism and the egocentricity of a population beset with shortages have changed Rossellini's collectivity into an angry, unwelcoming mob. But perhaps the most striking measure of the distance separating *Open City* and *Bicycle Thief* is De Sica's rejection of Rossellini's synthesizing conclusion. Where narrative events pointed ahead to the political and spiritual fulfillments of Rossellini's Christian–Marxist typology, De Sica's various semantic levels sharply diverge at his film's termination. The narrative remains inconclusive while the sociopolitical and philosophical levels reach the dead end to which the film's pessimism invariably leads.[22]

The same comments can be made on Chen's early films, where formal experiments become the means of expressing anger and frustration toward a collective belief, because Chen himself was an embittered witness of the disappearance of this collectivity. In *Yellow Earth,* his first film, cinematic experiments reinforce the multilayered ambiguity or irony toward Yan'an, portrayed as a utopia or fantasy space in the collective imaginary of peasants – as indicated by the happiest and most dynamic scene of the film, waist-drum dancing.

In the opening sequence, the beautifully written screen title summarizes the allegedly historical background of the film by emphasizing its sources: "Shaan-Gan-Ning base area [*genju di*]." This base appears only once throughout the entire film, in the scene of waist-drum dancing – right after the frightening scene of Cuiqiao's wedding night. This euphoric dancing scene is isolated from the rest of the film. Diegetically, it is justified only by the brief appearance of Gu Qing as one of the spectators. Contrary to any other sequences except for that of the prayer for rain, this series is characterized by dynamic movements. Five hundred dancers look like a stormy ocean agitated by ceaseless and passionate waves, in which everyone and everything, onscreen or offscreen, seems to participate, including the spectators, the sun, the land, the camera, and the entire team.[23] This scene forms a striking contrast with the previous shot of Cuiqiao's wedding night – the oppressive atmosphere, lifeless room, the ghostly black hand, and Cuiqiao's indescribable fear of the invisible husband. In an interview, Chen describes the exuberant scene of waist-drum dancing as "hyperbolic," "allegorical," and "symbolic." Interestingly, this happy location was so indefinable that Chen was forced to add a subtitle – "Yan'an" – to avoid censorship, following the advice of some well-intended colleagues.[24] The need to specify the location precisely indicates its indeterminacy. This scene is less realistic than fantastic – a utopian space. Fredric Jameson writes:

> The truth value of fantasy, the epistemological *bon usage* or proper use of daydreaming as an instrument of philosophical speculation, lies precisely in a confrontation with the reality principle itself. The daydream can succeed as a narrative, not by successfully eluding or outwitting the reality principle but rather by grappling with it, like Jacob's angel, and by triumphantly wresting from it what can precisely in our or its own time be dreamt and fantasied as such.[25]

The contrast between the desperate situation of Cuiqiao's marriage and the seemingly boundless happiness of waist-drum dancing creates the impression that this fantasy place vaguely defined as Yan'an is the only thing the suffering peasants like Cuiqiao may in their daydreams "wrest from the reality principle." However, this daydream cannot completely "succeed as a narrative," since the isolated scene of waist-drum dancing is not a narrative component but a fragment of an unachieved and unachievable narrative – that of communist salvation. An unbridgeable gap between the suffering peasant girl and the exuberant fantasy space fragments this ideological tale. Gu Qing's arrival and his descriptions of Yan'an life, whose positive effect is reinforced by some concrete details in his life-style, such as sewing, ploughing, and teaching Hanhan to sing, offer the only point of departure from which a peasant girl like Cuiqiao can dream of possible enhancement in her future life – just as new revolutionary lyrics appeal to peasants' sensitivity through their associations with familiar folk-song music. By ordering Eighth Route Army artists to create revolutionary lyrics on the basis of folk-song music, Chairman Mao and his party shrewdly tried to occupy the peasants' fantasy space with the reinvented revolutionary dream. This strategy may partly explain the victory of the Communist Party in China, because hope for realizing their dreams for a better life propelled a great number of peasants to participate in the Communist Revolution. Like the soldier in the film, the party failed to deliver on its promise to peasants, who helped it gain political power.

Peasants like Cuiqiao's father call folk songs "sour tunes" (*suanqu*), which means lyrics sung in the Shaanbei dialect. *Suan* (sour) can also be interpreted as sad. When Gu Qing asks the father how he could remember so many "sour tunes," the father responds: "If life is difficult, you will remember" (*rizi jiannan le jiu jixia le*). Folk songs in this case become metonyms of peasants' suffering. Can the old lyrics of suffering turn into the new lyrics of liberation? Is the new language able to change the peasants' fate, which has remained virtually unchanged for thousands of years of Chinese history? The only song with new lyrics is taught by Gu Qing to Cuiqiao's usually speechless brother, Hanhan. Just as the scene of waist-drum dancing is the only truly exuberant scene in the film, so Gu's revolutionary lyric is the only happy and self-confident song among many folk tunes in the film:

> Sickle, axe, and old cutter
> Opening a new road for workers and peasants
> Spotted cock stands on the wall
> All people's salvation must rely on the Communist Party

After listening to this song, Cuiqiao, like the peasants in the waist-drum dance, is exuberant. She runs as fast as possible with two heavy buckets of water – completely forgetting her worry and fear. Once she has reached her father's cave, she sees wedding gifts brought by the matchmaker – a reminder of her inescapable fate. A long take shows the dramatic change in her face: A bright smile freezes into an expression of indescribable fear, while the bright sunlight a moment ago fades in the darkness of the cave. As a result, the happy song only temporarily opens a fantasy space, whereas the dark and frightening reality she faces in the cave is unchanged and unchangeable, despite the beautiful but empty promise of the revolutionary song and its singer. The basic tone remains invariably "sour" and "sad" (*suan*) for the peasants' community.

Furthermore, even Gu Qing's new lyric is not necessarily so new. In the concluding sequence of prayer for rain, thousands of peasants repeat the same expression – "saving all people" (*jiu wanmin*) – only this time they address the dragon king instead of the Communist Party. Hanhan and Cuiqiao are the only ones able and willing to learn Gu's song, whereas numerous peasants keep their faith in the statue of the dragon king. In the final scene of prayer for rain, Gu Qing appears on a hill – as the symbol of the Communist Revolution in opposition to the dragon king. Everyone follows the statue of the dragon king, except for the young Hanhan, who runs against the crowd and toward his "elder brother" Gu. The slow motion makes him look even younger in the childish red dress sewn by his sister before her death. In contrast to the numberless naked chests of adult male peasants, the child appears so fragile, as if he were on the verge of being stepped on by those zealot peasants. Esther Yau writes:

When conventional meaning in that society has been fragmented and questioned within the text, Hanhan (as a textual figure) functions as the desire for meaning. One may venture to say Hanhan is the signifier of that meaning – an insight for history and culture with an urge for change, portrayed as a childish moment before inscription, before meaning is fixed at the level of the political and agrarian institutions. Therefore the silent, blank face, because to speak, to have a facial expression, is to signify, to politicize.[26]

This desire for meaning, this blank signifier, is necessarily fragile and isolated – as shown in the last shots. From the retrospective perspective of Chen and his generation, this so-called new meaning has already been seized by their fathers' generation, by means of the Communist Revolution. Unfortunately for them, it is not only empty but also destructive. The film concludes with Cuiqiao's off-screen voice, her song before she is drowned in the Yellow River. Since she does not have time to finish the last syllable of the lyrics, "All people's salvation must rely on the Communist Party," "Communist" (*gongchan*) without "Party" (*dang*) becomes a floating signifier. For example, the same word has been used by the Nationalist Party to accuse the communists of being the devils who force people to share their property and wives. The laudatory song for the party has become open-ended, which is doubly ironic. First, it again reminds the audience of the commonality between the dragon king, icon of the tradition, and the Communist Party, represented by the soldier. They are old and new dreams for poor peasants suffering from natural and human disasters. Second, people's salvation by the party is as hopeless as salvation by means of the dragon king – to which Cuiqiao's death attests. The future of China was represented by her childish brother, who welcomes the soldier as the "true savior" in the last sequence. How can we prevent this representative of the future from following in Cuiqiao's footsteps, namely, being drowned in the Yellow River while singing the laudatory song for the party? If Hanhan's last image represents a possibility for a new meaning, this meaning is definitively utopian in a Jamesonian sense:

Perhaps in a more Western kind of psychoanalytic language – with specific reference to the origins of Freudianism in hysteria – we might think of the new onset of the Utopian process as a kind of desiring to desire, a learning to desire, the invention of the desire called Utopia in the first place, along with new rules for the fantasizing or daydreaming of such a thing – a set of narrative protocols with no precedent in our previous literary institutions (even if they will have to come to terms somehow with our previous literary or narrative habits).[27]

This "new onset of the Utopian process" has motivated Chen and some of his classmates to experiment with "a set of narrative [filmic] protocols with no precedent in our previous [film] institutions (even if they will have to come to terms somehow with our previous [cinematic] or narrative habits)" – to paraphrase Jameson.

BIG PARADE

INDIVIDUALS IN RELATION TO THE DOMINANT FICTION

Chen Kaige's second film, *Big Parade* (*Da yuebing*), focuses on a group of soldiers who undergo a rigorous training program in a remote place for one year, in order to prepare them to perform flawlessly a drill routine of ninety-six steps in Tian'anmen Square during the national day parade. Supposedly, soldiers selected for this program are the best from various military units. Furthermore, in the course of training, those who do not perform perfectly will be eliminated, one after another. Although perfection in this case means to create an absolutely homogeneous appearance, soldiers have different personal interests in this game and adopt different attitudes accordingly. The only high-school graduate, Lü Chun, is openly critical of the parade as an empty political ritual. Li Weicheng, who is older than any soldier in the team, hides his fainting spells, hoping to grasp his last chance at promotion by participating in the parade. Section chief Jiang ties his bowlegs every night in order to avoid the unavoidable – his elimination from the team. The film shows how their individual needs are repressed and ignored, if not crushed, in the process of this collective training. By the end of the training, many soldiers have been eliminated from the final parade team, including Li and Jiang. The eliminated soldiers have suffered almost as much as the others, but without obtaining the promotions and honor granted to participants in the actual parade. However, at the suggestion of Commander Sun [Fig. 2], the leader of the training team, the names of those who left the training ground before the final stage are the first to be recorded on the flag of their regiment.

The prologue comprises a single lengthy helicopter shot, dollying through seemingly endless groups of soldiers who form clear-cut geometric lines on the immense training ground. This shot is introduced by a brief trumpet sound and accompanied by the monotonous rhythm of amplified footsteps. In this shot, each body is indistinguishable from thousands of others. The opening sequence, however, offers a different picture. The camera approaches the fragmented images of soldiers' bodies gradually, progressing from extreme long shots to long shots, to medium shots, to close-ups. The closer the images of individual bodies, the less sustainable the impression of the totality created by the crane shot in the prologue. The legs, arms, and bodies are carefully measured by the hands of mostly invisible army medical personal. In the following scene, every soldier receives a mandatory haircut – apparently in order to look identical to all the others. However, even in this small incident, rules are not necessarily respected. Liu Guoqiang, the young teenager from the South, hands a cigarette to the barber. The barber immediately understood his intention: "You *also* want to have longer hair!" Indeed, numerous cigarettes on his table prove that many other soldiers share Liu's desire to keep their look a little more individualistic – by convincing the army barber to alter the rule slightly, with the help of one or two cigarettes.

In front of well-arranged trucks, Commander Sun, who is also the teacher of the training team, briefly addresses his soldiers: "The significance of this training has already been explained by the leader. Thus, I won't repeat." What is this self-evident significance? No one seems to know the exact answer. However, a rhetorical question asked in a meeting by Lü Chun, the straightforward high-school graduate, seems to suggest a tentative answer: "Now, what period is this? Do you think that parade will warm up people's blood?" In other words, the party uses the parade with the futile intent of salvaging the dominant fiction by re-creating a symbolic image of people's unity under the party's flag, since its collective ide-

2. Commander Sun in *Big Parade,* directed by Chen Kaige (1986). COURTESY OF THE MU-
SEUM OF MODERN ART.

ology no longer "warms people's blood" during the 1980s. As Kaja Silverman
explains in her *Male Subjectivity at the Margins,* the dominant fiction, which
fetishistically equates phallus with penis, is the ideological basis of the symbolic
order in a patriarchal society.[28] Soldiers, as "manly men" (*nanzi han*) or as
"screws of the revolutionary machine" – to use a common expression in socialist China – are equivalent as basic elements in this rewriting of the dominant fiction. Several times in the film, "manly men" is used by various soldiers to refer
to themselves, as if it were the highest standard by which to judge individual
worth. To this extent, their manhood is related to their possible participation in
the parade, or determined by the approval of the dominant fiction. In one case,
a soldier's participation in the parade has even become the prerequisite for mar-
rying his sweetheart – a precondition imposed by his potential father-in-law. The
very fact that the significance of the training does not need to be explained grants
it authority, because authority requires only obedience but not understanding –
as Žižek points out.[29] The dominant fiction, in order to remain efficient, must not
be analyzed. However, as if to answer the unanswered question in Sun's speech,
the film itself is a process of analyzing its significance. By fragmenting and in-
dividualizing the apparently impeccably unified training team, Chen's film deconstructs this fiction.

Silverman writes:

We must remember that although the symbolic order determines to a significant degree the form which the dominant fiction can take, its survival is nevertheless keyed
to that ideological system, which depends in turn upon collective belief. A given symbolic order will remain in place only so long as it has subjects, but it cannot by itself
produce them. It relies for that purpose upon the dominant fiction, which works to
bring the subject into conformity with the symbolic order by fostering normative desires and identifications. When the dominant fiction fails to effect this interpellation,
it is not only "reality" but the symbolic order itself which is placed at risk.[30]

The big parade in Chen's movie can be considered a portrayal of the party's
attempt to re-create the dominant fiction in order to regain public confidence,
or "collective belief," in the party in postsocialist China. Is this attempt successful? More important, how do various subjects establish their relationships with
the dominant fiction by means of their participation in its symbolic reconstitution?

The film presents soldiers mainly at three different levels. First, on the training ground soldiers seemingly form a unified and homogeneous collectivity.
Viewed from a distance, hundreds of soldiers often seem an indistinguishable
entity. Second, in their barracks off-duty soldiers joke with each other, talk to
each other, or often take showers together. In comparison with shots on the training ground, these pictures, mostly in medium shots, emphasize individual differences. Furthermore, a soldier's individuality is often marked by a physical deficiency: for example, Hao Xiaoyuan's stutter and Jiang Zhenbiao's bowlegs.
Third, the use of several disembodied voices, Lü Chun's, Commander Sun's, and
Li Weicheng's, creates a space for their subjective positions. From three perspectives, they all to different degrees question the significance of the big parade
as well as their own public stances vis-à-vis the training. Unlike the physical deficiencies that single out some soldiers' objectified differences, these subjective
voices mostly distinguish the better-educated or more mature individuals from
the crowd.

Either objectively or subjectively, these individuals gain subjectivity through
their negative relations with the dominant fiction. In Žižekian words, a subject
comes into being through failures of subjectivization. These men are individualized because they fail to dovetail with the images of them projected by the dominant fiction, and to occupy the positions assigned to them in the chain of the
symbolic order. In other words, these subjects play important roles in the constitution of the dominant fiction as supporters of the symbolic order by disrupting
the same order. By means of intellectual skepticism or physical deficiencies,
these individual soldiers disrupt and at the same time help to defend the dominant fiction based on the myth of a unified nation under the party's flag as a
homogeneous collectivity, an impression that the future parade will supposedly
be able to re-create and reinforce.

Lü Chun is the first individual who speaks in a disembodied voice. He is also the only one who openly questions the meaning of the parade. During the first training day, he is singled out by Commander Sun for keeping a Walkman in his pocket. Ordered to return it to the dormitory, he makes a detour to the post office and inquires about a letter from the military school, instead of running back to the training ground immediately. After receiving his punishment from Sun – repeating the same physically demanding and monotonous movement thousands of times – Lü's disembodied voice criticizes the leader's training method. At the same time, Lü is also the only one who expresses explicit desire to leave the training ground, first in his voice-over, then in his public speech, by telling his leader that the only reason for him to stay in the army is to enter military school, since he failed the civil entrance examination for colleges.

In his quarrel with Commander Sun in a group meeting, after drawing a gloomy picture of the training ground, Lü's voice fades away, submerged by incomprehensible noises in the sound track. Then, a tracking shot sweeps the expressionless faces of his fellow soldiers. His last distinctive sentence is a rhetorical question: "Do you think that a parade will warm up people's blood?" This question is followed by Sun's voice-over: "As an educated soldier myself, when did I start to believe that I should be stricter with educated soldiers?" In other words, the commander of the team himself identifies with the rebellious soldier through their shared higher level of education. This male bonding also works in the opposite direction: Regardless of his skepticism toward the party's ideology, Lü cannot resist a more deeply rooted and much older human desire, the desire to be accepted as part of the group. As a result, he must stay with his fellow soldiers on the training ground despite the misgivings expressed by his individual voice.

To an extent, Lü's position is like that of Gu Qing's in *Yellow Earth* – he is a more educated outsider who critically judges the community based on his knowledge of the outside world. His skepticism is part of his educational package. Other soldiers, such as the loyal Section Chief Jiang, cannot even imagine what Beijing, the sacred city, looks like, whereas in Lü's disabused eyes anything unrelated to his own educational opportunity seems meaningless. To a lesser degree than in *Yellow Earth,* this slightly privileged outsider also partially exemplifies the directorial point of view in its ambiguous relationship with the dominant fiction. Despite himself, this outsider is also an active participant in the collective attempt to re-create the dominant fiction. Chen in his autobiography describes his own generation in relation to the Cultural Revolution:

Generally speaking, these youngsters were somewhat educated. The conflicts between their educational backgrounds and insignificant social positions, between their passionate dreams and the cold reality of the countryside, put them psychologically off balance. In addition, numerous vicissitudes in their lives and physically demanding farming work made them the angriest and most thoughtful generation of modern

China. They want changes and are able to face changes. As a result, they can be entrusted with the future. On the surface, it looks fairly promising. In reality, they have not brought substantial changes for the nation for several reasons. First, despite the size of the spatial and temporary exodus of a generation, the Cultural Revolution (which sent almost all the high-school-aged citizens to the countryside) did not search for culturally positive or progressive meanings. Second, even if this generation gained experiences by their sweat, blood, and youth, these experiences still belonged to an agricultural society. As a result, no true progress has been made. The source of their creativity is limited within a well-confined world of the self in the absence of any communication or comparison with the outside world. Probably for this reason, human suffering only produced another generation of much more enduring peasants.[31]

Like Chen Kaige himself, Gu Qing and Lü Chun can both be perceived as belonging to this generation of "much more enduring peasants." In other words, they are outsiders to a small confined community but insiders of a much larger confined community, namely, China. Despite their critical attitude toward the dominant ideology, their angry reflections on Chinese society and their own positions in this society are in the final analysis impotent, since they are intricately related to the dominant fiction – even if in a negative way. In Chen's films, male subjects, be they angry critics like Lü Chun or determined leaders like Commander Sun, are often as "impotent" as the dominant fiction, in which each of them is a willing or reluctant participant. Their anger partly expresses the frustration caused by their unwanted tie with a defective patriarchal order. At the same time, participation in their "impotent" mission is also the only way for them to stay in a cultural center. This self-contradictory desire to be a radical critic of the dominant fiction without losing his central position in the cultural space may partly explain Chen's pessimistic vision of culture. At the same time, this also marks the limits of his transgression.

In contrast to Lü Chun, Commander Sun offers a positive identification with the dominant fiction. As the organizer and orchestrator of the training program, he is the center of the training ground. Paradoxically, his voice is so like that of the rebellious soldier, Lü Chun, that sometimes it is initially difficult to distinguish between their voice-overs. As Sun mentions in a disembodied voice, he, like Lü, is an "educated soldier" (*xuesheng bing*). Three times in his private room, the commander listens to Western classical music – a trademark that contradicts his apparently unshakable revolutionary purity. Similarly, Lü has been secretly studying English with his Walkman. In both cases radios connect them to the West, representing individualism and modernity on this remote Chinese collective training ground.

Sun's relationship with Jiang Zhenbiao, the section chief, is at least ambiguous. Jiang had saved the commander's life on the battlefield, and Sun, to express his gratitude, initially lets Jiang pass the examination, despite the latter's obvious physical inadequacy – his bowlegs. During the last round of selection, Sun is finally forced to eliminate Jiang. His two contradictory decisions have made Jiang suffer almost the complete process of training in vain, without the benefit of participation in the final political ritual. If Sun identifies with Lü at an intellectual level by secretly questioning the dominant fiction that he himself supposedly personifies through his role as the leader of the training program, his relationship with Jiang is at a much more physical level. When Jiang found Sun gravely wounded in a pile of dead bodies on a battlefield, he carried his future leader on his back. The half-conscious Sun's unbearable pain made him bite Jiang's shoulder until it bled. This detail suggests a certain erotic implication in their relationship, which is further reinforced by two bathing scenes in Sun's bedroom. In the first scene, Sun offers to wash Jiang's back. They are both half-naked, and Jiang asks Sun, "What does Beijing look like?" Sun stops washing his friend, who after a while asks another question: "Would I be able to go to Beijing?" Obviously moved and disturbed, Sun hides his face by continuing to wash Jiang's back and answers "yes" while nodding his head forcefully – an implicit promise of Jiang's participation in the final parade, one that he fails to deliver in the end. In the second scene, after learning from Lü Chun how Jiang tied his bowlegs during the night in order to straighten them, Sun washes his legs with obviously strong emotions. A tilt from a close-up of Jiang's wounded bowlegs to a high-angle shot of Sun's emotional face near the legs intensifies erotic tension between the leader and the man who saved his life. During these two intimate scenes between Sun and Jiang, the radio in Sun's room plays cozy Western classical music. In the austere context of a Chinese military camp, Western music, which connotes "petit-bourgeois sentimentalism" (*xiao zichanjieji qingdiao*), contributes further to providing a romantic outlook to their relationship.

Apparently, Sun is an impeccable leader of the training ground, strict, cold, and determined – "as if he did not know how to smile," Lü's voice-over comments. On the one hand, at a superficial level, he identifies with the dominant fiction as a responsible guardian of the parade's success. On the other, he also gains his subjective voice through a negative relationship with this fiction at both intellectual and physical levels. Through his voice-over, Sun joins Lü as a critic of his own ideological belief. When Hao Xiaoyuan, the young peasant, refuses to attend his mother's funeral in order to stay on the training ground, Sun's disembodied voice questions the meaning of this loyalty, since "a person can have only one mother." At this point, his disembodied voice literally identifies him with Lü Chun's humanistic perspective.

In his farewell speech, Jiang passionately defends Sun's drastic training style. According to Jiang, since in the past Sun's insignificant gesture of lighting a cigarette in an ambush attracted enemies' artillery shells and caused the death of a great number of his fellow soldiers on the battlefield, Sun has decided to become a teacher in order to eliminate even the slightest undisciplined gesture on the part of less experienced junior soldiers in the future. In other words, he wants to teach them not to commit the same mistake as he did, in order to prevent future loss.

As a result, his initial identification with the dominant fiction is also based on a negative feeling of loss – he wants to negate his own past.

Unlike Lü Chun or Sun, Li Weicheng, chief of the detachment, is less educated: "I didn't spend much time in school, and did not have any chance to participate in the war" either, as he explains to Lü. This also means that he has hardly any chance to become an officer. Consequently, participation in the parade means even more to him than to his fellow soldiers: This will be his last opportunity for promotion. As at the age of thirty-five he is considerably older than his fellow soldiers, who are mostly in their teens or early twenties; Li is no longer as naïve and idealistic as Section Chief Jiang, whose highest hope is to see Beijing with his own eyes, or Hao Xiaoyuan, who wants to perform the national day parade on television for his dead mother. His goal is unequivocally practical: to grasp his last chance at promotion, even if this means cheating the leadership by hiding his illness. Partly due to his greater maturity in age, Li always behaves compassionately toward other soldiers. Unlike Lü Chun, he never explicitly criticizes the dominant ideology; but unlike Jiang and Hao, he never fully embraces the dominant fiction either. A wise resignation is probably the only definable trademark of his personality, which makes him respected by soldiers as well as by the commander. However, his personality is also determined by negative qualities in relation to the dominant fiction at the physical and ideological levels.

At the physical level, as the oldest soldier, his fainting spell is the only deficiency that could ruin the carefully prepared parade. At the ideological level, he is the only deliberate cheater. As he mentions to Lü, if he fainted in the bathroom a moment ago, he may also faint on Tian'anmen Square during the parade. Still, since it is his last chance for promotion, he prefers to take this risk. Knowingly he chooses his personal interests over the party's. Like Lü Chun's rebellious position and Sun's sense of irretrievable loss, Li's choice of betrayal provides him with a disembodied voice through a negative channel. It also enables him to act as a spokesman for all the soldiers near the end of the film, because he heroically subordinates his personal interests to the group's.

His emotional farewell speech also approaches the topic of the parade mainly negatively. It starts with a widely circulated Chinese proverb: "Good people do not become soldiers; good iron is not used for making nails" (*haoren bu dangbing, haotie bu dading*). As the end of Li Weicheng's speech, this proverb that negates any positive quality of soldiers is also negated by the speaker, who as a soldier himself represents everyone on the training ground at this moment: "Thus, I speak: Only good people do become soldiers." During his lengthy speech, soldiers' "goodness" is also proven negatively – examples of soldiers' suffering are given, such as physical pain caused by swelling legs; material losses are invoked, such as the tons of shoe nails used up on the training ground. Furthermore, unknown to his audience, this spokesman of all the soldiers on the training ground is himself excluded from the parade, since Li is on the verge of leaving his team. In this sense, Li himself exemplifies the negative logic that permeates his farewell speech – while negating, as well as being negated by, the dominant fiction. In his final letter of withdrawal, Li writes: "If I did not withdraw, I would not have considered myself as having truly participated in the big parade." Consequently, even his participation is negative. In the penultimate scene, the name of each absent soldier who was forced to leave the team in the process of training is written on the flag as a true hero of this mission. Furthermore, the film was originally supposed to end in a total negation of the political ritual, the parade. The concluding sequence, which had to be changed due to political censorship, was originally a long take of the empty Tian'anmen Square with a rising national flag, associated with footsteps on the sound track.

RESISTANCE AS A FORM OF PARTICIPATION

Although every individual in the film gains a subjective voice by assuming some negative relationship to the dominant fiction, this negativity is canceled out by each soldier's willing participation in the apparently empty political ritual, which aims at a reconstitution of this fiction. Paradoxically, instead of weakening the dominant fiction, the ambiguously negative relationship between the subject positions and the dominant ideology serves as a basis for a revival of the dominant fiction.

Žižek writes:

More to the point, this inner distance of the subject towards the totalitarian discourse, far from enabling the subject to elude the madness of the totalitarian ideological spectacle, is the very factor on account of which the subject is effectively mad. Now and then, Adorno himself has a presentiment of it – as, for example, when he implies that the subject "beneath the mask" who "feigns" his captivation must already be "mad," "hollow." It is in order to escape this void that the subject is condemned to take refuge in the ceaseless ideological spectacle – if the "show" were to stop for a moment, his entire universe would disintegrate. . . . In other words, madness does not turn on effectively believing in the Jewish plot, in the charisma of the Leader, and so on – such beliefs (in so far as they are repressed, that is, the unacknowledged fantasy-support of our universe of signification) form a constituent part of our ideological normality. Madness, however, emerges in the *absence* of such engaging beliefs, in the fact that "in the depth of their hearts, people *do not* believe that the Jews are the devil." In short, madness emerges through the subject's simulation and external imitation of such beliefs; it thrives in that inner distance maintained towards the ideological discourse which constitutes the subject's social symbolic network.[32]

This "automatic" participation in the political ritual, frequent in a totalitarian system, is far more dangerous and powerful than a movement based on subjects' deliberate choices, since the acknowledged inner distance between the subject and ideological discourse is the basis for the subject's renunciation of any reasoning and individual responsibility. Thus, "social Law assumes the features of a superego injunction," which means it is senseless, incomprehensible, and incommensurable with "the psychological wealth of the subject's affective attitude."[33] The superego directly appeals to "the subject's most intimate kernel of his being," to "enjoy." This externalization enables the subject to renounce the mediating function of this ego between the superego and id. Thus, the subject seriously participates in political rituals whose ideological basis the subject takes as a pure signifier, and not as an object of belief. This "simulation" that removes any psychological tie between the dominant fiction and the subject is more powerful than an act of faith, since any individual barrier or resistance against the superego is silenced and eliminated by the death of the ego. Following the same logic, the negation of each individual in regard to the dominant fiction does not diminish that fiction's power. On the contrary, it results only in a negation of the individual's own ego.

To a large extent, the Cultural Revolution can be considered a logical outcome of this faithless participation of millions of Chinese people, like the soldiers preparing for the empty ritual, the big parade, on the training ground in Chen's film. Their doubts about the meaning of such a parade lead toward the negation of their egos to the point that they give up any reasoning by subjecting themselves to a maddening logic of total negation, including the negation of the self. This logic is initially generated by the training program for the parade, which tends to negate any individual difference in order to achieve a fictive image of totality. Instead of reconfirming their individuality, the disembodied voices finally internalize the same logic by negating their own initially ambiguously negative positions in relation to the dominant fiction.

KING OF THE CHILDREN

BREAKING THE CINEMATIC (OR CULTURAL) FRAME

King of the Children (*Haizi wang*) is Chen Kaige's third film. Partly because of his new cameraman, Gu Changwei (the cameraman of his previous two films, Zhang Yimou, had become a director himself), certain cinematographic changes occurred. The camerawork is marked with long shots and extreme long shots, as well as an extensive use of natural light. Although Chen had usually paid special attention to manipulation of the sound track in his previous works, this film in particular uses sound track to create offscreen spaces at both the diegetic and conceptual levels. Some critics, such as Peng Xing'er, paid attention to another highly self-conscious feature in this film, manipulation of the frame.[34] In his interviews after *King of the Children*'s release, Chen equates the cinematic frame in this film with cultural restriction. According to his explanation, Chinese culture limits individual freedom, not only objectively but also subjectively, since individuals to different degrees internalize the cultural frame.

The screenplay is roughly based on a 1985 novella of the same title by a well-known writer of Chen's generation, Acheng. An "educated youth" (*zhishi qingnian*)[35] nicknamed Laogan'er ("old stick") for his thinness, who has been working as a farmer in the Yunnan border region for seven years, receives an assignment to teach in a county school – a job that releases him from everyday physical labor. Although, like most Chinese youth of his generation, he himself has not finished high school, Laogan'er is assigned to teach the upper level of junior high students. As in most educational districts during the Cultural Revolution, the school is completely in shambles. After he has started the first class, he suddenly realizes that his students do not even have textbooks. Laogan'er also learns from his student Wang Fu, who later becomes his favorite pupil, that a teacher's task in this class consists mainly of copying texts from a worn-out textbook to the blackboard. Then, students will copy the same text into their notebooks. After dutifully following this rule for a while, Laogan'er realizes that most students do not even understand what they are copying. In fact, they do not even know how to read or write at a basic level. Moreover, the textbook is saturated with useless revolutionary slogans that have little to do with students' everyday lives. As a result, Laogan'er decides to get rid of this official teaching method and focuses on teaching students how to express themselves through writing. At the end of three months, his students's writing skills indeed improve a great deal. However, his transgression of the official teaching method is reported to his superiors and perceived as politically subversive. As a result, the school fires him and sends him back to his old production team. Before his departure, Laogan'er leaves his dictionary to his favorite student, Wang Fu, who had been copying it every evening after school. On the dictionary he writes, "Do not copy anymore – not even the dictionary," as a testament for all his former students.

In Chen's film, constant use of long shots (almost 50 percent of the shots)[36] not only creates an impression that the camera eye is only a distant observer but also provides a certain freedom for people to escape the camera frame. In addition, the film rarely uses eye-line matching for conversations among adults. The speakers are often offscreen. If they are onscreen, the distance and the usually dim natural light (there is a minimum use of artificial lighting) make them appear less visible and definable. The first conversation between the team leader and Laogan'er, the protagonist, occurs in the "educated youth"'s dark dormitory. The team leader is outside the threshold, verging on the right border of the frame, whereas the protagonist sits quietly in the dark room on the left side. At the same time, the leader's voice indicates his offscreen presence, which is also suggested by his shadow, blocking part of the outdoor sunlight. In this scene, the certificate of the teaching assignment casually passed to Laogan'er by his boss puts him into a preconceived cultural frame – that of a schoolteacher – as a master who passes (cultural) knowledge to children.

Once in the school, although he is often shown doubly framed by windows and doors, either in his dormitory or in his classroom, Laogan'er becomes less constrained in his movements in front of his new boss, the principal Chen. His room in the school literally has three "frames": two windows and a door in which Laogan'er often situates himself, as if posing for a photo. A repeated image shows Laogan'er's face framed by the small window of his dormitory. Close-ups of this image look like an identity photo. In this image, he usually observes destructive acts: human acts destructive of the natural world (a forest fire) or cultural acts destructive of human nature (Wang Fu's copying of the dictionary). The film seems to evoke the feeling that various representatives of the Communist Party are less effectively oppressive, despite their power of punishment, than the invisible cultural frame. The protagonist can free himself to some degree from political restraints by refusing to follow official rules. It is more difficult, however, if not impossible, to free himself from the oppressive culture, because the invisible frame is internalized as part of the protagonist's psychological makeup, despite his rebellion against both political and cultural authorities.

On the one hand, the protagonist tries to escape the control of the frame by speaking from offscreen spaces. In order to avoid being identified with the frame, whenever he tries to establish some rules for his students in the classroom, Laogan'er shies away from the camera, apparently speaking from an invisible locus – outside the cultural frame. At the same time, he cannot escape the frame because even his room serves as a frame within a frame, which locates him within not only the cinematic frame but also the window or door frame of his small room. Laogan'er's onscreen activities often appear aimless and bored. One night, in the dim candlelight, he is reading the dictionary, doubly framed by the screen and his window. A close-up of his face by the window, lit by weak candlelight, is accompanied by ghostly voices reciting Chinese classics in a hellish atmosphere.

Before returning to his production team, Laogan'er visits the principal in his office in order to obtain his dismissal order. This scene is a reversal of the opening scene. This time, Laogan'er is on the threshold, thus inside but also outside the frame. By positioning himself somewhat out of the frame, the protagonist gains a greater degree of symbolic freedom. Earlier, the principal had suggested that he copy the official guidelines on how to teach the Chinese textbook. Instead of complying, Laogan'er visits his production team immediately after turning down this suggestion. The school as the place to pass on cultural knowledge imposes the cultural frame. The team where the "educated youth" remain closer to nature, by contrast, is associated with a degree of freedom. In this sense, for Laogan'er, returning to the team is also regaining his lost freedom by breaking away from the cultural frame imposed by his teaching position. As a result, he welcomes this decision, despite having to return to physically demanding labor. During his final encounter with the principal, Laogan'er's active role is reinforced further. Before leaving the school, he asks the principal for permission to keep the last compositions of his students. The principal, surprised by such a simple request, repeats his favorite cliché after praising Laogan'er's resignation: "Making trouble does not lead to a good end." Laogan'er interrupts his sentence with a sudden laugh. Visibly embarrassed, the principal stops and hesitantly asks Laogan'er, with a shy smile, as if he were a schoolboy unsure of his answer, "What? Isn't this correct?" The protagonist responds, "Yes, it's correct." This rare series of shot–reverse shots between two adult interlocutors portrays Principal Chen as a hesitant student caught in some mistake, and Laogan'er as a self-assured teacher who ironically and condescendingly gives the principal the answer he desperately needs.

As a result, his relationship with the authorities has been completely reversed. In the opening sequence, he receives his teaching assignment as an unexpected favor from the team leader, and allows the leader to put him within a cultural "frame" – defined by his educational background. At the end, Laogan'er gracefully accepts the principal's decision to remove him from the school by putting his boss within a particular ideological framework – defined by his repeated use of political cliché.

COPYING AND REPEATING

In the prologue, an extreme long shot of the mountain path that leads to the school lasts for exactly one minute. During this minute, the camera does not move, but the lighting and colors change from morning light to sunset. As Chen explains, the camera was set on the same spot from 6:00 in the morning to 8:00 in the evening for this one shot.[37] As in Su Dongpo's "Chibi fu,"[38] this image creates the impression of changeability in nature, which signifies the unchangeable by dint of its regularly repeated changes. At the same time, the school is always there, without the slightest movement, as "the representative of the most decadent and tenacious part of Chinese culture."[39] The penultimate shot of the film returns to the same setting – the mountain path leading toward the school – during a forest fire, which creates a sense of repetition reinforced at different levels throughout the film.

The students copy the texts on the blackboard, copied by the teacher from a worn-out textbook. In this context, the official method of teaching itself is portrayed mainly as a constant act of copying, be it textbook or teaching guideline as in Acheng's original fiction. What is more disturbing in the film, however, is that the act of copying is not limited to a particular historical moment, namely, the Cultural Revolution – contrary to Acheng's assessment in his work. Chen deliberately integrates the act of copying into a larger picture of Chinese cultural history by denying the distinction of "good" and "bad" acts of copying, a distinction upheld in the novella. According to Chen, despite the party's claim to subvert traditional culture, the practice of copying prevailing during the Cultural Revolution is only another version of traditional Chinese culture. In the novella copying the dictionary is a laudatory act, since it marks a return to the "true meaning" of Chinese cultural tradition, whereas in the film copying politically overcharged propagandistic texts on the blackboard is in the final analysis not so different from copying the dictionary. Both acts are executed in the dim candlelight of the classroom, suggesting that these acts could only darken the perspective of the future generation. Chen's criticism of copying is a double-edged weapon; it deconstructs both the Communist Party's claim to have revolutionized China and the traditionally nationalist claim of Chinese culture's everlasting superiority, which was overshadowed only by alien elements brought by communist power.

When Laogan'er's students are copying the textbook, we hear a female teacher's voice-over, followed by her students, reading another text that is absurdly ideological. Similarly, when Laogan'er is reading his dictionary, a multitude of faceless voices are reading various Chinese classics in ghostly darkness. The two kinds of faceless voices resemble each other in that they are both reciting nonsense – be it communist or classical. Furthermore, when Laogan'er is reading the dictionary at night in the dim candlelight, his face is almost invisible. This darkness reminds us of the other scene where the classroom appears almost empty except for several dozen candles, and we hear the amplified sound of copying on the blackboard as well as in students' notebooks. Later, their faces faintly appear in candlelight. When Chen tells an interviewer that these candles represent children's eyes,[40] he obviously has in mind a proverb popular in China during his formative years: "Eyes are the window of the soul." The children's souls, represented by candlelight, are emptied by the act of copying, through which they lose their independent ways of thinking. The same statement can be made about their teacher in the nightly scene of dictionary reading: His face is lost in the darkness, as if his individuality were submerged by the multitude of anonymous voices that repeatedly recite texts from a timeless past. Burdened by the repeated act of copying, Laogan'er's subjecthood becomes a locus remapping various past texts, which he "copies" during all his life – voluntarily, or more often, unwillingly and unconsciously. As a result, copying becomes a vicious circle that no one, including Laogan'er himself, seems able to escape, despite his increasingly lucid awareness of its destructive function. Finally, his subversive act against the prevailing practice of copying cannot be free from the object of his subversion, since even in his subversion he is still copying – probably from a different textual source.

When his friends from the production team visit Laogan'er in his classroom, they invite him to perform as a teacher for them. By this moment, since he has successfully started communicating with his students, Laogan'er has abolished certain rules. First, he has asked his students not to stand up when the teacher enters the classroom. Second, he's told his students not to put their hands behind their backs. In other words, he has abolished useless rituals in the classroom that tend to restrict students' independence. For this mock class, however, Laogan'er demands that his friends stand up and put their hands behind their backs despite the change in his actual class. In other words, this mock class is intended to ridicule the conventional teaching method as an exaggerated counterexample for his own teaching. However, when he pretends to use a well-known cyclical children's rhyme as his teaching material – "Once upon a time, there is a mountain. In the mountain, there is a temple. In the temple, there is an old monk. The old monk is telling a story. What does he tell? Once upon a time, there is a mountain. . . ." – this cyclical story, familiar to almost all the Chinese of Chen's generation, is immediately repeated by his friends, while Laogan'er happily performs in front of the blackboard with dynamic gestures that contradict the protagonist's usual subdued acting style. A moment later, a group of his students who happen to be eavesdropping learn the cyclical tale and repeat it loudly while walking away from the school. As soon as he hears the children's recital, Laogan'er's face suddenly saddens. His mock class is initially an indirect attack against the official teaching method in his school, as if to suggest that the students learn nothing except a cyclical, meaningless, and useless tale in the official educational system. By ridiculing this practice, the protagonist positions himself as an outsider to the official teaching system. However, his students' voices, which echo his mocking tale, serve as a mirror. Does he change anything substantially by making some alternations to the conventional teaching method? Because his subjective world is to a large extent determined by what he has learned (or copied) consciously or unconsciously from thousands of years of a cultural tradition, he cannot truly become a cultural outsider. In this sense, the caricature becomes a snapshot of reality, a reality from which he himself as a teacher cannot escape.

This pessimistic vision of an endless vicious circle leads to a culturally nihilistic gesture at the end of the film. The area around the school path is burned in an annual fire (the seventh after Laogan'er's arrival in this region) following the party's order, because regional party leaders believe that one needs to burn useless trees in order to plant useful ones. In the sound track, we can hear a mixture of sounds: cowbells, students' play, tree cutting, and the adults' and the children's voices reciting the cyclical tale. The image of burning mountains gradually fades, while all these sounds disappear as if they were burned in the fire – except for the sound of cowbells, which accompanies the camera returning to the empty classroom. A close-up of a character written on the blackboard, which Laogan'er inadvertently invented, water + cow, catches the viewer's attention in the final shot [Fig. 3]. In other words, all these sounds represent parts of culture, which Chen would like to burn out in order to have a fresh start. Ironically, doing so unintentionally imitates the gesture of destroying a forest – a gesture he repeatedly condemns.

A pertinent question has been asked by Chen himself in his *Playboy* interview: How can one distinguish useful trees from useless ones?[41] Paraphrasing this question asked by Zhuangzi, the Taoist philosopher more than two thousand years ago, one may also ask: How can one distinguish a "good" new culture from a "bad" old one by assigning a discontinuity between the past and the future? Who may occupy the moral high ground in order to perform the function of a judge? The Communist Party did play the role of judge by trying to replace traditional Chinese culture with a mixture of Marxism and Mao's pragmatism; but history attests to its failure. Can one still find a new kind of judge outside the realm of culture, as Chen claims in this film?

OUTSIDE LANGUAGE AND CULTURE

In one scene, Laogan'er listlessly waves his half-empty sleeves under a tree while listening to a minority folk song, sung in a language that he does not understand. Like the Chinese character he inadvertently created – cow (*niu*) + water (*shui*) – this song, repeatedly heard throughout the film from offscreen, represents the possibility of creating a new culture. This new culture, of which the incomprehensible song and unreadable character are indexes, must be free of the cultural burdens accumulated in the course of five thousand years of Chinese civilization.

Gilles Deleuze's explanation of "minor literatures" is helpful to illustrate this point:

They [some modernist writers in the West] do not mix the two languages, although many of them are tied to minorities as a sign of their vocation. What they do is actually inventing a minor use of the major language in which they express themselves completely: they minorize this language, just as in music where minor mode designs dynamic combinations perpetually out of balance . . . within limit, he [a writer] obtains his strength from an unknown voiceless minority. Making cry, stutter, murmur the language itself.[42]

Chen Kaige in *King of the Children* is questioning mainly through audiovisual language – making an attempt to break away from cinematic conventions in traditional narrative films. His attempt at subversion also aims to deconstruct further Chinese cultural tradition, which has heavily relied on its writings. Consequently, meaninglessness, such as the folk song and misconstrued character, especially fascinates the filmmaker. The most successful fruit of Laogan'er's unconventional education is Wang Fu's composition about his father, which is also the only heavily emotionally charged moment in the film. Wang Fu reads his composition, and his reading is immediately followed by the folk song, as if the song in an incomprehensible language were a continuation and extension of Laogan'er's successful education, which aims radically to renew Chinese culture. Interestingly, this change has to start with an attempt to create a brand-new language, as the May Fourth radical intellectuals had attempted at the beginning of the century, by "minorizing the language." Laogan'er concludes his classroom teaching by explaining the source and the meaning of his invented character, cow + water, as if he were initiating his students into a new culture. This resem-

3. Wang Fu singles out a character inadvertently invented by Laogan'er as not yet having been taught in *King of the Children,* directed by Chen Kaige (1987). COURTESY OF THE MUSEUM OF MODERN ART.

bles his last instruction to his favorite student, Wang Fu: "Do not copy anymore – not even the dictionary." To this extent, the subversion of traditional culture in Chen's film is primarily formal at different levels: linguistic, acoustic, and visual. As Terry Eagleton points out:

A radical politics can prescribe what must be done for this to occur; but it cannot prescribe the content of what will then be lived, for the content, as Marx says, goes beyond the phrase. All radical politics are thus in a profound sense formalistic. As long as we can now adequately describe the transformations our political actions intend, we have failed by that token to advance beyond reformism.[43]

In *King of the Children,* Chen invented an outsider to the teacher's "kingdom": a cowherd, a young boy, who stubbornly refuses to communicate with the teacher. From the beginning to the end, the boy remains a true cultural outsider, a stage no longer reachable for Laogan'er despite his conscious effort. Laogan'er's fascination with this outsider can be seen as evidence of the same kind of cultural nihilism as the final scene of the burning forest: Everything must start from zero in order to build a possible "paradise." As Chen explained, he invented this person as a symbol of "paradise," since the cowherd has direct contact with the world of nature, which Laogan'er has lost due to his entrance into "civilization."[44] To this extent, the cowherd represents the teacher's lost innocence, or an idealized and nostalgic image of the self, which gazes at his actual subjective world self-reflexively and critically. As Rey Chow points out, in this image of a child narcissistic desire is heavily invested, since the protagonist to a great extent represents the director's point of view.[45] Indeed, Chen Kaige's autobiography, *Tree of Dragon Blood* (*Longxue shu*), attests to the same kind of self-critical stance.[46] However, the process of identification with the projected image as a critical part of the self has not been realized smoothly. We can see this if we examine closely the relationship between the protagonist and the child, since this "self" has been definitively "lost" – to use Chen's own expression.[47]

Despite the director's repeated emphasis, in various interviews, on the cowherd's significance, the boy's footage in the film remains fairly limited. For this reason alone, the encounters between the teacher and the boy deserve some critical attention. The boy never appears without the teacher's implicit or explicit gaze. Throughout the film, they meet only four times.

The first encounter occurs during Laogan'er's journey from his production team to the school. On their way, Laogan'er and his friend Laohei are surrounded by trees, river, and mountains. Extreme long shots of beautiful scenery remind us of classical Chinese landscape paintings where human figures, usually small, are part of natural scenes. However, this landscape is not simply pastoral. On the sound track we hear birdsong as well as sounds of woodcutting, and onscreen the camera constantly cuts from idyllic scenes to striking images of burnt tree trunks. Despite the cowherd's closeness to nature, cowbells can also be heard among the sounds of nature destruction, and the cowherd appears among the images of such destruction. Furthermore, the camera seems to tease the protagonist, who cannot take his fascinated gaze away from the strawhatted boy, by showing only the boy's back in a soft-focused and dimly lit long shot. Shortly after, even this fuzzy image fades away and leaves Laogan'er alone on the screen.

The second encounter happens shortly after Laogan'er's arrival at the school. While he is copying one of the lessons from the textbook to the blackboard, Laogan'er again hears the sound of cowbells, which prompts him to create inadvertently the new character cow + water before he hastily goes outside to look. Again, a medium shot shows only the cowherd's back, disappearing over the horizon. The third encounter occurs after Laogan'er has changed the conventional teaching method by allowing students to write about what they have in mind and what interests them the most. This time, Laogan'er is finally able to talk to the child, although the boy still does not show his face. Laogan'er tries to teach the cowherd how to write; he invites the boy to study with him. The child responds by spitting contemptuously and rigorously shaking his head. Then he turns his back on the teacher. Gradually the boy is submerged in changing light and colors associated with the mysterious folk song. Although this child's world remains frustratingly inaccessible to the teacher, at each meeting Laogan'er seems to approach one step closer to him. If the cowherd represents the protagonist's lost self, as the director claims, this self is presented only abstractly, as composed of symbolic steps in the development of a narcissistic ego-ideal. As Rey Chow points out, Laogan'er's relationship with children substitutes for his relationship with women. The child then plays a role, traditionally assigned to women: that of a locus of narcissistic projection of male subjectivity.[48]

If this is the case, however, one can also find specific sociological explanations for Chen's preference for children over the opposite sex in this role of projection. Due to the puritanism of communist ideology in China, the usual cinematic image of the woman that was familiar to Chen Kaige and his generation in their formative years downplayed sexuality. A glamorous or sexually appealing woman may smack of bourgeois ideology in a socialist-realist context. Consequently, Fifth Generation filmmakers were more familiar with another kind of female image, of which Laidi, the townboyish female lead in *King of the Children,* is only a slightly caricatured reproduction. According to a strict socialist-realist standard, a woman could be beautiful, as in the eight Model Operas of the ten years of the Cultural Revolution, as long as her beauty was safely "desexualized" and "proletarianized," at least on the surface. By contrast, only an evil woman, such as a Nationalist or a Japanese spy, could publicly (or shamelessly?) display her sensuality or sexual appeal. Moreover, this display supposedly did not provoke any desire from male revolutionaries; it elicited only their class hatred for bourgeois corruption. Consequently, a "good" heroine in these operas was usually portrayed as tough, straightforward, daring, independent, and revolutionary. Her attractiveness could only be accidental, and she herself never paid much attention to her appearance. Naturally, these attributes more often than not remain rather superficial and limited, since they must be subordinate to the heroine's unquestionable loyalty to the party – as in the case of a good wife vis-à-vis her husband in traditional China. Like women's to-be-looked-at-ness in Hollywood films, the qualities of "new women" in socialist-realist cinema were themselves on display, although these qualities did overshadow some values of traditional femininity.

Obviously, this early education left a deep imprint in Chen's first films – as he mentioned in his interview with French journalists. As a result, Chen directed the narcissistic gaze not toward a woman but to an object relatively free from any ostentatiously erotic investment, the child. The only woman in the film, Laidi, is safely desexualized according to the perverse model of socialist-realist puritanism. She is not "beautiful," so that Chen's protagonist does not need to "be afraid of" her, since there will be no danger that "her charms make him forget other aspects of life" – as Chen candidly explains to a French journalist.[49] In other words, Chen's portrayal of women shows the legacy of socialist realism: Sex and work (or whatever is serious in this world) are in conflict with each other.

Understandably, as a tomboy clone Laidi does not seriously arouse the teacher's desire, but the cowherd does so in her place, because Laogan'er's desire for the child, unlike that for a woman, is supposedly free from any sexual implication. (Fortunately for Chen, pedophilia was not a fashionable term, or even a recognizable one, in China during the 1980s.) Moreover, this choice is further justified because among Chinese radical intellectuals, children have been serving as the metaphor for China's future since the beginning of this century, as in the May Fourth movement. Everyone in China probably is able to recall Lu Xun's final sentence in his story "Diary of a Madman": "Save the children."[50] Moreover, the child as a metaphor reminds us of Mao's well-known expression "a piece of blank paper on which one can draw the newest and the most beautiful picture in the world." Thus Chen's fondness for this metaphor also reveals an intellectual heritage from his radical forefathers, despite their ideological difference – cultural nihilism. However, one similarity exists between the figure of the woman in the Hollywood tradition and that of the child in Chen's film: Both remain objects, albeit objects of the narcissistic gaze and of self-projection. As a result, when the protagonist finds his "self," his fascination with this object disappears. As Chen explains in an interview:

In the course of his teaching reform, we can observe that the "king of the children" becomes more human, without having recourse to the cowherd's spiritual world. Moreover, he tries to make his students become members of a potentially healthier society. During his teaching career, he does what he can do, that's enough. As a result, when the cowherd appears in front of him for the last time in the film, we hear only the sound of cowbells, without music and cows. This means that the king of the children no longer feels fascinated by them. Although the cowherd and cows represent my ideal of paradise, I hope that people will not be seduced by the illusory world of fantasy. I am for a positive attitude of life: People should do something in the world of reality.[51]

The cowherd functions as a trope for an escape from reality. At the same time, the world of reality is the location that defines male subjectivity: One should live, not like a child living in a fantasy, but like a soldier tested by a battlefield. In his final encounter with the cowherd, Laogan'er reaches an equal footing with the object of his previous fascination, not through fantasy or escapism but by means of his self-cultivation firmly situated within social reality. In their previous three encounters, although the teacher, step by step, reduces the distance between himself and the child, the cowherd remains always aloof and never returns the protagonist's fascinated gaze. By contrast, during their last meeting, the cowherd looks back. A series of shot–reverse shots cut from the child to Laogan'er, crosscutting with surrounding images of burned tree trunks. It is then that the boy, in a dramatic reversal, unknowingly copies an action from the teacher's past: urinating for the cows. (Earlier, during his last class, Laogan'er explains to his students how he inadvertently came to invent the character cow + water because he overheard cowbells, which reminded him of his own past. When he had herded cows in his production team, Laogan'er used to urinate for them: They loved to drink human urine for its salty taste, and these cows had become extremely loyal to Laogan'er.)[52]

At the end of this last of the cowherd scenes, a close-up shows the child looking back – without his straw hat. This uncovering demystifies this object of fascination, which no longer attracts the protagonist's intensely desiring gaze. The sublime object, to use a Žižekian term, returns to its everyday position as a common country boy with a dirty face.[53]

Chen's three early films studied in this chapter were all made prior to his stay in the United States at the end of 1980s. They represent one of the most daring efforts in formal experiment not only in his own filmmaking career, but also in the history of Chinese cinema. In all these films, Chen has created a conceptualized visual language to criticize the dominant ideology. On the one hand, the cinematography in his early works, defying filmic conventions, is hauntingly beautiful. On the other, despite its apparently radical outlook, his conceptualized criticism fails to go beyond the discursive practice of its target, communist ideology, since it assumes the same iconoclastic gesture toward China's past as did the May Fourth movement, whence the Communist Party emerged. This gesture still embraces an implicit cultural hierarchy inherent in the discourse of modernity, namely, division between backward traditional China and the progressive modern West. To this extent, the limitation of his criticism of the dominant ideology stems from his uncritical attitude toward the discourse of modernity, which has in various forms dominated the ideological and intellectual stage of twentieth-century China.

2

ALLEGORICAL AND REALISTIC PORTRAYALS OF THE CULTURAL REVOLUTION

TIAN ZHUANGZHUANG: *ON THE HUNTING GROUND; HORSE THIEF; BLUE KITE*

Tian Zhuangzhuang's two consecutive minority films, *On the Hunting Ground* (*Liechang zasa*, 1984) and *Horse Thief* (*Daoma zei*, 1985), are two of the most visually striking experimental works created by the Fifth Generation film-makers. An important quality of these two films is their visual accuracy. Melvyn Goldstein, a prominent anthropologist studying Tibetan culture, told me in a phone conversation that, as a close observer of this culture, he was deeply impressed by the verisimilitude of Tian's portrayal in *Horse Thief* of Tibetan nomad life at the beginning of the century. However, he also added that despite the film's visual accuracy, the selection of its images conveys a misleading impression of Tibetan culture overall – a negative impression.[1] The same claim can be made concerning Tian's other minority film, *On the Hunting Ground,* made one year before *Horse Thief.* The Mongolian life-style is portrayed in such a realistic fashion that the film looks even more like an ethnographic documentary. At the same time, the main activity, hunting, is fictional in contemporary inner Mongolia. As a result, the filmmaker had to stage this activity completely. As in *Horse Thief,* the staged hunting also conveys a negative image of the community it purports to represent. Mongolian hunters are shown shooting at smallish animals, such as ducks and rabbits, with disproportionately powerful rifles. The frequent use of slow motion in these scenes emphasizes further the agony of these innocent animals. In an interview in 1993, Tian claimed that these two minority films, along with his then recently completed film *Blue Kite* (*Lan fengzheng*), were the only works truly belonging to himself, since he had compromised too much with people on his team while making other films between these.[2] In terms of both subject matter and visual qualities, however, Tian's *Blue Kite* seemingly has little to do with his two minority movies, made almost a decade earlier. With modest means and unpretentious cinematography, it tells the story of a boy growing up in Beijing amid political movements. Censored by the Chinese government prior to its final editing and released in the international market in 1993, *Blue Kite* can be considered the first Fifth Generation film devoted to the negative effects of political movements on Chinese people.

What motivated the Han Chinese filmmaker to make such visually accurate pictures about minority cultures, which are at the same time subjective and/or fictional? To what extent does *Blue Kite* differ from his two minority films? Why does the director single out his two minority films, made earlier in his career, along with his final film, *Blue Kite,* as his only "own works" despite their differences? These are some of the questions that I shall address in this chapter.

ON THE HUNTING GROUND

REALISTIC IMPACT OF RULES ON A FICTIONAL GROUND

Tian's minority film, *On the Hunting Ground (Liechang zasa,* 1984), bears an astonishing resemblance to documentary. At first, the Mongolian language was not translated into Mandarin, although the film addresses a specific Han audience, familiar with film culture and completely alien to this language. Due to objections from reviewers, Tian unwillingly added the offscreen voice of a male interpreter, who translates male and female, old and young voices with an equally monotonous tone. Like the title, written in the Mongolian language, the Mongolian culture in the film is objectified through this impassive voice, which serves mainly as a signifier of something more significant: the Han culture. Tian claimed that he was interested only in the Han Chinese society while making minority films.[3] Furthermore, this documentary quality is also put in question by the very title of the film: *Liechang zasa,* a hybrid combination of Mandarin and Mongolian, means rules (*zasa* in Mongolian) on the hunting ground (*liechang* in Mandarin). Despite the documentary appearance, these rules are fictional in contemporary Inner Mongolia, since collective hunting activities are themselves inventions of the filmmaker in this specific geographical and historical location.[4]

Both Tian Zhuangzhuang and Chen Kaige have shown a strong interest in the impact of social institutions on individuals – especially in their earlier works – partly due to their still-fresh memory of the traumatic experiences of the Cultural Revolution. However, at the beginning of their careers they expressed the same interest in different forms, as both tried in their own ways to break away from conventions of traditional narrative films. Chen's approach was much more conceptual, whereas Tian's was more visual. *Zasa,* the Mongolian word for "rule," stands as the very embodiment of this interest. The introductory shot of ruins of ancient palaces gives these rules an origin: the Mongolian nation as unified by Genghis Khan. In the following scene, a group leader on the hunting ground, Jirguleng, explains these rules in detail to other hunters. His explanations provide these rules with a hybrid nature by combining ancient Mongolian culture and current Chinese state policy. The first rule – a hunted animal belongs to the owner of the dog that first grasps it – seemingly has its origin in ancient times, since it appears free of any current political implication. By contrast, the two other rules – the care of childless aged people and the prohibition of shooting at state-protected animals – appear to belong to the era of the People's Republic of China, because they use a contemporary politicized vocabulary. By combining supposedly ancient Mongolian rules with those of contemporary China, the film suggests that these apparently exotic rules do not separate the Mongolian community in the film from the political reality of the Han Chinese audience. After all, the film addresses only a limited Han audience, despite the exclusive use of the Mongolian language.

The story line is deceptively simple and sketchy. Against the rule, a hunter named Wangenzabu takes possession of a deer that was first grasped by the dog of Bayasiguleng, a hunter from a neighboring village. By chance, a passerby happens to witness his transgression and reports it to the legitimate owner. Bayasiguleng angrily reports the thievery to Wangenzabu's village chief, Jirguleng. As a result, according to a traditional ritual of punishment, Wangenzabu's mother publicly whips her transgressive son and forces him to kneel down until next morning in front of a tree trunk to which the deer head is nailed. Wangenzabu's public humiliation angers his elder brother Taogetao, the manager of the cooperative shop, and triggers a series of vengeful acts against Bayasiguleng. The animosity between the two men intensifies to the point that, armed with sickles and knives, men in the two neighboring villages almost battle over the use of a piece of grassland. Moreover, this animosity also destroys the male bonding between Wangenzabu and Jirguleng, although the latter just saved his former friend from a wolf den at risk of his own life. At the end the film, partly through the intervention of their wives, the male community of Mongolian hunters finally reconcile by kneeling down one after the other in front of the tree trunk.

From the very beginning, the film portrays hunting as transgression of the peaceful coexistence between the natural and human worlds, as a series of slow-motion, high-angle medium shots highlight the agony of hunted animals. Those defenseless animals, deer, rabbits, pheasants, and ducks, form a striking contrast with hunters on the backs of their fast-running horses, armed with powerful rifles, and accompanied by merciless dogs [Fig. 4]. Captured by eye-level fast tracking shots, Mongolian hunters move in different directions, relentlessly chasing animals. Since the hunting activity itself is fictional, the choice of animals with particularly innocent looks as targets for such a furious hunt should be interpreted as intentional – especially because more harmful animals, such as wolves (performed by dogs), are used in another episode. Constant cross-cutting between the dark-lit hunting ground and the village full of sunshine further indicates the gratuitous nature of this activity, since the village scenes seem to suggest that animal husbandry and agriculture have already provided villagers with ample self-sufficiency. Furthermore, hunters do not have any reason to use such powerful weapons to hunt animals like rabbits. Still, the film purports to present Mongolian hunting activity as part of production, not as leisure. This apparently aimless activity more effectively focuses our attention on one aspect, violation of nature by the community purely for the sake of violation. Slow-motion shots of hunted

4. Mongolian hunters in *On the Hunting Ground,* directed by Tian Zhuangzhuang (1985).
COURTESY OF THE MUSEUM OF MODERN ART.

animals, helplessly exposed to hunters' guns (and the film's camera) at their most
vulnerable moments, further intensify this violation. At two different levels, this
violation questions the value of a human society. First, from the very beginning,
the law on which the society is founded is a double-edged weapon. Despite its
acknowledged intent to reinforce the human bond, its self-contradiction is also
a constant source of conflict and division in the community. Second, at a more
fundamental level, certain social activities tend to violate the natural world gra-
tuitously, without any visibly beneficial effect on the community.

By its arbitrary nature, the rule itself invites transgression. One can say that
the simple story line in *On the Hunting Ground* focuses on the transgression of
the ancient Mongolian rule, the alleged foundation of Mongolian civilization, that
bases the ownership of a game animal on whoever dog touches the animal first.
However, since the owner is not the dog but the hunter, who arrives not necessarily simultaneously with his dog, it is up to the first arriving hunter to decide
whether he respects the rule or not if his dog fails in this competition. If the hunter decides to keep the game, the winning dog cannot appeal this decision for its
absent master, since it cannot speak the language in which this rule is articulated; and because the danger of being caught is relatively small, a hunter is often
tempted to violate the rule. In the film, an initially benign transgression of an

essentially arbitrary hunting rule leads toward increasingly severe transgressions of male bonding. This series of transgressions destroys means of production, threatens human lives, and drives the community to the edge of collapse.

Furthermore, Tian's film endows the dual nature of this law with a universal flavor by reminding audiences what happened recently in their own society – that is, mainstream Han society. During the Cultural Revolution, self-contradictory political rules often led to destruction of traditional human ties, as did *zasa* in the Mongolian hunting community. These rules engendered conflicts among neighbors, former friends, and close family members by pitting them against each other, while triggering selfishness in human beings by promising rewards or promoting fear. One can see the story of the fictive Mongolian hunting rule as an allegory of recent Chinese social history. Since all actions are reprehensible one way or another if interpreted from the basis of self-contradictory rules, those who tried to impose punishment on others according to the rules of the moment may have committed a punishable act according to a different rule later. These punishments imposed by their own peers provoked endless factional fights among people in the same workplace, the same neighborhood, and the same family. During the Cultural Revolution, party policy changed constantly. Often these changes invited people to target different factions. A faction that had been politically correct yesterday according to one policy could be condemned today as "enemy of the people" – equivalent to a political death sentence. At a different level, members of these targeted factions are also like pitilessly hunted animals in the film. Victims of destructive political activities, capitalists, rich peasants in traditional China, intellectuals, officials, and finally various sections of Red Guards, were in turn helplessly exposed to public humiliation and the whim of arbitrary rules. The contrast between arbitrary and faceless political power and its defenseless victims is as striking as the difference between the powerful hunters and helpless animals. Tian explains in an interview: "By making movies about minority people, I can more truly reflect the life of Han people."[5] As a result, by looking at minorities "objectively," the absent subject, the Han culture, can project its own image onto a mirror refractively.

Confusion caused by arbitrary law intensifies conflicts among hunters. The most intense conflict in the film is a confrontation between the people of the two neighboring villages on the grassland. Led by their vengeful chief, Bayasiguleng, his fellow villagers provocatively cut grass on the grassland assigned by the government to Jirguleng's village. The camera focuses alternately on the two groups, both armed with knives, whips, and guns. The initially benign transgression of the hunting rule concerning an insignificant individual possession, a deer, leads toward a much more dangerous transgression of grassland, collective property crucial to villagers' livelihood. The lengthy close-ups of various weapons further dramatize the tension. Interestingly, this film uses almost no close-ups of human faces, but largely those of objects, animals, and occasionally, fragments of human bodies. This practice creates an impression that impersonal objects are more

5. Women in *On the Hunting Ground*, directed by Tian Zhuangzhuang (1985). COURTESY OF THE MUSEUM OF MODERN ART.

important than human subjects. This further reinforces the objectification of minority characters in the film. For example, fragments of anonymous bodies are portrayed at the same level as animals and things, as shown in a series of neatly arranged shots in the last hunting sequence: From a changing oblique angle, three hunters throw saddles on their horses. The camera focuses on the same dynamic movement of each saddle, which repeats exactly the same curve three times in a row. In each of these shots the camera shows the hunter's back in motion only briefly. The short, evenly paced, precisely controlled movements create a dehumanizing effect, as if these hunters function only mechanically, as part of a huge machine.

WOMEN'S INTERVENTION AND COLLECTIVE GUILT

Women in the film are mainly portrayed as mothers [Fig. 5]. Their activities are usually limited to motherly functions: breast-feeding, inquiring about another woman's stage of pregnancy, and disciplining their adult sons. Thanks to their motherly instinct, women succeed partially in domesticating hunters' drives toward violence. Their interventions, passive as they might appear, are crucial in keeping the masculine community from collapse. At the same time, these women themselves can also be subject to violence. When Jiruleng's wife tries to prevent him from risking his life to save Bayasiguleng's in the wolf den, he kicks her forcefully in public. Except for the first scene of ritualistic punishment, this is the only instance of violence directed at a human body in *On the Hunting Ground*. However, Jiruleng's violent gesture against his wife (despite his apparently mild temperament) also marks solidarity with his male friend – solidarity of male bonding. If the hunting community serves as a metaphor for human society, women in this society are beyond any doubt marginalized – they are a cushion to violence in the male community.

During the last hunt in the film, Gerile, Bayasiguleng's wife, rescues Taogetao's sick mother from her burning house in the village. Out of gratitude, the shop manager admits to Bayasiguleng a series of vengeful acts: throwing a wolf pup into the latter's sheepfold, for instance, and accusing him falsely of stealing buffalos in the name of Jiruleng, Bayasiguleng's former best friend. After this confession, the shop manager voluntarily performs the ritual of self-punishment by kneeling in front of the tree trunk – the same ritualistic punishment, imposed by Bayasiguleng upon Taogetao's brother Wangenzabu at the very beginning of the film, that first spurs Taogetao's numerous vengeful acts, and thus drives the entire drama in the film. However, Bayasiguleng now realizes that he has wrongly blamed his best friend Jiruleng, who had saved his life at the risk of his own. As a result, he visits Jiruleng, to whom he admits his thievery on the hunting ground of the latter's deer. In other words, he has committed exactly the same violation for which he had demanded punishment for Taogetao's brother at the beginning of the film. Then, Bayasiguleng joins Taogetao in kneeling before the tree trunk.

Immediately before this scene of final reconciliation, when Taogetao knocks on Bayasiguleng's door in order to thank Gerile for having saved his mother, Bayasiguleng at first refuses to open it. Gerile then welcomes Taogetao despite her husband's objection. It is her feminine forgiveness toward her husband's enemy that makes the ensuing scene of reconciliation among male hunters possible. The rule that regulates the male community must be softened by its marginal members, women; otherwise, the male community could not survive the violence generated by the arbitrary nature of this rule. Women's interference is portrayed in the film mainly as motherly – asexual and altruistic – whereas the hunting rule represents the Name of the Father in a Lacanian sense, or cultural authority, in a patriarchal society.[6] From the very beginning, the hunting rule is materialized in a dead tree trunk, a phallic symbol, to which a dear head is nailed. In the last scene Jiruleng, before joining the group, takes away the deer head, thus leaving an empty bloody mark on the trunk. At the end, the hunters are bound together only by a collectively self-inflicted punishment. Their relationship with the tree trunk in this sense is purely negative, as acknowledging collective transgression serves as the basis for their reconciliation. At the same time, the rule's effectiveness depends on women's intervention: Wangenzabu's mother was the first one to impose punishment on her disobedient son. Morever, although the sons finally accept their own responsibility and take their punishment into their own hands, as conscious and mature citizens, this is only after a wife intercedes with her womanly compassion. In other words, despite the phallic symbol of the rule, its implementation is also a process of feminization through women's mediation at different stages. If we take the director's words seriously, the Mongolian hunting rules in this film, like other elements in minority culture, should directly or indirectly "reflect" on a center that is apparently absent, namely, the Han culture. In this case, the Han cultural authority goes through a double process of marginalization in its cinematic representation: It is first symbolized by a marginal culture and, second, partially implemented by the marginal gender within that minority community.

The final reconciliation is expressed exactly in the form of collective acceptance of individual guilt. Taogetao, Bayasiguleng, Jiraguleng, and Wangenzabu, all four male protagonists in this film, successively kneel down by the tree trunk. Bayasiguleng, who once imposed punishment on Wangenzabu according to the hunting rule, voluntarily accepts his own punishment in the same form for exactly the same reason, taking a deer first grasped by the dog of another hunter. The subject of punishment becomes subject to the same punishment. After listening to Bayasiguleng's confession, Jiraguleng removes and discards the deer head from the trunk and joins Bayasiguleng in the ritual of self-imposed punishment. His action is followed by that of Wangenzabu. Jiraguleng's act of freeing the tree trunk of the deer head redefines the phallic symbol. As a result, this symbol has become universal. At the same time, through the bloody mark left on the phallic tree trunk, this gesture also suggests castration. The *zasa,* symbolized by the trunk, functions as a unifying force only negatively, through commonly acknowledged transgression against it – or through feminization or castration. In the next sequence, images of this group of hunters kneeling before the phallus are repeatedly shot from various angles. On the sound track, their images are accompanied by ritualistic music, in order to provide a religious aura. Then, the camera cuts to a title screen in which Genghis Khan's initial edicts are restated in standard Chinese writing. At the same time, superimpositions of the tree trunk multiply the symbol of the patriarchal authority – with its bloody mark of castration. The final scene uses the same introductory footage of ruins of the Mongolian palaces. The ancient rule, with its origins in these vanished palaces, is rejuvenated by the renewal of male bonding.

To a great extent, the fictionality of hunting activity and the doubly fictional hunting rule allegorically suggest the implicit presence of an absent subject, the Han Chinese. In the same vein, the problematized male bonding in the film can be considered an allegorical search for Han male subjectivity. This search also questions the validity of the foundational rule of patriarchal society, the rule of private ownership, based on which patriarchal society and, to a certain degree, male subjectivity are defined. Perceived as relatively transparent due to its allegedly primitive nature, the Mongolian community is supposedly not governed by a complicated civil code as is the Han society. Since Tian repeatedly expressed his disinterest in the minority community itself, and his interest in reflecting on the Han society through a projection onto the minority community, within limits one can also interpret the hunting rule as a metaphor for the foundational law in patriarchal society. At an empirical level, like the numerous self-contradictory rules during the Cultural Revolution, this rule is also by nature arbitrary. Its arbitrariness generates an endless circle of violence in the patriarchal community, despite its supposed function of maintaining order. In the final analysis, the rule can function only negatively – by means of a commonly shared sense of guilt among its members. Moreover, the Mongolian hunting rule that serves as a metaphor for the Han cultural authority can be considered a negation in itself, since from the outset this apparently neutral vehicle, minority culture, already marginalizes the mainstream Han Chinese society that it reflects. The intervention of the opposite sex feminizes this rule, and thus further marginalizes it.

As both participants in and victims of the Cultural Revolution, Tian's generation struggled at the end of this political movement to redefine their roles. Like the community of the Mongolian hunters, they were also divided and confused. Refusing to resort to the simplistic theory of self-victimization, as did many post–Cultural Revolutionary literary and cinematic works at this time,[7] some Fifth Generation directors, such as Chen Kaige and Tian Zhuangzhuang, tried to reflect on their traumatic experiences at the beginning of their directing careers. This task is actually more difficult because victims were not necessarily innocent. As Chen Kaige wrote in his autobiography: "During the Cultural Revolution, I suffered; I watched others suffer; I also made others suffer. I was part of the mob."[8] Partly because of their roles in the mob and partly because of their own deeply emotional and personal trauma, they had trouble speaking directly about their experiences during the Cultural Revolution until it was well over, during the 1990s. Prior to this emotional and ideological cooling-off period, they tended to approach the same subject only obliquely. Tian chose minority cultures as convenient vehicles by means of which he could approach a recent history of his own emotionally charged past. Tian's generation had a relationship with the dominant ideology in China similar to that of the Mongolian hunters in the film. Although they were punished by this ideology, they were also its products – not only because of their roles as Red Guards but also because of their education. Only through transgression and acknowledgment of collective guilt could they change the nature of the dominant ideology by discarding the bloody head – as Chen Kaige did in his autobiography.

HORSE THIEF

SKY BURIAL

Horse Thief (*Daoma zei*), Tian's next film on minorities, which came out the following year, at first glance appears much less documentarylike than *On the Hunting Ground.* Unlike in *On the Hunting Ground,* a great number of close-ups in *Horse Thief* focus on human faces: either individualized faces such as those of the protagonist and his family members, or anonymous faces as part of a collective, such as those of monks in the scenes of sky burial. Paradoxically, instead of intensifying emotions, facial close-up creates further a distance between the audience and the world onscreen, since these faces themselves are intensely objectified. The film portrays the life of a Tibetan named Norbu and his family. Although its story line is seemingly stronger than that of *On the Hunting Ground,* *Horse Thief* challenges its viewers more because most of its religious scenes are often loosely related, if not unrelated, to the diegetic world.[9]

Taking into consideration the great proportion of religious scenes, the film develops almost on two separate fronts: a feature on Norbu and his family, and a documentary on Tibetan religious rituals. Paradoxically, instead of creating a deeply religious atmosphere, the quantitatively and qualitatively impressive footage of religious rituals in this film reinforces the impression of objectification. Since the religious world is somewhat isolated from the narrative chain, a number of Chinese film critics have complained about how difficult it is to make sense out of this "documentary about customs."[10] Since its distribution, only two copies of *Horse Thief* have been sold in the Chinese market.

This film presents the life of Norbu, a Tibetan living on the margins of the Qinghai Province during the 1920s and relying on horse thievery to support his family. Because he robbed several Muslim messengers of governmental gifts for a temple, Norbu and his family are expelled from the tribe by the headman. Partly due to hardship in exile, his two-year-old son Tashi falls ill. Despite all their prayers, Norbu and his wife Dolma fail to save their son's life. After burying his body in the snowy land, Norbu and Dolma start a long and strenuous pilgrimage journey, by the end of which his wife has become pregnant. Since Norbu believes that his first son's death results from a divine punishment, he decides to steal no longer. In order to keep his promise, the horse thief is reduced to the lowest job, serving as a surrogate for the evil river ghost in a religious ritual, which no one else would do despite its financial incentive. (Even the actor playing Norbu was reluctant to perform this role, as he was afraid of contempt from his community.)[11] As a result of his job, the tribe is even more determined to refuse Norbu's plea for a possible return. As worse comes to worst, Norbu is forced to sell his beloved horse, which until this point has followed him everywhere. Afterward, he returns to its new owner's tent to bring his horse some food for the last time and bid the animal farewell. Taken as a horse thief again, he is severely beaten by the new owner. On a stormy night, Norbu sends his wife and the child away on the back of a stolen horse in order to save the life of his newborn son, while he himself commits suicide in front of the tower of sky burial.

The film's tendency to isolate religious scenes from the narrative chain reinforces the impression of Norbu as a lonely individual disconnected from the world. Despite his sincere desire to connect with the world through his religious faith, he is essentially left alone in a state of alienation. At the same time, the human community is disconnected from the natural and religious world as well. This fundamental sense of disconnection is from the very beginning illustrated by the introductory sequence of sky burial. At a certain point in the filmmaking, Tian even thought about changing the title to "sky burial," due to the central position occupied by this sequence.[12] In this repeatedly used sequence, the tower of sky burial is located in the extreme left side of the frame, almost as a vanishing point. A series of close-ups in a rapid and monotonous rhythm tracks impassive faces of a group of lamas, reciting sutras. The same gesture, the same neutrality, and the same clothing, make these faces appear barely distinguishable one from another. In the following scene, the evenly paced tracking shots present some hawks occupying the previously empty space of the ground in front of the tower. Since the camera follows an equally cold and indifferent rhythm, the images of sacred birds maintain an almost seamless continuity with the close-ups of the monks' faces. In this prologue of sky burial, tower, monks, and hawks are used as equally important signs in the construction of the religious ritual. The camera pays commensurate attention to each of them. Each is shot in isolation. Symbolically, the tower represents social institutions; monks, human community; and hawks, the natural world. At the same time, they are also isolated from each other in their shared neutrality and indifference.

The film presents three sequences of sky burial, often using exactly the same footage, each one closer than the last to the hero of the narrative world, Norbu. In the introductory sequence, the sky burial for an unknown individual offers a seemingly universal version of this religious ritual. Then, in the middle of the film, from Norbu's impassive perspective, the film presents the sky burial of the headman's father. Norbu himself is excluded from the ritual, and his gift has been disdainfully rejected by the headman because it came from an impure source, his thievery. As a result, as an unwelcome intruder, Norbu sits alone, watching the ceremony from a distance. Granny and the father of Norwe, another horse thief, earlier spoke of their belief that sacred hawks would send the soul of the headman's father to heavens by eating his flesh. However, they believe, since Norbu and Norwe sin against heaven through thievery, the divine birds will certainly refuse to eat their bodies after their death; hence their souls will never be able to reach the heavens. As if to contradict this prediction, in the last sequence the image of Norbu's dagger, drenched in blood and abandoned on the snowy ground, suggests his suicide near the tower of sky burial. Presumably, hawks perform their duty of sky burial for the horse thief, although monks, unlike in the two previous scenes, are conspicuously absent. Norbu's implied suicide near the tower deliberately challenges the common faith in his community according to which a former horse thief is not entitled to sky burial – as Granny explained earlier. At the same time, this challenge is also an expression of unshakable faith in religious salvation.

THE CONTINGENT NATURE OF NAMING

More than half of the footage of *Horse Thief* is devoted to religious rituals.[13] Except for the three recurrent scenes of sky burial, most scenes appear loosely related or unrelated to the story line.[14] Unlike other decorative rituals, one of those scenes, the ritual of releasing the sacred sheep into the mountains, stands out as a marker in the evolution of Norbu's faith. At first, he mentions this ritual to his son, Tashi, suggesting that he will bring the boy to participate in it when he reaches adulthood; but Tashi dies soon after this conversation, and Norbu's promise is unkept. After he is beaten by the new owner of his horse, who mistakes his innocent visit for a tentative horse thievery, Norbu discovers Granny's remains on the snowy ground. Ironically, despite her lifelong devotion, her flesh has been eaten by wolves instead of divine birds. Deeply disappointed by this scene, Norbu chooses to kill a sacred sheep he encounters on the snowy steppes in order to save the life of his second son, born soon after Tashi's death. Like his first son, the innocent sheep must die for others' sins. At the same time, the earlier ritual release of sheep becomes a reference point for Norbu in his changing relations with religious as well as worldly authorities. He tries to conform with the law by giving up horse thievery; but since the community, instead of protecting him, continues to reject him for his past transgression, the law in a sense forces him to return to his old profession in order to survive. Despite Norbu's effort toward redemption, his name is irrevocably associated with horse theft in the eyes of his community. Rebelling against the power of this act of naming, Norbu finally rejects the sheep's sacred title by treating it as an ordinary animal, existing only for its food value as meat. Having thus desublimated the sacred sheep, Norbu hopes that he may eventually save his family in the name of an irrevocable outcast.

Whether trying to change his fate by making a honorable living or by rebelling against the invisible authority that condemns him in his previous occupation, Norbu is doomed to fail. He needs the community to survive, but its unchangeable perception and labeling of him as "horse thief" overpower him, defining him as an eternal outcast. His hard-earned honorable life-style cannot alter his permanent status, and the killing of the sacred sheep resolves only the most urgent survival problem at the moment for his wife and child. Named an outcast, Norbu can never return to the community – a condition that makes the survival of an individual family difficult, if not impossible, especially taking into account their difficult natural environment. At the same time, the need to save his family from a pressing disaster further reinforces Norbu's outcast status in a vicious circle: Since the community refuses to grant him any rights to normalcy, his only choice is to commit illegal or dishonorable acts.

In another ritualistic scene, Norbu is paid to play the role of the river ghost – a job he accepts to avoid horse thievery, since his family, now in exile, desperately needs money to survive. Although this job brings some temporary relief to his family, it also makes his situation even more difficult: The perception of him as the surrogate of the evil ghost further precludes his return to the tribe. Norbu is forced to sell his last possession, his own cherished horse, for the sake of his family. When he is violently beaten by the buyer of his horse and falsely accused of horse thievery, the accusation serves as an ideological interpellation that puts the final stroke on Norbu's fate. Norbu's good intentions – his rejection of his past in order to conform with social and religious rules, and his desire to see his beloved horse for a last time – ironically further identify him with evil, condemning him to permanent exile. Thus exiled on the steppes, Norbu finally recognizes that "horse thief" will always be his name and, regardless of his own intention, his only possible livelihood. However hard he tries to change this name, the perception of the Other will never change because of the contingent nature of the act of naming.

Žižek makes an interesting remark on this subject:

It is because the Real itself offers no support for a direct symbolization of it – because every symbolization is in the last resort contingent – that the only way the experience of a given historic reality can achieve its unity is through the agency of a signifier, through reference to a "pure" signifier. It is not the real object which guarantees as the point of reference the unity and identity of a certain ideological experience – on the contrary, it is the reference to a "pure" signifier which gives unity and identity to our experience of historical reality itself. Historical reality is of course always symbolized; the way we experience it is always mediated through different modes of symbolization: all Lacan adds to this phenomenological common wisdom is the fact that the unity of a given "experience of meaning," itself the horizon of an ideological field of meaning, is supported by some "pure," meaningless "signifier without the signified."[15]

Norbu himself has become victim to this "pure, meaningless 'signifier without the signified.'" "Horse thief" as a title is following him and haunting his family, not because of what he is doing, but because of what he did at a certain moment in his past. This name determines his present mode of existence, despite his rejection of his previous life-style. This radically contingent nature of naming becomes the Real to which he must constantly return in spite of himself. Even the sale of his last possession, his horse, uncannily leads him to return to his old profession, since his later farewell visit simply reconfirms his label of horse thief in the eyes of the Other. In this regard, the Tibetan horse thief is not unlike numerous "counterrevolutionaries," "rightists," and other kinds of "enemies of the people" during political movements in China. They often died precisely because they carried burdens of "radically contingent acts of naming,"[16] just as Norbu dies at the end of the film for this ineffaceable name of "horse thief." For example, during the Cultural Revolution the well-known writer Laoshe drowned himself in a lake. By first surrounding his body with Chairman Mao's poems, meticulously copied by his own hands, Laoshe believed that he could prove that he was not a counterrevolutionary, as he had been accused of being. Neither Laoshe's suicide nor Norbu's death succeed in washing away their humiliating titles. On the contrary, their deaths only make the titles even more undeniably theirs. Norbu finally does steal horses in order to save his son's life; thus he ends his life having identified with this title. Likewise, according to the official definition of suicide during the Cultural Revolution, Laoshe's suicide has been taken as proof of his antiparty political stance.

The label of horse thief pits Norbu against the symbolic world of religion and social institutions despite himself. His acts, intended to conform with the demands of the Big Other, invariably lead to sins not because of his behavior but rather because of the perception of the Other based on a contingent act of naming. Precisely because this label is independent of his own intention, Norbu can only reinforce his bond with it. In the final analysis, his only way to "please" the Big Other is to conform to its named expectation, even at the price of his life. The vicious circle of punishment continues to affect his family even after his death, leaving his wife and baby in poverty and starvation. At the same time, Norbu's traumatic experience with the world of religion makes him a true believer, according to a Lacanian definition.

Žižek writes:

The only real obedience, then, is an "external" one: obedience out of conviction is not real obedience because it is already "mediated" through our subjectivity – that is, we are not really obeying the authority but simply following our judgment, which tells us that the authority deserves to be obeyed insofar as it is good, wise, beneficent. . . . Even more than for our relation to "external" social authority, this inversion applies to our obedience to the internal authority of belief: it was Kierkegaard who wrote that to believe in Christ because we consider him wise and good is a dreadful blasphemy – it is, on the contrary, only the act of belief itself which can give us an insight into his goodness and wisdom. Certainly we must search for rational reasons which can substantiate our belief, our obedience to the religious command, but the crucial religious experience is that these reasons reveal themselves only to those who already believe – we find reasons attesting our belief because we already believe; we do not believe because we have found sufficient good reasons to believe.[17]

After being beaten by his horse's new owner, Norbu discovers Granny's remains on the snowy ground. Despite her lifelong devotion, instead of receiving a well-deserved sky burial, her body becomes the food for hungry wolves. In the past, socialist-realist films would have portrayed this moment as ideological enlightenment, when a religious believer finally realizes the deception of his gods. For example, in *Serfs (Nongnu)* – a propaganda film made in 1960 after the crackdown on Tibetan rebellion – Tsangba, the mute hero, sees the High Lama try to hide guns inside the giant statue of Buddha, despite his claim to be peace-loving. Then, in order to eliminate a witness, the lama attacks Tsangba and tries to burn his body along with the temple. Saved from the burning temple, Tsangba, after a lifelong silence caused by a religious punishment during his childhood, pronounces his first words: "Chairman Mao." He is transformed from a victimized Buddhist believer to a liberated follower of the Communist Party. Tsangba's enlightenment coincides his disillusionment with the deceptive nature of religion. If *Horse Thief* were a socialist-realist film, Norbu's encounter with Granny's remains should have been the moment for his ideological enlightenment, since her lifelong devotion does not seem to prevent the gods from treating her body mercilessly. Following the same logic, from this point he would have renounced his religious faith to become a revolutionary. What makes Tian's film particularly interesting is that instead of becoming a disbeliever, Norbu's belief deepens and takes a different form. Tian explores the mechanism of a belief system through its repeated trauma, beyond any individual comprehension. At the same time, this different approach does not necessarily reveal much more sensitivity to the Tibetan culture. It reflects more on the experiences of Tian's own generation encountering Mao and his party during the Cultural Revolution and other political movements. Although Norbu is driven to kill the sacred sheep and to steal the horses to save his wife and second child, he also sacrifices his own life near the tower of sky burial, literally dying for his belief. For him, death at the tower of sky burial is enough for his salvation. In this sense, the ending is not truly a rebellious gesture but rather a radical act of faith in religious salvation.

As Žižek explains in the above-quoted paragraph, "external" obedience is the marker of a true faith, be it religious or communist. Norbu's traumatic experience with religious faith can be taken as an emblem of the faith in Chairman Mao and the party during the Cultural Revolution. Most people who lived through the Cultural Revolution in China, including Fifth Generation directors, were to different degrees traumatized. However, their traumatic experiences did not stop them from actively participating in this movement – even if only "externally." Precisely the externalized faith demonstrated by numerous traumatized subjects served as the engine for this political movement. Chen Kaige once used an interesting simile to describe the Cultural Revolution: For him, it was like the Wheel of Fortune, where almost everyone could play the role of enemy of the people. At any given moment, the percentage of people's enemies should not surpass 5 percent of the population, as Mao stated repeatedly during this political movement. Thus, the rest of population could cast their stones at this small percentage of people's enemies without feeling implicated. Thanks to the ever-changing map of the stone-casting crowd, collective trauma perpetuates itself infinitely among the

Chinese population. As a result, at the end of the Cultural Revolution almost no individual had escaped his or her turn of the Wheel.[18] Despite the increasingly shared disillusionment with the dominant class and ideology, a great number of Chinese continued to cast stones at various targeted groups *as if* they were truly enemies of the people. In short, to some degree they actually brought the collective trauma upon themselves, by their externalized faith, since the Cultural Revolution was indeed a mass movement to the point that its long-lasting development would have been impossible without the constant reconstitution of a massive stone-casting crowd. As a result, victims were not necessarily innocent, and victimizers were not free of suffering. In this context, the faithful followers were often punished not because they heroically betrayed their faith, but rather because their unjustified punishment by the Big Other was one of the best proofs of their unconditional faith – just as in Norbu's case. Like the horse thief, they could not truly betray their faith, precisely because it was fundamentally externalized – free of their subjective interpretations.

SPECULARIZATION OF THE MALE BODY

Since the publication in 1975 of Laura Mulvey's influential article "Visual Pleasure and Narrative Cinema," it has become almost a truism to say that visual pleasure is generally associated with the female body as the object of the male gaze in the Hollywood classic tradition, although later feminist film scholars have contributed to refining Mulvey's initial argument. According to Mulvey, the male subject projects his own lack onto this object of visual pleasure based on a presumably fundamental gender difference. This projection enables him to suture his subjectivity through a process of differentiation and identification.[19] Some films made by well-known Fifth Generation male directors seemed prima facie to deny this generally accepted assumption concerning gender hierarchy in narrative films. To different degrees and in different forms, in these films the object of the projection of lack has been mainly the male body, which is often defective – such as in Chen Kaige's *Big Parade* (*Da yuebing*), where the female body is virtually absent. Even in most of Zhang Yimou's films, famous for their visual exploitation of the female body, castration anxiety always leaves its ineffaceable marks on the male body. In the same vein, the specularization of Norbu's body in *Horse Thief* can be considered a telling example. Taking into account these directors' usual indifference toward women's issues, it is difficult to take this gender change in objects of projection as a product of their heightened consciousness of women's emancipation. In fact, this change reflects an uneasiness toward the gender situation in China, especially earlier in their careers. Caught between a traditional belief in male superiority and the reality of women's obligatory participation in the work force, male subjectivity is constantly in crisis during the 1980s in China. For some Fifth Generation directors, the specularization of the male body, either physically defective or ethnically marginalized, has become a substitute for that of the female, in order to avoid certain awkward subjects in gender relations.

The scene of Norbu's collecting sacred water for his sick child provides an interesting example. In order to save his son Tashi's life, Norbu visits the Buddhist temple to collect sacred water. Five of the seven long takes in this sequence focus on Norbu's immovable body. The first close-up highlights a tile on the roof from which water slowly drops into a pot on the ground. The second shot shows a corner of the temple. Further on the right side of the frame, Norbu stands under the roof. In the next medium shot, the camera cuts to Norbu's body in a canted frame. From an oblique low-angle perspective, his body appears in a painfully precarious position, as if he were on the verge of losing his balance. Furthermore, his body looks more like a sculpture than a living being, a status that suits its temple background. The next close-up presents Norbu's face and right hand in a high-angle shot. In a fixed position, his right hand lifts the container over his head in order to collect each drop of sacred water from the roof. The next shot concentrates on his bare feet, standing motionless on the ground. The sixth shot returns to Norbu's face and hands, but from the opposite angle. The last shot once again shifts to the pot on the ground. Throughout this sequence, the initial lengthy duration of each shot seems prolonged by the monotonous water-dripping sound. Apart from the first and last shots, each of the five long takes in the middle carefully studies part of Norbu's body. The intense scrutiny of Norbu's fragmented body represents his emotional stage – torn by anxiety concerning his only son's life. The specularization of Norbu's inner feelings turns his subjective world into visual spectacle. At the same time, the fragmentation of his body objectifies him and distances him from audiences. Similar to the disjunct views of various details of the temple, Norbu's body is portrayed as one of the numerous artifacts of Tibetan religion presented in this film.

Despite the film's apparent effort to portray religious rituals as truthfully as possible, this portrayal remains nevertheless fragmentary and ambivalent, partly because what is truly at stake is not the specificity of a religion but rather its symbolic dimension in relations to an individual as the representative of the dominant ideology or social institution. Another example is a series of jump cuts in the scene of Norbu's disposal of Tashi's body in front of the tower of sky burial. A long shot of the tower cuts to an extreme long shot of Norbu's back in the snow. With the body of his son in his arms, the father stands on the immense steppes covered by snow, appearing disoriented, lonely, and helpless, as if he himself were about to be swallowed by this overwhelmingly indifferent natural world. A close-up of Norbu's motionless face cuts to a long shot of the hero's back as he slowly bows forward to set his child's body on the snowy ground. Then the camera returns to a close-up of Norbu's face. This sequence concludes in a long shot of his back in a similar position. The lengthy duration of each shot further emphasizes the contrast between the close-ups of his face and the long shot of his back. Although the object, Norbu's statuelike body, remains the same, each picture shot from a different angle appears isolated from the rest, as if his body had been fragmented into unrelated images. In a discussion of *Horse Thief*, several Chinese film critics objected to the separation between religious scenes and narrative development.[20] In my opinion, the differences between the two lines of development in the film are not great when one considers the intense specularization of Norbu's body, as if it were part of religious ritual. This specularization associates Norbu closely with religious ritual not at the level of a subject of faith but as an exotic and aesthetic visual object. In other words, Norbu is not mainly a narrative subject, but an object of specularization.

A sequence of superimpositions that multiply Norbu's and Dolma's bodies reinforces this impression. After Tashi's death, Norbu is determined to live an honorable life in order to redeem himself. For the same reason, he and his wife Dolma engage in a long and strenuous pilgrimage to Lhasa. During this journey, they both constantly kowtow in the direction of the holy land, flattening their bodies on the ground. While shooting this sequence, Tian jokingly asked his photographer, Hou Yong, "Do you believe that this sequence will earn you a position in the film history of the world?"[21] In this sequence, shot from different angles, close-ups of the couple's fragmented bodies are superimposed on long shots of the complete bodies captured with changing perspectives. Their superimposed body images are further superimposed with geographical locations. In the background, the green color of the steppes has gradually been replaced by a warmer reddish tone of a barren land. This land is slowly covered by snow. Then, the reddish color remains, but the somehow flat barren land fades out to the mountains. Finally, the multiplied bodies of the two pilgrims are superimposed with scriptures, sculptures, and colorful bricks on the roof of the temple – their final destination. The film concludes its series of superimpositions and focuses on Dolma in the temple, who reveals to her husband her pregnancy. As a result, the series describes a circle, from the death of their firstborn son to the conception of the second. If Norbu considers Tashi's death as a punishment for his sinful past, Dolma describes her pregnancy as a gift from the Buddha, rewarding them for the demonstration of their unshakable faith.

During this sequence, Norbu and Dolma simultaneously emerge from all directions. At the same time, the changes of their positions and of geographical locations make their body movements seem even more monotonous and repetitive. Wherever they are and from whichever direction they come, Norbu and Dolma perform the same movements. Due to the 360° shots of their repeatedly performed rituals, the pilgrim couple often gives the impression of remaining on the same spot, although changing background settings suggest geographical displacements. Their movements remain unchanged within changing sceneries. Because of the mechanical pace and monotonous repetition of their movements, the changing scenes only reinforce the impression of the two "automatized bodies."

Rey Chow writes:

Being "automatized" means being subjected to social exploitation whose origins are beyond one's individual grasp, but it also means becoming a spectacle whose "aesthetic" power increases with one's increasing awkwardness and helplessness. The production of the "other" is in this sense both the production of class and aesthetic/cognitive difference. The camera brings this out excellently with mechanically repeated motions.[22]

Like the body of the laboring-class hero in Chaplin's *Modern Times* and the female voice of Olympia, the mechanical doll in E. T. A. Hoffmann's short story "The Sandman"),[23] in Chow's analysis, the excessive specularity of the Tibetan couple leads toward a dehumanization of their bodies, which become "automatized." Their bodies are multiplied through excessive superimpositions, as a "*mise-en-scène* of modernity par excellence," to use Chow's expressions.[24] Similar to the "comic effect" produced by the automatization of the working-class body in Chaplin's film, and the seductive charm brought about by the mechanization of the female voice in "Sandman," the objectified bodies of the Tibetan couple are used to construct a visualized Other whereby the Han Chinese director deconstructs the established power of the Han cultural and political center. In this sense, the Tibetan horse thief is "feminized" as the culturally inferior Other, exposed to the impassive gaze of the Han subject. Regardless of its gender, the "feminized" object of a minority culture is even further distanced from the mainstream male subject than a woman of his own ethnic group would be.

BLUE KITE

DISAPPEARANCE OF PRIVATE SPACE

In an interview, Tian claimed to have made *Blue Kite* (*Lan fengzheng,* 1993) for his fortieth birthday.[25] He also considered this film "his only serious work" since 1985, the year in which he made *Horse Thief.* In an earlier interview, Tian had perceived his Tibetan film as the best one that he had ever made.[26] Deeply frustrated by the poor reception of his favorite film – only two copies were sold in China – Tian told me that he was unable to take filmmaking seriously for a long period, namely, 1986–92.[27] When he approached forty in 1992, Tian felt pressed for time and decided to direct *Blue Kite,* based on the screenplay by Xiao Mao.[28] In 1993, *Blue Kite* was censored by the Chinese government prior to its final editing, and it has never been publicly released in China despite its relative success in the international market. The editing was done in Tian's absence, but according to his directorial notes, by Japanese technicians in Tokyo.

On the surface, this film differs considerably from Tian's two early minority works. Unlike those, *Blue Kite* is shot from a highly subjective point of view. The film, mainly based on the life story of a boy from Beijing named Lin Dayu or Tietou (Iron Head), presents the world from his perspective. Along with his mother, Tietou lives through the most important political movements in the history of Communist China, that is, the Anti-Rightist Campaign in 1957, the Great Leap Forward in 1958, and the Cultural Revolution in 1966. His mother, Chen Shujuan, loses her three successive husbands during these political movements. Tietou's father, Lin Shaolong, sent to a labor camp in a border region as a rightist, is killed by a falling tree while chopping wood. His "uncle," Li Guogdong, falls in love with his mother partly out of guilt (during the Anti-Rightist Campaign he had reported his private conversation with Lin and another friend). Soon after his marriage to Shujuan, Li dies of liver failure partly due to malnutrition caused by "three years of natural disaster" – a convenient name for the economic disaster caused by the Great Leap Forward. Tietou's later stepfather, Wu, suffering from severe heart disease, dies during the Cultural Revolution after humiliation and torture at the hands of Red Guards. The film is divided into three segments, each of which has a title written in a childish hand: "father," "uncle," and "stepfather" – successive fathers for the protagonist.

Despite its highly subjective perspective, *Blue Kite,* like the two minority films, reveals a concern with one fundamental problem: individuals facing a powerful social institution.[29] Power may be represented by the hunting rules in the Mongolian community, as in *On the Hunting Ground,* or by religious authority in a Tibetan tribe, as in *Horse Thief.* As he repeatedly stated in his various interviews, Tian is mainly interested in the form of power that directly affected his personal life or that of his generation, the power of the Communist Party in the course of political movements. In this sense, *Blue Kite* is a direct expression of his concern, whereas the two minority movies approach it allegorically. This power had great impact on Tian's childhood and formative years, as it did in the case of the protagonist Tietou. Partly because almost two decades had separated Tian from the traumatic experience of his generation, the director felt comfortable enough to deal with this part of history in film. In contrast with the monotonous and impersonal voice-over of the anonymous Mandarin interpreter in *On the Hunting Ground,* Tietou's boyish voice in *Blue Kite* narrates "my" story, in a world often observed from the child's perspective. Moreover, the child's handwriting in the title and subtitles further suggests Tietou's subjective input.

Unlike the two minority movies, *Blue Kite* approaches the impact of political oppression on individuals like the director himself straightforwardly, and audiences can easily identify with the protagonist. Relatively free of the visual tours de force of Tian's minority films, *Blue Kite* roughly classifies various individuals' relations to the party's power matter-of-factly, in terms of space – that is, a person's relation to state power varies roughly in accordance with the space that he or she occupies at a given moment. The further one is temporarily situated from political power's direct control, the better one is able to enjoy life. By contrast, the closer one is to the power center, the more unbearable life is. Following the same logic, *Blue Kite* shows how the party gradually extends its power from official space to the private home. There are four primary categories of spatial relationship in this film: first, private space or home; second, public space such as a shared courtyard, neighborhood lane, street, or train station – spaces between the party's uninterrupted political control and possible intimacy within a family; third, official space, such as workplaces and prison cells, where the party's power is overwhelming; and fourth, the space of freedom on the margins of society.

HOME: THE LAST SHELTER OF INTIMACY

From the protagonist's point of view, two locations can be called "home": the two-room house that witnesses his parents' marriage and his own birth, and his maternal grandmother's house, where his widowed aunt and two bachelor uncles live. Both houses are situated in traditional Beijing-style courtyards "with houses on four sides" (*sihe yuan*), shared by several neighboring families. In his parents' house located in Ganjin ("dry well") Lane, Tietou spends his first three happy years with his own parents and his early childhood with his mother, Chen Shujuan. After the father's death, she is briefly married to the loving "uncle," Li Guodong, in this place. At the same time, Tietou often visits his grandmother's house. Since Tietou is the only third-generation member in this extended family, his grandmother, aunt, and real uncles all treat him like their own child.

The two-room house rented by Chen Shujuan and her first husband, Lin Shaolong, right before their marriage, serves as one of the major settings for the first two segments: "father" and "uncle." During these segments, the mother sporadically enjoys brief moments of happiness. In her first marriage, she appears deeply in love with Tietou's father; in her second marriage, she and the "uncle" have a mutually caring relationship. At the end of the second segment, after Li Guodong dies, the mother and son move out of this house forever. In its empty rooms, they leave behind them sad memories, represented by the guest register of Tietou's parents' wedding. At this point, most people, including his father and "uncle," who signed their names on the list a decade ago, have either died or disappeared during consecutive political movements. Thus, the list, currently buried in a pile of garbage, serves as a witness of the destruction of individual spaces by the political regime.

In this space, even Tietou's parents' highly politicized wedding ceremony offers many endearing features. The wedding preparations start with a crane shot of the courtyard plunged in a bluish tone, while a radio announces the death of the Soviet leader, Joseph Stalin. Ironically, the Communist Party, which perceives traditional mourning rituals for dead parents as "feudal," implicitly imposes a similar mourning upon Chinese citizens for a foreign communist "father." Consequently, Tietou's parents feel that they need to mourn this foreign "father" for two months before they can perform the wedding ceremony, in order to express their unconditional support for the regime. This incident adds a comic twist: On the one hand, this delay further intensifies the couple's expectations for the wedding, especially taking into consideration that premarital sex was criminalized in the Mao era. Tietou's voice-over jokingly comments, "That's how the date of my birth was delayed for ten days." On the other hand, this scene also shows that from the very beginning Shujuan's private life has never been intentionally in conflict with the dominant ideology. On the contrary, everyone seems to support the party the best they can. The wedding ceremony provides a good example. First, the groom and the bride bow to Chairman Mao's portrait – the party leader occupies the position of the father in a traditional Chinese ceremony. Then, when the participants request that the couple sing a song, they choose one praising socialist China. In a long tracking shot, all the participants cheerfully join the couple in singing this song, which goes like this: "In our great socialist motherland, youngsters improve their lives everyday, and old people become younger and younger."

In the following sequence, the groom and the bride playfully perform a traditional wedding ceremony after the departure of all the guests. In contrast with the dominant blue tone in the rest of the film, the bride's flushing red Chinese dress with large embroidered flowers brightens the room. This red dress, according to Shujuan, "cannot be worn outside" (*naer chuande chuqu ne*). It can be shown only in this private space, and at a brief moment of a playful return to a lost past. As a counterdiscourse against the bloody color of revolution (the Chinese national flag and party flag are both supposedly colored by the blood of revolutionary martyrs), the red color in this film occasionally returns to its precommunist Chinese tradition – symbolizing happiness and good fortune. However, the brief nostalgic moment of happiness appears particularly fragile, as if it might be disrupted at any moment under the intrusive gaze of the Big Other. Even the least politically threatening intruder, Madam Lan, the private landlady, makes the couple feel somewhat ashamed of their jubilation.

The warm light engendered by the newlyweds suffuses Shujuan's two-room house throughout the film's first segment. While the grandmother bathes the baby Tietou, Shujuan smiles to her husband Shaolong, who is outside under a similar reddish soft light. The happy father gazes through the window at his beautiful wife and healthy child. After Shaolong's death, the warm light seldom returns to this corner. The visits of Li Guodong, the "uncle" and surrogate father for Tietou, occasionally bring warmth to the family; but almost all of his visits have a sad, if not disastrous, ending, as if the house no longer had room for personal pleasure. During one visit, in front of the ominous handkerchief that served as the wedding guest register – most of whose signatories have either died or disappeared – Guodong confesses to Shujuan the sad truth that it was he who reported to the leader a conversation with her dead husband and another friend. Although Shujuan forgives him wholeheartedly, thanks to her grasp of the nature of political movements through these years, his relentlessly exaggerated guilty feelings anger Shujuan to the extent that his next visit ends in a vehement quarrel. Political movements, which pit even the best friends against one another, create an impossible atmosphere for the communication between the two lovers. During another visit, while playing with Tietou, Guodong falls from a chair due to liver pain, a symptom of his hepatitis – the disease that, aggravated by malnutrition, will later claim his life.

Shujuan chooses Guodong as her second husband partly because of his fatherly love for her son. As if to prove this point, the couple's interchanges are often perceived from Tietou's perspective, giving the impression that the child is present at each of his mother's encounters with his "uncle." Furthermore, their wedding picture includes all her neighbors. In a crane shot of the courtyard, almost twenty people participate in this picture taking – quite a contrast to the traditional (if supplemental) wedding intimately enacted between Shujuan and Shaolong. Not surprisingly, it is difficult to distinguish the "uncle" from the rest of the crowd in the photograph, especially because all the men, including the groom, wear inconspicuous dark blue suits. The last scene of Guodong in the house ends in his second fall, which leads to his death in hospital a month later.

The other place Tietou knows as "home," Shujuan's mother's house, offers a warm family ambiance. At the grandmother's house, family members are usually sitting around the dinner table. If Shujuan's home is portrayed as a private corner, the grandmother's house represents Tietou's maternal extended family. On the evening of Shujuan's first wedding, Shaolong is surrounded by his bride and her extended family at the dinner table. In contrast to the impressive visual manipulations in Tian's minority movies, this scene focuses on individual psychology, subtly portraying each member's distinct personality. The grandmother anxiously asks why Shujuan has not worn the traditional dress she made for her; in other words, she wants her daughter to play the role of a traditional bride, that is, to appear as beautiful as possible. Her old-fashioned motherly desire is bound to be frustrated, however, because in the new historical period being pretty is less important than being revolutionary. Moreover, since femininity in a traditional sense contradicts with the image of a revolutionary woman, Shujuan has no choice but to wear subdued clothes in order to look like a "new woman." For example, Shujuan's elder sister, a communist cadre who devotes her life to the revolution, always dresses in dull blue. Her language is as dull as the color of her dress, full of political clichés. At this family banquet celebrating her sister's wedding, she describes her sober and unfortunate marriage in a Yan'an grotto, which resulted in the death of the groom on the battlefield shortly after the wedding. At the end of the sister's story, the camera cuts to a close-up of Shujuan's hand grasping Shaolong's tightly under the table – secretly congratulating each other for their good fortune of living in a much happier society. (Ironically, a similar fate will befall the newlyweds shortly after their marriage; but whereas the sister's husband died for his ideal during wartime, as a glorified revolutionary martyr, Shaolong will die senselessly during a peaceful period, as a humiliated political outcast.)

The elder brother Shusheng, also at the banquet table, has the most common sense in this family. (Probably for this reason, he will soon become blind.) Once a Nationalist military pilot, he had brought a fighter jet to the Communist Party. As a result, his status as a "democratic gentleman" (*minzhu renshi*) – that is, a member of a different party who firmly supports the communist regime – makes him to a degree immune from the party's strict political control, to which other, common Chinese are subject. This relative freedom allows Shusheng occasionally to voice frank criticism to his family members against successive political movements. At Shusheng's request, Shaolong timidly calls his mother-in-law "mama" for the first time. Thus the elder brother concludes the ritual in which the extended family accepts Shaolong's membership.

In the first section of the film, this traditional family seemingly establishes a model for the future generation. While bathing the newborn Tietou, Shujuan's mother, with a beaming smile, tells the baby: "In the future, you will also give life to such a big, fat boy." However, political movements interrupt this continuity of the family tradition. In Shujuan's second and third marriages, most of her extended family members are absent. Near the end of the film, another wedding celebrated in the same family compound offers a completely different picture.

When her younger brother Shuyan briefly returns to his mother's house from the border region in order to have his wedding, only Tietou, Shusheng (who has lost his sight by now), and the grandmother are present. In other words, the participants in this family celebration include a child, a handicapped person, and an old lady. Any "normal" adult member is either dead, such as Shaolong, or tied by political obligations, such as the elder sister and (by then) Shujuan. Contrary to the loving relationship between Tietou's parents a decade earlier, Shuyan remains distant from his bride throughout the sober wedding ceremony. The images of Shuyan's wedding form a striking contrast to those of Shujuan's early in the film, where everyone happily participates in the ceremony as a close family, and Shusheng urges Shaolong to call his mother-in-law "mama." At Shuyan's wedding, on the other hand, the few family members who attend seem utterly uninterested. The only person who displays enthusiasm is the bride herself, who, without any invitation, repeatedly calls each one "mother," "brother," or "nephew." Each one, being named in such an artificially familiar tone, reacts uneasily to her overzealous initiative. In contrast with the newlyweds' passionate hand holding under the table a decade ago, the physical distance between Shuyan and his bride seems unbridgeable. As an indifferent observer of his own wedding, the groom listlessly lies in bed and watches his bride run around in the kitchen or the courtyard, busily ingratiating herself with every member of his family by doing all kinds of house chores. Shuyan's wedding dinner is highlighted by exchanges of negative comments about the bride between the groom and his malicious nephew behind her back. Shuyan even approves Tietou's debasing remark about the bride's looks, by telling him not to follow his example in the future.

Moreover, he admits to his nephew that in a sense he was forced to marry her, since his previous girlfriend was dismissed by his local party leader due to her politically incorrect background.

Between these two marriages, Shujuan's and Shuyan's, politics has succeeded in destroying the happy image of the extended family. Not only does Shujuan's two-room house never get the chance to develop into as warm, secure, and affectionate a family space as her mother's house, but even the atmosphere at her mother's house fades away due to the increasing intrusion of political movements.

PUBLIC SPACE

Tietou plays with other children in the courtyard and the lane, an intermediate zone situated between school and home. Although from the very beginning in this kind of public space the atmosphere is not as warm and sweet as in a traditional home, it is also much less threatening than in an official institution or workplace (*danwei*), since neighbors at least occasionally offer each other friendly assistance. On the one hand, the courtyard resembles a traditional extended family. The children in the courtyard play together and neighbors help each other. For example, after three years of economic hardship caused by the Great Leap Forward, all the neighbors come out on the eve of the Chinese New Year in 1961 to share dumplings and celebrate the end of this ordeal. On the other hand, since even in a private household family members cannot preserve their emotional ties under constant political pressure, its apparently friendly atmosphere is understandably more fragile. Physically, this zone has no roof to cover itself from the threatening "obscene" gaze of the symbolic father, the party. Emotionally, neighbors are not tied biologically as in a family. As if the film intended to prove this point, political turmoil constantly disrupts the children's happy games. As a toddler, Tietou already witnesses how the director of the street committee (*jiedao weiyuanhui*) forces the landlady, Madam Lan, to participate in a meeting – as a member of the "bourgeois" class, she is a political underdog. In this sense, the courtyard also resembles society in general in that, despite its analogy to a traditional family, it has its own political scapegoat, the landlady. Furthermore, Tietou himself suffers political discrimination when a group of schoolboys beat him in the lane simply because they learn of his father's status as political outcast. Fortunately, his neighbors rescue him.

In terms of atmosphere, the train station can be considered a larger version of the courtyard and the lane. Due to its function as an intersection between home and the distant world, the station witnesses the separation and reunion of family members in the heart of political movements. When Tietou is three, his father leaves him and his mother behind in the train station in order to travel to a labor camp in a remote border region – from which he never returns to his family. At the same place, Tietou also welcomes his mother returning from the countryside

6. Mother and son in *Blue Kite,* directed by Tian Zhuangzhuang (1993). COURTESY OF
PHOTOFEST.

after three months of "voluntary" farming work [Fig. 6]. Like a thermometer, the
train station measures changes of political temperature. Tietou's father leaves the
station wrapped in the gloomy atmosphere of the Anti-Rightist Movement. By
contrast, his mother returns to Beijing in the heart of the Great Leap Forward,
accompanied by overzealous revolutionary songs and slogans, and surrounded
by numerous red flags. Finally, during the departure of Shusheng's former girlfriend, Zhu Ying, at the beginning of the Cultural Revolution, the station exemplifies the chaotic state of the entire country: Red Guards jump in and out of the
train from windows, and no one dares to object. A loudspeaker broadcasts a monotonous revolutionary song. Shusheng, who has by now lost his sight, waves
goodbye to a stranger before his sister redirects his hand toward Zhu Ying, who
has just returned from her prison. At the same time, we hear Tietou's voice-over:
"I don't know why Aunt Zhu Ying was arrested or released. I asked her. She said
that she didn't know too well either. This remains a mystery for me forever."
Mysteriously, Zhu Ying comes and goes, and is finally swallowed up in the anonymous crowd at the train station. No one knows what will happen to her, including her onetime boyfriend. However, this no longer matters: as she had asked
him before, during his visit to her in jail, "What does it matter whether you can
see me or not?" Since the entire country is overwhelmed by collective madness,

individual tragedy becomes ordinary and insignificant, part of everyday life. Not a single person can avoid his or her tragic fate, if arbitrarily targeted by the political power. Neither private home nor public space will offer refuge.

OFFICIAL SPACE

Workplaces are threatening spaces in the film because they are officially controlled by the party and represent the origin of all political movements. Shusheng once receives a visit from his girlfriend, Zhu Ying, while working in an airplane hangar. A dark bluish light dominates the immense hangar, which appears particularly impersonal. Once the warehouse opens, sudden exposure to daylight makes him temporarily lose his sight – a sure sign of glaucoma, the cause for his future blindness. This ambiance is similar to that at the textile factory where Shusheng visits Zhu Ying. She has been transferred to this factory from her army drama troupe in order to punish her for her refusal to dance with a party leader – possibly a sexual harasser. The two work units create an extremely oppressive and prisonlike atmosphere for the lovers, foreshadowing the destruction of their happiness by the party's arbitrary power. Immediately following these two scenes of their respective workplaces, each of the lovers encounters the most difficult moment in his or her life. After Zhu visits him at the hangar, Shusheng learns of his glaucoma. In order to connect his loss of sight to political oppression by the state, the doctor who examines his eyes tells Shusheng that he should by all means avoid anxiety and anger, which would likely lead to his blindness. After Shusheng visits Zhu's textile factory, she is arrested. When he visits her next, her unit is no longer simply prisonlike but an actual prison. In a similar gloomy blue light, Zhu faces Shusheng in her cell. A backlit close-up makes the former star actress look almost like a zombie, with her disheveled hair and lifeless voice. The atmosphere in her cell, however, is not substantially different from that of their respective workplaces.

If these workplaces seem like prisons in normal times, they are certainly much more frightening during political movements. In the library where Shaolong works, during the Anti-Rightist Campaign the party secretary asks workers to denounce more rightists among them, since the number is still too small to fulfill the party's quota. At this moment, Shaolong has an urge to go to the restroom. The following deep-focus shot exposes Shaolong standing on his return and facing the silent gaze of his colleagues on both sides of the seemingly endless conference table. Since everyone felt too embarrassed to accuse a colleague falsely in his or her presence, Shaolong's brief absence provided his coworkers the opportunity to meet the party's mandatory quota while sparing them the embarrassment of confronting him on the spot. As a result, his basic need at an unfortunate moment turns him into a public enemy – a rightist. In another deep-focus shot, Shusheng and his fellow army officers are sitting on two sides of a similar long conference table while their party secretary reads the list of newly select-

ed rightists. One officer shoots himself in the head as soon as the secretary pronounces his name. His body falls heavily on the floor, and blood flows abundant-
ly from his lifeless head.

MARGINAL SPACE

In the course of the film, private space is increasingly invaded by political
movements to the extent that home has gradually become contaminated by ideological and political oppression, which prevails in the official space. At the end
of the film even a private conversation between mother and daughter must be
censored within the confined home space in order to avoid looming persecution.
As a result, in this heavily ideologically constraining world, freedom can be created only either in a fantasy or a marginal world. This world cannot be shared
by everyone or projected in any place, since politics has invaded most space and
occupies everyone's mind. Children can still project their fantasies in the sky
through a sense of identification with airborne toys or birds, whereas old housewives living on the margins of social politics can occasionally throw a commonsensical gaze at the dominant ideology by innocently pointing out its absurdity.

Even when Tietou is only a toddler, he already expresses a desire for freedom. During the Great Leap Forward, sparrows are considered to be one of the
"four harmful animals" (*sihai*), along with flies, mice, and mosquitos. Sparrows
supposedly diminish the harvest in China by eating grain in the field, and so must
be eliminated. Following the party's logic, hundreds of people in Tietou's neighborhood, as in the rest of the country, try to catch as many sparrows as possible.
They create a great noise with gongs and cymbals to induce disoriented sparrows to fall from the sky. One of them falls in the hands of a neighboring boy,
who gives it to Tietou at his request. Although Tietou claims that the bird escaped
from him, a previous shot shows that he deliberately releases it as soon as the
little sparrow reaches his hands. In another association of boy and bird, Tietou
also learns a song from his mother at a very tender age. In this children's rhyme,
Tietou compares himself with a baby crow, who grows up in order to feed his
mother in her old age. This song, repeated constantly, becomes the film's theme
song.

Toward the end of the film, private space, previously associated with the soft-
focused warm light, is increasingly overwhelmed by the cold blue tone prevailing in institutional spaces to the point that every place looks equally depressing.
Furthermore, the household of Tietou's stepfather, Shujuan's third husband, appears cold, impersonal, and institutional from the very beginning. As a high official of the Communist Party, understandably his home is free of bourgeois or feudal sentimentalism. Unlike the two houses with limited spaces, Wu's spacious
mansion is divided into large private rooms. Confined in his or her segregated
space, each family member has almost no chance to disturb others in his or her
clearly assigned duty and space – Wu with his official documents in his office,

Tietou with his homework in his room, and Shujuan with her cooking in the kitchen.

However, before the very end, the warm reddish light returns at least once – not inside the house, but in an open space. An event accidentally breaks the distant atmosphere in Tietou's new family. During a visit to the family of the stepfather's son, Wu's granddaughter, Niuniu, a cute five-year-old girl, inadvertently helps Tietou establish an emotional tie with his stepfather by persistently asking her "little uncle" to fly a kite for her. Although Tietou, who is only eight or nine years older, initially does not want to accept such a "foolish name" (*bie xiajiao*), he finally yields to Niuniu's stubborn request. When Tietou takes Niuniu to the Yuanmingyuan Garden, they fly a blue kite under a sky colored by a beautiful sunset. This happy moment creates a utopian space that allows the two children momentarily to escape from the oppressive political movement that increasingly dominates everyone's life. Furthermore, the kite in this movie represents a father's tie to his child, a tie constantly undermined, if not destroyed, by political movements. A decade earlier, Tietou's father had demonstrated his affection to his son by promising to make a new kite for him, since the old one was stuck in a tree. Now Tietou himself assumes a father's role by repeating to Niuniu the same promise, word for word. The kite expresses the children's desire to escape from political oppression, although this desire cannot prevent it from ruining their lives. However, this symbolic fatherhood does not last long: When later he returns from school, Tietou asks about Niuniu. Wu explains that he has sent Niuniu away, since he is worried about his granddaughter's safety at the beginning of a political movement – the Cultural Revolution. Like his father a decade ago, Tietou never has the chance to keep his promise to his "niece." From this point on, however, the relationship between the stepfather and stepson improves considerably, to the point that Wu finally becomes fatherly toward Tietou.

Interestingly, in *Blue Kite,* any man who assumes a father's role, including the adolescent Tietou in his symbolic role for his "niece," will sooner or later be victimized by the party's political movements. In this sense, political movements serve as instruments for the Communist Party to eliminate any possible father figure besides the abstract party icons, such as the name of Stalin and the portrait of Chairman Mao. Through this symbolic father figure, state power invades private space by usurping the traditional position of the family authority. As a result, family in this film is portrayed as fatherless: In Tietou's family alone, three successive fathers are eliminated by political movements. Behaving like a father, even only symbolically as in Tietou's relationship with Niuniu, also provokes life-threatening punishment, like the protagonist endures at the end of the film.

Although the sparrow released by Tietou may continue to enjoy its limited freedom, none of the human beings in this film seems capable of escaping the fate of a captured bird. Consequently, some external obstacles always prevent Tietou from fulfilling his desire for freedom. even in his fantasy world. Three times, Tietou's kites are stuck on top of trees. The repeated image of stuck kites suggests how difficult it is for an individual to escape from the ironclad control of the police state – even in an imaginary world. In the concluding shot, Tietou lies unconscious under a broken kite stuck on a tree branch, after being beaten severely by a group of Red Guards – viewers are not sure whether he is dead or alive. In the end, fantasy space has also been eliminated, and a dreamer is harshly punished for his dream. The blue kite, stuck and broken over the protagonist's motionless body, symbolizes the fate of this innocent dreamer in a totalitarian society where individualistic desire is often criminalized. Following the same logic, a space that allows such a desire deserves elimination. As a reminder of the past happiness, the film concludes with the children's rhyme about the baby crow in Tietou's childish voice.

Nevertheless, if private spaces, including the children's fantasy world, are drastically reduced, if not eliminated, by the intrusive gaze of political power, politics is also ridiculed by the innocent observation of some old ladies. These ladies are mostly housewives – a rare species in socialist China, because it is mandatory for any woman of the younger generation to participate in the work force, for both ideological and economic reasons. As a result, these ladies are the only people able to keep a certain distance from the party's propaganda in the workplace. They are a leftover species of traditional China. This distance allows them to preserve a certain amount of common sense, because to a degree they still live in a traditional past, which is not completely dehumanized by daily political struggles in contemporary society.

When Shaolong explains to Madam Lan that they decided to hold the wedding on March 8, the official women's holiday in China, Madam Lan answers: "Even number is good. It is auspicious" (*shuangshu hao, jili*). Her ignorance of the ideological implication enables her to (mis)interpret their decision in a traditional way – as a symbol of happiness. In fact, her (mis)interpretation is closer to a commonsensical understanding of a wedding, since future happiness should be much more important for the engaged couple than the vague ideological significance of an official holiday. When the radio announces Stalin's death (a reminder of Hou Xiaoxian's movies, whose trademark is using radio broadcasts to mark historical events), Granny – an old neighbor and Tietou's future baby-sitter – asks innocently, "What's the face of this guy? What did he do in his life?" Her question inadvertently points out a simple fact: In reality a foreign leader's death has nothing to do with the life of a young Chinese couple on the verge of getting married. Consequently, the couple's decision to postpone the marriage as a gesture of mourning in accordance with the dominant ideology cannot be more absurd, judged from a commonsensical perspective. During the Cultural Revolution, as a party official, Shujuan's elder sister repeatedly undergoes struggle-sessions. Shujuan's mother comments to her daughter, "She has spent her entire life doing revolution, why does she still need to be revolutionized?" (*gele yibeizi ming, hai ge?*) This apparently politically innocent question lays bare the madness inherent in the logic of Mao's party: In the name of revolution, everyone must constantly face the danger of becoming the party's political enemy, including the most faithful members of the party.

In this chapter, I have studied the three films that Tian claimed were truly his own:[30] two minority movies, *On the Hunting Ground* and *Horse Thief,* and one film about Beijing during the Cultural Revolution, *Blue Kite.* In his two minority movies, visual effects are often dazzling. At the same time, both films reach a degree of verisimilitude that characterizes ethnographic documentaries. In both films, the camera stays mainly objective. As a result, minority characters, Mongolians and Tibetans, are observed from an external point of view. In *Blue Kite,* by contrast, the director devoted his attention to individual emotions and psychology, as well as interpersonal relationships. Moreover, the world of the film is often observed through the subjective perspective of Tietou, the young protagonist.

One can explain these differences in terms of Tian's personal experiences. The Han Chinese director is an outsider to both the Mongolian and the Tibetan cultures, whereas Tietou's life experience in *Blue Kite* to a great extent resembles his own, as Tian explained to me in his interview. Having grown up in Beijing, like Tietou, Tian himself is indeed an insider of the "lane and courtyard culture." In both cases, the camera seems to reflect accurately the director's positions in the respective cultures. Furthermore, from 1986, the year he made *Horse Thief,* to 1993, the year for *Blue Kite,* Fifth Generation filmmakers underwent radical changes. *On the Hunting Ground* and *Horse Thief* were sponsored by the state-owned studios Inner Mongolian and Xi'an in the mid-1980s. At the beginning of the open-door reformist policy, Xi'an Studio was famous for its support for formal innovations. In this context, box-office failure would not greatly effect the financial situation of the filmmaker's socialist "iron bowl." By 1992, since the film industry in China had become market-oriented, box-office value had become predominant in measuring a film's success or failure. At the same time, well-known Fifth Generation directors started seeking investments from multinational corporations. In this case, their works depended even more on commercial success in a global market. Understandably, the antinarrative and experimental tendency in Tian's minority films can no longer survive in the new world.

Since the relative commercial success of Zhang Yimou's first three movies in the international market, most Fifth Generation directors have multiplied their efforts to make conventional narrative films, often by re-creating eroticized and suffering images of Chinese female beauties in the early 1990s. In this respect, Tian's *Blue Kite* bears many characteristics of its time. Nevertheless, Tian followed the Zhang Yimou model[31] more discreetly than most of his colleagues – such as Chen Kaige, for example, who wholeheartedly embraced this model in his *Farewell My Concubine* (1993) and *Temptress Moon* (1996). Although Tian's film was forbidden in China, ironically, it was one of the few films made by Fifth Generation directors during this period that tried genuinely to address the Chinese audience despite its focus on the global market. Unlike most films in the Zhang Yimou model, *Blue Kite* avoided ritualizing Chinese tradition. Furthermore, Tian's antitraditional fervor at the early stage of his career was toned down, possibly thanks to the influence of Hou Xiaoxian (who is a good friend of his). Unlike in his earlier films, traces of traditional Chinese culture in *Blue Kite* are portrayed in a relatively positive light.

Nevertheless, despite their different outlooks, all three of these films by Tian have one point in common: They all question the effect of political power over individuals through various institutions – as Tian repeatedly stated in his numerous interviews. In the final analysis, all these institutions are metaphors for one form of power: that of the Communist Party. *Blue Kite* presents a straightforward picture of this power through the portrayals of various political movements, despite its somewhat schematic and simplistic structure.

Tian explains what motivated him to make *Horse Thief:*

The reason I want to do this film now is that Chinese politics is somewhat religious in nature. I'm going to link social reality with religion. Communism is a kind of religion. This is what I want to reflect in my film, because what we have gone through in the recent past has deepened our understanding of politics.[32]

In other words, Tibetan religion allows Tian to question the political culture in the mainstream Han society allegorically, since religion becomes the equivalent of communism. This political culture was responsible for some of the most traumatic experiences in the life of his generation. Like other well-known Fifth Generation directors, Tian was deeply influenced by the Cultural Revolution and other previous political movements during their childhood and formative years. Until 1993, however, no one among them had made a single film devoted to the trauma of this historical moment. Tian was the first Fifth Generation filmmaker to portray this period exhaustively in his *Blue Kite,* after it had become a relatively distant past. Subsequently, Chen Kaige's *Farewell My Concubine (Bawang bieji,* 1993) and Zhang Yimou's *To Live (Huozhe,* 1994) followed the same course by focusing on the traumatic effect of political movements on Chinese people.

Interestingly, Tian's first film, *Red Elephant (Hong xiang,* 1982), made at the request of the Children's Film Studio, also focuses on a minority group. In this film, several Dai children of an elementary school search for the legendary red elephant in the Sishuanbanna forests. Although it is not as visually striking as his two later minority movies, *Red Elephant* nevertheless underlines the director's fascination with minority cultures. During his interview with me, Tian explained this fascination in terms of his own straightforward personality. Since the Han society appeared too complicated to his taste, the filmmaker felt much more at home in a relatively primitive community. However, despite his claimed affinity with ethnic minorities, Tibetans and Mongolians in his best-known films are portrayed in an objectifying fashion, whereas Han characters are granted much greater subjective voices in *Blue Kite* and other films. Furthermore, Tian also explained that, compared to such colleagues as Chen Kaige and Zhang Yimou, he felt much more reluctant to impose his will upon his crew members. As a result, the quality of his films often suffered to the point that the director had a hard time accepting them as his own. However, Tian did not seem to feel reluctant to demand that his minority actors follow the directorial intention – occasionally even against their religious faith.[33] That may partly explain why the two more artistically mature minority films are his most visually successful works, since they are "truly his," to use his words. Because minority actors, unlike their Han counterparts, are relatively free of subjectivity in the director's eyes, they can carry his signature more forcefully and efficiently.

During the 1980s, partly because a profound disappointment in mainstream culture brought about an ideological vacuum in post–Cultural Revolution China, some writers and filmmakers used minority cultures as critical weapons against the dominant culture. For example, Ma Yuan and Ma Jian, two well-known writers of Tian's generation, both specialized in fictional works on Tibetan culture. Zhang Nuanxin, a Fourth Generation director, made a film *Sacrificed Youth* (*Qingchun ji*) in the mid-1980s. From the subjective perspective of a Han "educated youth," the film portrays the Dai community in which a city girl spends her formative years during the Cultural Revolution. In all three cases, minorities are portrayed with a touch of differential racism – that is, they are used as a relatively shapeless mirror to send a critical image of the Han mainstream culture.[34] To a degree, some of the "western films" (*xibu dianying*)[35] (including Chen Kaige's *Yellow Earth* and Zhang Yimou's *Red Sorghum*), belong to the same category, taking into consideration these areas' great distance from the geopolitical and cultural center in China.[36] Despite the various techniques used to portray minority cultures, one fundamental condition remains constant: An insurmountable gap exists between the center and its margins. These Chinese authors, proud of their close ties with the mainstream culture despite their openly acknowledged admiration for the "primitive" cultures, portray these cultures as the Other. Thus, these cultures do not exist on their own merits – except as "difference" from the mainstream Han culture – since their critical power originates precisely in their irreducible difference. Negatively, this difference nevertheless reconfirms the centrality of the Han culture by the subordinated roles of the marginal cultures.[37] Not surprisingly, this reconfirmation of the Han culture's centrality through a negative channel was intricately related to the resurgence of nationalism during the 1990s.

Étienne Balibar states:

The discussion of this controversy (as of other similar controversies to which we might refer) is of considerable value to us here, since through it we begin to grasp that the connection between nationalism and racism is neither a matter of perversion (for there is no "pure" essence of nationalism) nor a question of formal similarity, but a question of historical articulation. What we have to understand is the specific difference of racism and the way in which, in articulating itself to nationalism, it is, in its difference, necessary to nationalism. This to say, by the very same token, that the articulation of nationalism and racism cannot be disentangled by applying classical schemas of causality, whether mechanistic (the one as the cause of the other, "producing" the other according to the rule of the proportionality of the effects to the cause) or spiritualistic (the one "expressing" the other, or giving it its meaning or revealing its hidden essence). It requires a dialectics of the unity of opposites.[38]

What happens to China during the 1980s and 1990s neatly corresponds to Balibar's assessment. A "differential racism" expressed in a number of literary and cinematic works of the 1980s was indeed followed by a popularized nationalism during the 1990s. This intricate connection between racism and nationalism can be traced back to the Nationalist Revolution at the beginning of the century, which to an extent initially based its agenda on the Othering of the Manchu ethnic group, from which the rulers of the Qing dynasty had originated.[39] In this sense, the "dialectics of the unity of opposites" between nationalism and racism has been inherited from the discourse of modernity imported to China at the beginning of the twentieth century. In both cases, the negative identity of the self is based on an Other defined by insurmountable differences. All these differences from the Other, be they imaginative or realistic, serve to reinforce a relatively homogeneous notion of cultural identity. Precisely because this notion is largely fictional, the only criterion on which it can rely is the differences of the Other. Understandably, regardless of how favorably contemporary Chinese authors may apparently view minority groups' "cultural differences" from the Han society, with few exceptions they have never touched either the subject of political oppression of minority groups by the Chinese government (as in the case of Tibetans, Mongolians, and Muslims), or the problem of the blatantly discriminatory attitude toward these minority groups among Han nationals.[40] At the same time, their own attitude remains in step with the widely accepted prejudices against these cultures in the mainstream Han Chinese society.

For example, Tian's confessed love for minority cultures notwithstanding, his visually accurate pictures cannot help portraying these groups in a negative light – backward and primitive – a snapshot commensurable with the generally accepted view of them among the Han Chinese. Minority characters are not truly granted subject positions and voices, since their expressions must primarily serve their allegorical functions as criticism of communist ideology in the mainstream Han Chinese society. Consequently, despite their astonishing quality of ethnographic documentary, Tian's minority films fail to bring the cultures they portrayed closer to their audiences, who are usually not familiar with them. Instead, they inadvertently reinforce the distance between these cultures and spectators. These characters' sense of alienation, through which the film intends to illustrate the negative effect of the communist power in the Han Chinese mainstream society, makes them appear even more alien to us. Although Tian is indeed fascinated with minority cultures, his attitude toward them still reflects a prevailing "differential racism" among most Han Chinese intellectuals.

Part II

IN SEARCH OF TRADITION IN
THE MIDST OF MODERNIZATION

3

FROM A VOICELESS FATHER TO A FATHER'S VOICE

HOU XIAOXIAN: *A TIME TO LIVE AND A TIME TO DIE; CITY OF SADNESS; THE PUPPETMASTER*

Jiao Xiongping, a leading Taiwan film critic, writes, "Hou Xiaoxian has constantly tried [in his films] to search for an origin of Taiwan history."[1] If we look closely at his films, however, we have the impression that this origin has much stronger connections with his personal experiences than with a general sense of national history. At the same time, in a different context personal experiences are not necessarily in conflict with what Jiao calls national identity, since Hou Xiaoxian, whose family immigrated to Taiwan during the late 1940s, shares an ambiguity toward his own identity with a great number of "mainlanders" (*waisheng ren*), despite his close ties to the regional culture. Literally, *waisheng ren* means "outsiders to the [Taiwan] province," although these so-called outsiders have resided in Taiwan for half a century. Originally, both mainlanders and the Taiwanese (*bensheng ren*) were from China, the only difference being their date of arrival, either before or after the Japanese occupation. This artificial line of demarcation was used to justify the minority rule of the Nationalist government over the majority of Taiwanese at the beginning of its power, since the Taiwanese had supposedly been "enslaved" (*nuhua*)[2] by the Japanese colonizers for half a century.

Furthermore, the Nationalist government, initially led by recent mainland immigrants, considered Taiwan culture to be an insignificant part of the great Chinese tradition. In the past, few officially sponsored scholarly works have been devoted to regional history, whereas a great number of them have contributed to Confucian, Daoist, Buddhist, and traditional Chinese historical studies in Taiwan. The most exhaustive historical work on Taiwan prior to the end of martial law in 1987 was written in Japanese by Shi Ming, an expatriated activist in the Taiwan independence movement.[3] This book was censored in Taiwan until the late 1980s. Because of its emphasis on orthodox traditional Chinese origins, situated in an unreachable and politically segregated land, official culture has been rooted in a nationalistic dream, the dream of returning to the mainland, perceived as the ultimate cultural center. The longer the Nationalist government has remained in Taiwan, the more unrealistic this dream has become. Meanwhile, during the

1960s and 1970s the Taiwan economy became increasingly prosperous, whereas the political struggles within the Communist Party led the mainland toward social upheavals and economic disasters. After Jiang Jingguo became chief of the Executive Yuan in 1972, political power started gradually shifting from the hands of the mainlanders to the Taiwanese. Under these circumstances, the officially defined identity centering on the mainland culture has become increasingly irrelevant, whereas an awareness of a Taiwan identity, different from the official definition of that of the Chinese, has become pronounced. A case in point is the Native Soil literature (*xiangtu wenxue*), which, during the 1970s, focused on the everyday life of the common people in Taiwan.[4] To a large extent, Hou's films, especially the early ones, can be considered an extension of this literary form because of their focus on ordinary local people's experiences. Furthermore, Wu Nianzhen, a well-known Native Soil writer of the 1970s, has written a great number of Hou's screenplays.

Nevertheless, Hou's notion of a Taiwan identity is different from the official definition of the identity of the Taiwanese (*bensheng ren*). As a descendent of a mainland family, and thus by definition a mainlander or an outsider to Taiwan, Hou Xiaoxian is torn between his official identity and his actual experience of growing up among his Taiwanese friends in the less industrialized South. His language and culture are far more distant from the orthodox Chinese culture than from the local culture, largely because as a child he preferred street activities, mainly conducted in Taiwanese, to the Mandarin-speaking school education. Some of Hou Xiaoxian's films can be seen as steps in overcoming the apparently unquestioned difference between the mainlanders and the Taiwanese. I argue in this chapter that his ingenious search for a reconciled identity has often taken the form of a search for a father figure, capable of replacing his own silent and debilitated biological father from the mainland, portrayed in his autobiographical film *A Time to Live and a Time to Die* (*Tongnian wangshi,* 1985). Later, a strong father figure emerged in *The Puppetmaster* (*Ximeng rensheng,* 1993). At a spiritual level, as a powerful father deeply rooted in the local culture as well as in the traditional Chinese value system, Li Tianlu, the film's protagonist, helps the director come to terms with his personal history as an outsider in his own land.

VOICELESS FATHER: A TIME TO LIVE AND A TIME TO DIE

A Time to Live and a Time to Die, Hou's autographical film, descibes how Aha (Axiao in Mandarin), who represents the director during his childhood and adolescence, grew up in a mainlander family, surrounded by the local Taiwanese culture in the South. In this film, Hou uses various "natural" frames. From the beginning, the introductory shot is framed by the entrance of a house, in front of which is written "Dormitory of the Gaoxiong District Administration" (*gaoxiong xianzhengfu sushe*) – a sober image of an impersonal residence, which is subsidized by the government for its employees. Inside, the dormitory appears depressingly compartmentalized. Associated with the images of this home, Hou's matter-of-fact voice-over emphasizes the "theme" of his film, namely, his childhood memories, especially "impressions of [his] father." The director's emotionless tone creates an illusion of a private conversation carried on with friends and acquaintances, instead of an address to the public.

Despite its apparent realism, the film is self-conscious about its filmmaking process: It constantly points out the camera's presence through reframing. The static camera is compensated for by the movements of characters doubly framed by a number of doors and the camera itself. The first person to enter this *mise-en-abyme* of frames is the narrator's father. While Hou's voice-over singles out his father as the most important person in his childhood memories, a medium shot places him in a bamboo chair while the voice-over explains how his family moved to Taiwan. From this point on, the father becomes barely separable from this chair. At the same time, the chair is supposedly bought for its transient quality, since the father initially did not intend to stay long in Taiwan. As he can never return to the mainland, the furniture bought for temporary usage has become a symbol of his life, which the chair has ironically outlived. Although the director's voice-over emphasizes his impressions of his father, these impressions appear slim and elusive. After Aha, the first-person protagonist, has passed the junior-high-school entrance examination, his mother asks him to report this good news to his father, who apparently values only book learning, as in the Confucian tradition. This is the only time in the film that the father and son speak to each other. However, since the father rarely communicates with Aha and his siblings, he fails to understand his son's news. Only after the mother has translated Aha's Mandarin into Hakka does the father finally grasp the son's words. Although Aha's adolescence constitutes the most important part of the film, the father dies of tuberculosis when the son has not yet left childhood.

Nevertheless, from a different point of view, the claim that Hou's voice-over made at the beginning of the film may be taken literally. This film is indeed "especially about [his] impressions of [his] father" – not about his presence, but rather about his absence. Like the introductory shot of the empty bamboo chair, a metonymy for his body, the father gives a lasting impression through the transient nature of his life, or his heartfelt absence. In most cases, the father is immovable and speechless. The only scene in which he speaks is introduced by a radio announcement on the air battle over Taiwan Strait between the Nationalists in Taiwan and mainland Communist Party forces in 1958. While the father is speaking, the radio announcer continues to describe the battle. The only common denominator between the father's speech and the radio announcement is death. Symbolically both speeches represent versions of a dying culture, a culture that has lost touch with the everyday life of the local people. The radio announces the death of a national hero who deliberately flew his plane into a communist enemy, threatening the lives of his fellow fighters. Meanwhile, the father talks about the strange death of a relative on the mainland decades ago. The father's narration trivializes the official voice by pointing out how distant the heroism promoted by the government is from the everyday life of people in Taiwan, be they mainlanders or Taiwanese. At the same time, it also demonstrates how distant the father himself is from actual life. Even a death is meaningful for him mainly because it happened in an irrevocable past and in an unreachable land.

As in the case of Aha's unsuccessful communication with his father concerning his junior-high-school admission, all contacts between the father and son in this film are mediated by female voices. In other words, women's interventions in the family preserve the father's voice, which is also compromised by the process of preservation. Furthermore, physically the father has to depend on the mother's care because of his sickness. Several years after his death, the mother bitterly explains to her daughter in an extreme long take, prior to the daughter's marriage, that she had taken care of the now deceased father for twenty years after their marriage. Then the mother advises the daughter to think very carefully about her fiancé's health before deciding to marry him, in order to avoid falling in the same trap as her mother. After the mother's death, the daughter reads the father's autobiographical writings. Many years after his death, then, his descendants are finally able to understand his feelings toward them. Their father avoided them because he was afraid of infecting his children, not because he was unattached. In his lifetime, the father never directly expressed either his love for his children or his longing for the mainland – apparently his two passions. However, if his daughter's reading reveals his fatherly love posthumously, while he is still alive his longing is expressed indirectly by another voice, that of his mother (Grandma to Aha). According to the protagonist's memories, the father is extremely filial to his mother, who is equally attached to their hometown on the mainland. Furthermore, the *xiao* in the names Hou Xiaoxian and Axiao (pronounced Aha by Grandma in Hakka) means "filial piety." Grandma [Fig. 7] frequently tries to journey to her home district on the mainland, a physical journey that parallels the father's intellectual one in their shared imaginary. Whenever she gets lost, she orders a rickshaw driver to take her to the mainland. Instead, the driver always sends her home to collect payment from her family members. The repeated association with the old-fashioned vehicle portrays Grandma in a slightly humorous but touchingly nostalgic light. Like the outdated means of transportation, she is living in a spatially and temporally distant place, precommunist mainland China. In this respect, the father resembles his mother; but he keeps his thoughts to himself, whereas his mother unabashedly enjoys living in the undivided world created by her childlike imagination.

Another example from Grandma's experience may illustrate the minority status of the father's dialect among the Taiwanese. In a small teahouse, Grandma, speaking Hakka, asks the owner, an old Taiwanese lady, where the Meijiang Bridge is. (This bridge is actually in her hometown, on the other side of the Taiwan Strait.) The old lady asks a young waitress, who no doubt learned Mandarin in school, to interpret her words. Instead, the waitress asks the owner what

7. Grandma in *A Time to Live and a Time to Die*, directed by Hou Xiaoxian (1985). COUR-
TESY OF THE MUSEUM OF MODERN ART.

Grandma meant. The owner answers, "Even you can't understand. How can I?"
This little anecdote, viewed from Aha's childish perspective, reveals how comic
the grandmother's search for a place on the mainland might appear to a child,
and how sad her isolation seems to the film's adult audiences. By insisting on
walking to this bridge, she believes that she will be able to return to her hometown across the ocean. Even if the bridge were in Taiwan, she would have had
trouble to find it, since she would not have been able to ask directions from most
local people in Gaoxiong. She lives entirely in her own fantasy world, disconnected from geographic and material realities. This world is exemplified by Hakka, the dialect spoken by the previous generations of this family. In a sense, the
grandmother's search for an imaginary place by means of a dialect incomprehensible to the majority of the local population symbolically represents the father's own world.

Furthermore, as the most important means of the father's expression, writing has subsumed the father's life: He has turned down opportunities for business and military service, which might have offered him and his family a better financial situation, because he is interested only in reading and writing. Writing, which exemplifies the traditional Chinese culture in this context, does not help the father either on a practical level or on an intellectual one. During his lifetime, the father always had difficulty in making ends meet on his meager state employee's salary. As a result, neither his daughter nor his eldest son, who have inherited the father's interest in learning, can obtain college educations, for financial reasons. Since Hou repeatedly distinguishes "the feminine inside from the masculine outside spaces" (*nan zhuwai, nü zhunei*),[5] his father's refusal to become integrated into the local culture reduces him to a feminized space within the family.[6] Consequently, his written expressions become meaningful only through the mediation of the "natural" insiders, women.

Unlike his other siblings, Aha has not inherited his father's passion for books. A sequence emphasizes Aha's difference from the rest of the family: While the mother is punishing Aha for stealing money from her purse – for a "rascal" street activity, gambling – his sister is trying to stop Azhu from reciting multiplication tables at the dinner table, since his excessive diligence endangers his health. Unlike most of his family members, such as his father, dead of tuberculosis, and the protagonist's elder brother, Azhong, who is too thin to be drafted, Aha is muscular and masculine. He rarely stays in the house; when he does, he stealthily reads erotic materials while masturbating in his bedroom. This is his only reading experience in the film. Furthermore, for no apparent reason, he has chosen the surrounding wall as his personal entrance to the household; the hero barely uses the gate during the entire film. This "personal entrance" symbolically transgresses the boundary of his family and allows Aha to go beyond this limited physical, cultural, and linguistic space.

After his father dies, his sister sends Aha to take a bath. From the bathroom, he hears his mother's desperate cry at his father's deathbed. In the following shot, Aha has become an adolescent, standing approximately at the same position in the frame (though now outdoors). These successive shots show two images of Aha looking intensely at the right side of the screen – one as a child and the other in his midteens, as if he had grown up at a glance. In the first shot, the child looks at his father for the last time. In the second, the adolescent covetously watches a peddler conducting successful business deals: Aha and his Taiwanese-speaking, street-smart buddies plan to squeeze money from the peddler. In the first shot, the child's space is narrowly limited by the four walls of the cagelike bathroom; in the next, the adolescent stands in open space. These two shots thus imply that the moment of his father's death coincides with the end of his childhood, since the physical absence of fatherly authority liberates the hero from the last restriction of the physical and cultural boundaries of his family. The father seems symbolically dead long before his physical death, since he inhabits a geographically distant and culturally uprooted world – mainland China before 1949 – like Grandma in her endless imaginary journey to the mainland. His physical presence in the household serves only to preserve a respectable appearance. This appearance is not strong enough to make Aha accept the father's value system, but it is strong enough to hold him within the limits of decorum. After his father's death, Aha's activities expand even further outside the household. Since the language used beyond the family compound is mostly Taiwanese, which derives mainly from oral tradition instead of the classroom, the open spaces also represent for Aha a cultural alternative to his father's writing culture.

As a child, Aha has never understood the longing for this distant place shared by the older generation. When his grandmother asks him to accompany her on the mainland, he asks: "What are we going to do back at the mainland [*hui dalu zuo shenmo*]?" In another scene, the Nationalist government's slogan "Regain the mainland" is turned into a game by Aha and his classmate. However, Aha does indeed once accompany his grandmother in her imaginary return. Grandma's trip is not terribly different from the playful scene of Aha's classmates' faking a Nationalist attack on the mainland, although she reveals greater gullibility in her own game than do the children. At the end of their trip, Grandma teaches Aha how to play with a kind of round tropical fruit (*bali*) that they find on the road. In a later sequence, he uses the same skill with billiard balls to irritate further a retired mainland soldier, who is already angry at the "little rascal" for the latter's refusal to mourn the deceased vice-president, Chen Cheng – an important symbol for the mainland political culture. In that scene, then, the game that marks Grandma's nostalgic trip turns into an expression of Aha's indifference toward the same culture. Aha is the only one in his family who chooses the open spaces and local culture. He is the only one in the family who speaks Taiwanese. The Taiwanese song he sings to express his lovesickness sounds like a foreign language to his family: One of the lyrics, "I can no longer live," is misinterpreted by his Mandarin-speaking and better-educated sister as "selling bronze." In this sense, Aha himself is a family outsider whose best-known language appears alien to the rest of the family.

Several times in the film, the camera associates the hero with an isolated shot of an electrical pole. With its impressive height under the blue sky, and its wires extending to infinity, the electrical pole becomes a powerful phallic symbol. This symbol is in striking contrast to the father's world of compartmentalized, low-ceilinged, dark rooms. The electrical pole or "pole of electric wires" (*dianxian gan*) also serves as a symbol for the cinema or "electric shadow" (*dianying*), which relies on electricity (*dian*). The grown-up Aha, the narrator or director, has indeed chosen a medium closely related to this masculine symbol in the film. By means of cinematic representation, the son rearticulates the father's voiceless presence. Thanks to his cinematic art, the father's writing, otherwise buried within the family circle, goes far beyond the walls of his household and even beyond the open space of Aha's childhood. Electricity, or technology, brings the story of

Aha's childhood not only to the Taiwan people, indigenous or formerly expatriated, with whom the father rarely communicated, but also to international audiences, who can appreciate this story visually despite the language barrier. In spite of his silence, the father still symbolizes limits and authority for the son. His absence paradoxically points out his importance, the importance of his lack in Aha's life. To this extent, the film is not only a cinematic rearticulation of the father's writing from a child's perspective, but also an articulation of the child's longing for a father figure.

A *Time to Live and a Time to Die* represents a son's version of his father's story. Hou chooses cinema as his means of expression, a means considerably different from writing. In this film, various dialects, Hakka, Mandarin, and Taiwanese, coexist not as representatives of isolated cultures but as components of an embryonic shared contemporary Taiwan culture. Instead of speaking from the father's perspective, the film replaces the father's voice with the son's, often portraying the protagonist's point of view. However, because the story presented by the son in his film is fragmentary, his point of view does not truly restore the fatherly authority; instead, it only emphasizes the absence of a father's voice in his childhood.

DEAF-MUTE HISTORICAL WITNESS: CITY OF SADNESS

A *Time to Live and a Time to Die,* as just noted, is often shot from the protagonist's subjective perspective, which is associated with the director's voice-over. In *City of Sadness (Beiqing chengshi,* 1989), by contrast, the camerawork is mostly objective. The film is the first work in Taiwan that dealt with the February 28 Incident, which had been a political taboo for four decades. On February 28, 1947, the Nationalist government suppressed the Taiwanese popular uprising through a bloody crackdown on the eve of its political exodus.[7] In Hou's film, the main witness of Taiwan history from 1945, right after the Japanese capitulation, to 1949 is a deaf-mute photographer, Lin Wenqing. Unlike Aha, the protagonist of Hou's autobiographical film, whose family immigrated from the mainland in 1948, Lin Wenqing is the youngest son in his aged father's large Taiwanese household, which includes the families of Wenliang's three brothers. He is the only sibling who has a separate space. The second brother, formerly a medical doctor, disappeared in South Asia while serving as a soldier in the Japanese army; his wife, who worked as his nurse, is eternally awaiting his return in her father-in-law's household. Wenqing's oldest brother, Lin Wenxiong, is the leader of a local gang. His third brother, Lin Wenliang, worked for the Japanese in Shanghai before 1945. Shortly before the end of the film, Wenxiong is killed in a gang fight, Wenliang loses his sanity, and Wenqing is arrested for his political activism. In the final scene, the only people left at the family dinner table are the old man, the madman, and children. Women, who are as usual excluded from the table except as men's servants, have in Hou's films rarely counted as independent individuals.

Both Aha in *A Time to Live* and Wenqing in *City of Sadness* are witnesses of family and social history. As a historical witness, Lin Wenqing even shares some of Aha's traits. First, both characters are identified with the director. In *A Time to Live,* Aha, who shares Hou Xiaoxian's given name, identifies with the "I" of the director's voice-over in the opening and concluding sequences. Although *City of Sadness* does not have a first-person narrator, Wenqing also vicariously plays Hou's role, though to a much lesser degree. For one thing, there is a close tie between Wenqing's career as a still photographer and Hou Xiaoxian's as a filmmaker. For another, they are connected by a surrogate figure – a photographer called Rascal Xian (Zhuge Xian, or Dekehen in Taiwanese), an actual nickname for the director Hou Xiaoxian. When, early in the film, Wenqing is too busy to return home for the celebration of the birth of Wenxiong's son, the first male descendant among the next generation in the entire family, he is playfully replaced by this surrogate – who, according to Wenxiong, is supposedly the best photographer in the village (just as Hou Xiaoxian is arguably the best filmmaker in Taiwan). Rascal Xian later disappears as soon as Wenqing shows up.

Second, both Aha and Wenqing have great difficulty communicating with their fathers. In Aha's case, the father is isolated from his family and society by his illness and cultural alienation. In *City of Sadness,* the father cannot write, whereas writing is Wenqing's only means of communication, due to his deaf-mutism (acquired in a childhood accident). As in *A Time to Live,* writing as an activity also bears some feminine traits. Except for Wenqing, who uses writing as a replacement for *parole,* none of the living male family members can write. By contrast, writing in the family appears to be women's only distinctive occupation. The film often is narrated by the offscreen voice of Wu Kuanmei, Wenqing's girlfriend and later his wife, who constantly writes and reads her diary. Axue, Wenxiong's daughter, writes letters to different people during various family crises. To this extent, Hou's attitude toward writing corresponds to Gilles Deleuze's description of literature as a constant process of becoming, or a dispersal of the illusion of a consistent self, since "this becoming does not go to the opposite direction, and one does not become Man, as long as man presents himself as a dominant form, which pretends to impose on everything in the world."[8] Writing, as a process of becoming, is tantamount to the loss of subjecthood or to feminization in its constant dissemination (since only men count as subjects in Hou's film). As a result, writing generally plays a negative role in Hou's films, because the Taiwan director is for the preservation of masculinity.

Just as the sister in *A Time to Live* reads the deceased father's autobiographical writings, and thus speaks for her voiceless father, so Kuanmei in *City of Sadness,* by reading her own diary out loud, indirectly gives voice to Wenqing's thoughts. By using a silent-movie title screen as the means of communication between the two lovers, Hou provides a nostalgic aura to their romance. However, this romance of the two major witnesses of history, paradoxically disconnected from historical surroundings, is not well balanced. The male character's words, despite his muteness, are followed and subjectified by occasional point-of-view shots. The female character's words, despite the diary format, are only secondary to the preceding images, or simply serve as footnotes for the images of the male character's actions.

Aha in *A Time to Live* is a son who tries to distance himself from his father's mainland official literary culture in order to be integrated into the Taiwanese native oral culture. However, despite the protagonist's familiarity with local culture and language, on formal occasions – such as the director's offscreen voice in the opening and concluding sequences – the "I" still uses Mandarin, indicating his official tie to the mainland culture through his father. In other words, the grown-up Aha, Hou Xiaoxian, is not yet an insider of Taiwanese culture, in spite of his ability to speak Taiwanese and his familiarity with the culture. Wenqing, by contrast, is legitimately a Taiwanese insider, although he cannot speak Taiwanese or any other language. Correspondingly, in *A Time to Live* the social history provides only a vague background for the family history, whereas in *City of Sadness* the social history becomes comparatively prominent.

In *A Time to Live,* the father's voice is strikingly absent: He has become an empty symbol, permanently linked to his flimsy bamboo chair. In *City of Sadness,* the father's voice is not only ignored by his sons but even considered annoying, because his voice is portrayed as morally deficient. In the middle of the night, Wenxiong wakes up from a nightmare and starts a monologue about his childhood memory of his father. Sent by his mother, Wenxiong was following his father, a gambling addict, in order to prevent him from gambling away the money obtained by pawning the mother's golden necklace, since the family was awaiting this money to exchange for food. For his own gratification, the father tricked his son and tied him to an electrical pole in the middle of a cold winter night. The father went to gamble freely, and young Wenxiong would have died of cold in the deserted street if a passerby had not by chance seen him. Even in middle age, Wenxiong still frequently has nightmares, dreaming about his father's abusive behavior to him during his childhood. In this anecdote, the father–son relationship has been reversed: Not only can the father not educate and discipline the son by using his fatherly authority; as an addicted gambler, he needs to be disciplined by his son, although the son's effort fails. The depraved father used his strength and shrewdness to abuse the son for his own gratification, to the detriment of the whole family. Consequently, Wenxiong is traumatized by the father's irresponsible behavior for the rest of his life.

In the following sequence, the camera cuts from the medium shot of Wenxiong's monologue in the night to an extreme long shot of mountains and a river, accompanied by the voice-over of Chen Yi, the Nationalist governor of Taiwan at that time, in his radio announcement in February 1947. Violent conflicts be-

tween the Taiwanese people and the mainland government led to a bloody crackdown on the Taiwanese activists by the Nationalists. Mountains and rivers in the
Chinese language serve as a metaphor for the nation (*heshan*). In this context,
the nation becomes a macrocosm of Wenxiong's household. The two sequences
suggest that the small space that confines Wenxiong's father and his family is
analogous to Taiwan as a nation. In the February 28th Incident, the Nationalist
government's betrayal of the Taiwanese people, despite its representative Chen
Yi's official promise of leniency, is at a much more macroscopic level compara-
ble to Wenxiong's father's treason toward his son. Like Wenxiong's irresponsible
father, the Nationalist government cheats the Taiwanese with an unkept promise.
Like Wenxiong, the Taiwanese are traumatized by a "father's" irresponsible action against defenseless "children" for the sake of personal gratification. In fact,
the Taiwanese were compared to helpless children by Wenxiong himself in an
earlier scene. His comparison, rhymed in Minnan dialect (Taiwanese), later becomes a slogan for the Taiwanese (*bensheng ren*) for voicing their frustration:
"The most pitiful people are the Taiwanese. No one cares about us, everyone tries
to oppress and humiliate us." "Care" (*teng'ai*) is commonly used to describe parental affections in Chinese.

At the same time, the comparison of the father of a large Taiwanese household
to the Nationalist government undermines the portrayal of the Taiwanese as victims in this important historical incident, since they are not only helpless sons
but also oppressive fathers, as in the case of Wenxiong's father. Furthermore, the
only dangerous situation in the political conflicts presented by the film is created
not by mainland Nationalists but by Taiwanese dissidents: A group of Taiwanese
mistake Wenqing for a mainlander and are prepared to torture him, but Kuanrong, his future brother-in-law, comes to his rescue. Without Kuanrong's intervention, he would have lost his life at the hands of his fellow Taiwanese, who
wrongly interpret his uncommunicativeness as a sign of mainland identity.

Lu Kuang, a Taiwan film critic, points out: "*City of Sadness* at best can be
taken as an amplified version of *A Time to Live and a Time to Die*. This reminiscence of a repressed past allows the film to create the original state of an individual self."[9] In other words, social history has been individualized as a background
of a family history to the point that its social dimension has been obscured. In
fact, historical accuracy does not seem to have much weight partly due to the
choice of the main historical witness, who is deaf-mute. Since Wenqing's perspective is at best ambiguous, if not self-contradictory, historical representation
in the film is logically evasive. His ambiguity greatly exemplifies that of the director's "individual self." As a mainlander who grew up among his Taiwanese
friends in the less industrialized South, Hou has been trying to integrate himself
into Taiwanese culture through his efforts to speak a different dialect, to form a
different circle of friends, and to focus on aspects of life different from those of
his strictly mainlander family background as portrayed in *A Time to Live and a
Time to Die*. His journey from mainland China to Taiwanese culture is paralleled

by that from his family compound to the streets in his autobiographical movie. However, Hou remains "Chinese" in the most traditional sense, since his vacillating cultural identity is made possible only through a weakened presence, if not absence, of a fatherly authority in his mainland family. In other words, because his biological father was powerless due to his cultural alienation, Hou has no choice but to look for an "authentic" father figure powerfully rooted in the native culture. Only such a father figure can legitimize the son's integration. Otherwise, the son's Taiwanese voice would be marginalized, as in the case of Aha and the director's voice-over in *A Time to Live,* or silenced, as in the case of Wenqing in *City of Sadness.* As the search for a father figure takes precedence over a collective identity, it is not surprising that even a historic and epic topic takes on the dimension of a family history in Hou's film, in part because of the central position granted the presence (or absence) of the father.

Explicitly or implicitly, Wenqing's witness status is underlined throughout the film. For example, in his house, several intellectuals discuss politics. After severely criticizing how the Nationalist government handles Taiwan affairs, these intellectuals predict that important conflicts between the government and local people will soon occur. One of them suggests that Journalist He, sitting at the table, will be the historical witness (*jianzheng*), then proposes a toast to the witness (*jing jianzheng*). Meanwhile, instead of showing He, the camera shifts to Wenqing's face in the left corner of the room, distant from the discussion table. This mismatch of sound and image suggests that the historical witness is not the journalist He, using his pen as a political activist, but the photographer with his faithful "voice" – Kuanmei, whose face serves as a somewhat out-of-focus background for her lover. In other words, the history witnessed in this film is less political than personal, because it is filtered through the combined perspective of a couple who are so concentrated on their personal romance that they are completely oblivious to passionate political discussion in the same room. Furthermore, they are logically excluded from the circle of these political activists, Wenqing by his hearing impairment, Kuanmei by her gender. If these intellectuals, as the film implies, are the major participants in the February 28th Incident, Wenqing is no doubt an outsider. He is present at their meetings as an observer but absent from their activities. Furthermore, since he cannot hear what his activist friends talk about, he can witness history only visually.

Interestingly, at this moment his written discussion with Kuanmei inadvertently mocks these idealistic intellectuals. While listening to Beethoven, Kuanmei explains to Wenqing in writing that the music is based on a legend in which several fishermen, intoxicated by the beautiful voice of a siren, perish in their sinking boat. Like the fishermen in the legend, these intellectuals devote their lives to a beautiful but intangible ideal, which will seductively lead them to destruction.[10] In other words, a female mythical seducer has become a metaphor for their lofty cause. The world of these intellectuals (played by writers, such as Wu Nianzhen, scriptwriter; Zhang Dazhao, famous novelist; and Zhan Hongzhi, film critic), is essentially confined to a room with good food, wine, and idle chatter.

Three sequences of these intellectual gatherings are shot in the same room. The third (just discussed) ends in a flashback to Wenqing's childhood, before the tragic incident of his hearing loss. After Kuanmei explains the meaning of the melody to him, Wenqing describes his childhood to her in writing. Thus the music, which has just linked the passionately idealistic intellectuals in the room to the self-destructive fishermen in the legend, also serves as a transition, leading toward the romantic and individualistic world of the lovers, symbolized by the nostalgic music of traditional opera in Wenqing's memory.

While Wenqing evokes his childhood to Kuanmei in writing, a low-angle shot of an opera singer dressed in traditional Chinese clothes appears, followed by a shot of Wenqing at the age of six or seven, whose point of view we've just seen. According to his writing (an onscreen title), traditional opera was the young Wenqing's love. His teacher, angry about the boy's passion, predicted that he would become an actor (*xizi*). (*Xizi* is a pejorative term referring to any performing artist in traditional China.) Because soon after this an accidental fall from a tree deprived Wenqing of his hearing, the teacher's prediction has never come true. However, at a different level, one can still say that Wenqing is closely related to the performing arts through his profession as photographer: In his vicarious connection with Hou Xiaoxian through their camera, he is indeed involved with performing arts, not as a traditional opera singer, but as an onscreen "spokesman" for the filmmaker.

By means of Wenqing's childhood love for traditional opera – the regionality of which has been downplayed – Hou indirectly identifies his art, cinema, with a vaguely specified traditional performing art. In this art, Taiwanese identity has not yet undergone the painful separation from its Chinese origin. This moment of enjoyable "pure" art is complemented by Wenqing's hearing, now lost. At the same time Wenqing, plunged in his nostalgia for a past of timeless music and unimpaired hearing, witnesses the current intellectuals' gathering through the perspective of his camera – a fragmentary and evasive perspective, similar to the representation of the February 28th Incident in Hou's film.

Hou is a passionate promoter of Taiwanese language and oral culture, and his "authentic" Taiwanese people, uncontaminated by an outside or literary culture, must be portrayed differently from the intellectual activists in this film, who are supposedly compromised by their association with writing culture. In an interview, while explaining his weakness for Taiwanese music, Hou Xiaoxian expressed his desire to "show the same kind of mixture in [his] films as in Taiwanese music, the mixture of vagabondage, sensuality, romance, gangster mentality, Japanese style, and dynamism."[11] Despite his desire for integration, then, Hou still perceives the local culture as an exotic mixture. In the same vein, local people in his film are still portrayed as an exotic Other, whose passions are seemingly uncontrolled and uncontrollable.

In *City of Sadness,* this exotic Other is personified by Lin Wenxiong, Wen-qing's oldest brother, the gang leader shot to death by a rival gang member short-ly before the end of the film. Wenqing is even more distant from his brother than from his intellectual friends. From the very beginning, he refuses to return to the household to celebrate the birth of Wenxiong's first male child, either as a fam-ily member or as a family photographer. Since writing is his means of commu-nication, and his brother never shows any ability to write (we are not even sure if he is literate), their communications are extremely limited. On one occasion, however, Wenxiong – after being scolded by his jealous wife for his relationship with his concubine – angrily yells at Wenqing. Although in this scene Wenqing serves only as an outlet for his brother's frustration, it is so unusual for Wenxiong to communicate with his brother that he apparently forgets Wenqing's deafness. Once his wife reminds him of this, Wenxiong realizes that his brother was unable to understand a single word of what he was saying; so he impatiently asks his daughter Axue to put his scolding in writing.

Wenqing seems uninterested in what happens to his family, despite his rela-tion to them. He visits his family members only on ritualistic occasions – funerals or weddings. Wenqing is at least willing to participate in the activities of his in-tellectual friends, but his physical condition reduces him to the role of passive historical witness for them. In his relationship with his family, however, he is an involuntary and mostly indifferent witness, one who has no choice because of his blood tie. In both cases, his testimony of history is limited to the visual realm in the strictest sense – as snapshots taken by his camera. In the course of the film, Wenqing constantly remanipulates and perfects these pictures. In other words, he does not simply witness history, but also changes it, embellishing its images as an artist does – indeed, as does the director of this film.

In this sense, *City of Sadness* portrays the activities of Wenqing's intellectual friends partly as products of his artistic creation and remanipulation, from which the artist keeps a certain distance. By contrast, Wenqing's family members (typ-ically, only men count, as in the case of the intellectual activists) take prominent roles in the narrative development because of their physicality and activity.[12] Nevertheless, their actions share a common ground with the intellectuals' chats in their fundamentally useless and self-destructive nature. Moreover, their ac-tions, viewed in dramatic lighting and limited to three or four selected back-ground settings, are often reminiscent of theatrical performance. This dramatiza-tion forms a striking contrast to Hou's usual low-key style, as in *A Time to Live and a Time to Die, Dust in the Wind* (*Lianlian fengchen,* 1987), and *All the Youth-ful Days* (*Fenggui laide ren,* 1983). As a result, it lends their actions an artifi-ciality – as in the case of intellectual activities presented by Wenqing's snapshots.

At the same time, the usual static camera movement in Hou's film also con-tributes to reinforcing this theatrical style. Most of the gang fights – fighting be-ing one of the major activities of Wenqing's brothers – are presented in extreme long shots and in relatively dark light. Viewed from a distance and in darkness, participants in these gang fights often look like puppets. Furthermore, contrary to his practice in previous films, Hou's casting of several movie stars (including Hong Kong–born superstar Liang Chaowei as the protagonist) calls even more attention to the film's performance nature. Unlike in *A Time to Live,* where emotional ties are subtly and lyrically portrayed, such ties are virtually absent from *City of Sadness.* In *A Time to Live,* the lack of communication between father and son is bridged at the end by the sister's reading the father's autobiography. In *City of Sadness,* on the other hand, family relations are portrayed objectively. Consequently, a script initially centered on family history is transformed into a kind of gangster movie, and some critics compare *City of Sadness* to *The Godfather.*[13]

THE FATHER'S VOICE: THE PUPPETMASTER

The Puppetmaster (Ximeng rensheng, 1994) is one of Hou's cinematographically most interesting films. It is based on the biography of a famous octogenarian folk artist in Taiwan, Li Tianlu, who spent his whole life performing puppet shows, throughout the political changes of the twentieth century. Unlike *City of Sadness* and *A Time to Live and a Time to Die,* this film creates its own narrative continuity by extensively using the narrative voice of Li Tianlu, the puppetmaster himself. As Hou explained to his editor, "The film should be edited in accordance with the narrator's expressions." In other words, he intended to create an emotional continuity centered on the aged artist. Five actors play the roles of Li Tianlu, or Alu, at different ages: the one-year-old baby, the child at six or seven years old, the boy in his early teens, the grown-up Alu, as well as the octogenarian artist Li Tianlu in person. Among these actors of different groups, the aged Taiwanese artist as himself leaves the deepest impression on the audience, since Li's narration structures the entire film. At the same time, the film uses a lot of long shots, long takes, and natural light. As a result, in the indoor scenes, which dominate the film, the features of various people are often barely distinguishable. Hou claims that, for want of experience, few of his Taiwanese-speaking actors, mostly nonprofessionals, truly know how to act. Consequently, the director prefers to use long takes and static camerawork in order to put them at ease.[14] However, in *Puppetmaster,* the long takes of Li Tianlu's narration are unusual; they look like footage from a documentary based on interviews of a single person. At the same time, images in flashbacks serve only as a somewhat evasive background for Li's narration.

Like Lin Wenqing, the historical witness in *City of Sadness,* Li Tianlu reminds us of the director himself at a professional level. If Wenqing is linked to Hou through his camera, the puppetmaster and the director are related in their linkage to performing arts. Hou states in one of his interviews: "Traditional Chinese performing arts, despite their various genres and regions, have in fact the same contents, and essentially express the same spirit."[15] In this film the puppetmaster occasionally also performs and directs traditional Chinese opera. Following the same logic, if one can easily shift from one kind of traditional Chinese opera to another, the line of demarcation between two performing arts, film and tradition- al opera, also becomes somewhat blurred. Furthermore, the character *xi* (perfor- mance, play, show) in the Chinese title can be used to describe not only Li's life as performance but also Hou's film. The fact that Li Tianlu has played the patri- arch in some of Hou's other movies (including the abusive, gambling father of *City of Sadness*) further facilitates the move from traditional arts to cinema.

In contrast to to deaf-mute Wenqing in *City of Sadness,* Li Tianlu speaks per- fectly "authentic" Taiwanese. His performance in *The Puppetmaster* is primarily a linguistic one, based on improvisation and unmediated by writing (as Li is il- literate). In *A Time to Live,* which the director's offscreen voice claims is based on his childhood impressions of his father, the father almost never speaks except posthumously through his autobiographical writing. In *The Puppetmaster,* how- ever, the story is not based on the vague and incoherent impressions of a child about his father, but on the narration of the "father's" precise and confident voice, speaking in an "authentic" Taiwanese language.[16] It is Li's explanations, his pow- erful voice, that provide meaning and structure to the otherwise dreamlike scenes of *The Puppetmaster.* Moreover, each of his appearances occurs in exactly the same setting as was shown in the previous sequence described by the aged artist – as if there were no barrier between the two chronologically separated worlds. In this sense, Li's narration has become "diegetic," thanks to its overwhelming significance in the film. Furthermore, since the narrative act becomes both the essential form and the content of the filmic structure, one may even say that nar- ration itself has become the most important action in the film. Images, in this con- text, become decorative and secondary. The narration, which ties fragmentary images together, functions not only as storytelling but foremost as a performance (*xi*) in itself. For example, the film constantly crosscuts the images of Li's story- telling, onscreen or off, with staging of his puppet shows, as if Li's professional and narrative performances were interchangeable.

According to Li's narration, after following an opera troupe to Taizhong, leav- ing his wife and children at home for financial reasons, Alu meets a prostitute named Lizhu. They become lovers. After Li describes their first encounter, the camera brings us to his lover's apartment. There, the young lady skillfully lights Alu's cigarette with a match between her lips. This act is carefully watched and commented on by Alu's friend, Fanshuzi, as in the case of a staged performance. In the next scene, at Alu's request, she poses for a photo, accompanied by cheesy Japanese music. Furthermore, in the third sequence, Lizhu herself stages a per- formance exclusively for her lover. One night, she pretends to visit her mother for an urgent matter, and one of other the prostitutes, Jinhua, tries to seduce Alu during her absence. Alu passes this test by turning down Jinhua's advance, and Lizhu reappears to reward her lover's loyalty. Immediately after this test, Alu borrows money from his lover, who is rich, for his performing troupe. Amid all these performances, audiences may wonder to what extent Alu's demonstration of loyalty may also be a performance aiming at financial gain. In the next shot, Li in person, the aged Alu, appears on Lizhu's bed, talking about the development of their relationship and how he would like to limit it to being a "temporary couple" (*lushui fuqi*), an expression used to describe a stage couple. According to this description, all the scenes concerning their romance can be considered various forms of performance. Li's narration of their relationship has become a script, which she follows, performing various roles. Largely thanks to her performance, Lizhu is the only relatively important woman in Hou's film. In reality, the most important woman in Li's life, according to his memoir, is not this girl but a teahouse owner, whose low-key personality prevents her from performing the same showy role as Lizhu the prostitute. For this reason alone, Jinluan, teahouse owner, never appeared in Hou's film.[17]

The Chinese title, *Ximeng rensheng,* translates literally as "Life as Performance and Dream." As a matter of fact, the film often gives the impression of leveling extradiegetic narration, diegetic plots, and performance. As already noted, Li frequently describes his past in the same setting as in the flashback where this past supposedly occurred several decades ago – as if, despite the change in his appearance, time had no impact on his life. The narrative act that purportedly occurs decades later immediately follows the flashback, in the same setting and with the same lighting. Thus each performance of decades ago becomes the continuation of, or introduction to, the performer's current narration. This purposeful anachronism erases much of the distance separating extradiegetic presence from diegetic past in the film. It creates an artificial continuity among chronologically discontinuous elements: images of Li's past experience, his present narration, and his previous performance. In short, various empirical, narrative, and performing elements in Li's life contribute to underlining the narrator's central role in this film. This narrative center is carefully orchestrated by a highly selective directorial point of view – as Hou explains in one of his interviews:

My selection of fragments from Li's life is highly subjective. It is absolutely impossible to reproduce Li's generation's attitude toward life through theatrical or cinematic performance. Consequently, I selected actors who might possess some traits of his personality from different age groups. Then, I made changes according to their personal situations. As a result, the films shows the perspective from which I understand his attitude toward life and the value system of his time. . . . There are two perspectives in this film, one belongs to him, the other to me. His perspective is encapsulated in mine.[18]

By effacing boundaries, be they chronological, generic, or ontological, the director makes the protagonist's perspective part of his own. Despite its central position in the film, Li's perspective is reframed, manipulated in order to represent the directorial point of view through his "highly subjective selection." As Li explains, his puppet theater is named by a man versed in classical Chinese as

"Truthful Art" (*Yi wanran*), because according to this traditional scholar the puppets look like real people. Not only are the puppets like real people, but real people often take the place of these puppets in the film. Following the pattern of experience, narration, and performance (or experience, performance, and narration) in this film, performance can be located either on a small puppet stage or on the stage for traditional opera, depending on circumstances. Li, in the three scenes of traditional opera, has been a spectator, an amateur performer, and finally a professional actor as well as director. The puppet and opera shows are interchangeable according to a consistant structural pattern in Hou's film; they are also linked because on both occasions Li's voice can be heard from the stage. Alu's past stage voice forms a continuum with Li's current narrative voice (onscreen or off) in the film. Moreover, Li Tianlu describes his past with numerous dramatic gestures, reminiscent of traditional performing and oral arts. Consequently, his stage performance in the past can hardly be distinguished from his current narrative performance, because they are all situated in the same cinematic space. Following this logic, the line of demarcation between the on- and offscreen performance worlds has also been blurred. In the same vein, Hou's own film about Li's performing and narrative arts can be considered an extension of the latter's life and art. However, this extension is often beyond Li's own comprehension, as the aged artist has confessed on different occasions that he did not even understand most of Hou's other films in which he performed roles. In Li's autobiography, he emphasizes the significance of puppet art in his life. In Hou's film, this art has taken on a much more symbolic dimension, which bridges gaps between various genres of performing arts, such as differences between puppets and real people, the traditional and the modern, the regional and the Chinese, as well as the onstage and the onscreen.

After the Japanese colonists hire the puppetmaster to perform propagandist shows, in order to recruit Taiwanese soldiers for the Japanese army, Li ceases to perform onstage in the film. From this point on, the stage drama is gradually replaced by the life drama. In the final sequence, a group of Taiwanese demolish Japanese airplanes in order to sell the scrap metal. This scene is portrayed in a dramatic light. Then, Li's onscreen voice recalls that he asked these Chinese why they demolished airplanes. According to him, their answer was: "If not, how can you get money for your shows? With metal we obtained from airplanes, we got money from scrap dealers. Since our local gods are powerful, we express our gratitude by theatrical performances. Thanks to their blessings, our Taiwan can now be restored from the hands of the Japanese." Compared with the other diegetic scenes, which are usually darkened and somewhat evasive, the concluding aircraft-demolition sequence is similar to one of the film's theatrical performances – well-lit and relatively sharp-focused. To a degree, this sequence can be taken as a type of theatrical performance, in which the actors are no longer puppets or opera singers but historical figures themselves. Ironically from Li's perspective, Taiwan history, in which the government changed hands from one kind of outsiders to another, looks like an endless drama (*xi*) – inconsistent and sense-less. Following the logic of the airplane demolishers, this part of the historical drama is staged for Li's theatrical performance, which finally brings about histor-ical changes through its function as ritual of respect for the local gods. The pow-erful gods accordingly effect the removal of Taiwan from the hands of the Jap-anese. In other words, history and drama are not only analogical but also chained to the same causality. By elevating Li's performance to the level of Taiwan his-tory, Hou glorifies his own cinematic art, which "encapsulates" the Taiwanese artist's perspective in his directorial point of view.[19]

The father in *A Time to Live* is powerless; the father in *City of Sadness* lacks moral authority. Unlike them, various father figures in *The Puppetmaster* gener-ally behave in fatherly ways toward their descendants, except for Alu's father when recently remarried. The grandfather, for example, is emotionally capable of communicating with his offspring. The bond between him and his potential granddaughter-in-law suggests a possibly stronger bond between him and his grandson, Alu. Moreover, father–son communication is not as totally lacking as in the two earlier films, despite the conflicts between Alu and his father, which are mainly to be blamed on the meanness of Alu's stepmother. At the end of his life, Alu's father changes his attitude toward his son. Disregarding his wife's pro-testations, the father gives all his puppets to Alu, who uses them to establish his own puppet theater. Furthermore, despite his claimed passion, Alu himself gives up his lover, Lizhu, mainly for the sake of his wife and child. Even a friend of his, a Japanese officer, in order to please him, chooses to play the role of a caring father for Alu's son Ahuang and spares the boy from a lawsuit. The care that the officer gives Ahuang indirectly indicates how much Alu cares about his son, be-cause attention given to the son has become the only effective means for this out-sider to foster the father's friendship. At the same time, the relationship between Alu and his son also reminds us of that between the actor Li Tianlu/Alu and the director Hou Xiaoxian himself, whose friends and colleagues have referred to them as spiritual father and son. *The Puppetmaster,* according to these observers, is largely the product of Hou's filial respect for his Taiwanese surrogate father.[20]

In *A Time to Live,* Aha's father barely speaks because he is isolated as an out-sider to the local culture and language. In *City of Sadness,* the illiterate father of the large Taiwanese household (played by Li Tianlu) cannot communicate with his deaf-mute son, who vicariously represents the director as cameraman and his-torical witness. In *The Puppetmaster,* Li Tianlu onscreen communicates to his spiritual son offscreen by means of his narrative performance, selected and re-framed according the directorial point of view. In other words, the father's narra-tive and performing arts, part of traditional local culture, are made much more effective by the son's cinematic art, the product of modern technology. By allow-ing his art to be "encapsulated" in a new frame, Li Tianlu acknowledges the legit-imacy of his spiritual son's cinematic art. Li's mastery of puppet art becomes a proof of Hou's cinematic excellence. By being framed within this essentially alien technological world, the traditional Taiwanese artist also encapsulates the cinematic art and its master, his spiritual son, Hou Xiaoxian, into the world of regional art and local culture.

Puppet theater, mainly a regional art in Taiwan, does not specifically separate itself from traditional Chinese opera, on which all the pieces presented in the film are based, except for one Japanese remade piece. By choosing Li's performance and narration as the legitimation of his own integration into the Taiwanese culture, Hou does not need to face the painful dichotomy of Chinese and Taiwanese cultures. Because his integration is endorsed by a Taiwanese artist who also personifies the Chinese tradition in his culture, arts, and value system, Li's spiritual son of the Taiwan cinema can escape from the current conflicts dividing the mainlanders and the Taiwanese. Unlike Aha in *A Time to Live,* whose integration into the local culture is also a severance from his father's culture, or Wenqing in *City of Sadness,* who cannot truly integrate into his father's local culture because he communicates only in writing, the traditional Chinese culture of Hou's biological father, reinterpreted by the Taiwanese voice of his spiritual father, becomes itself integrated into the native culture. In other words, a father's voice finally allows Hou to reconcile with his alienated father's culture and his own otherwise "unfilial" assimilation.

Among all the Fifth Generation and Taiwan New Cinema filmmakers, Hou Xiaoxian emphasizes personal history the most. He has made films on his own life story (*A Time to Live and a Time to Die*), on those of his two screenwriters, Wu Nianzhen's (*Dust in the Wind* [*Lianlian fengchen*]) and Zhu Tianwu's (*A Summer at Grandpa's* [*Dongdong de jiaqi,* 1984]), as well as on that of one of his actors (*The Puppetmaster*). The latter three individuals are all of Taiwanese background. As a "mainlander," Hou in his filmmaking is also making a personal journey toward his integration with the local culture. In the course of this journey, he often blurs different boundaries, be they artistic, professional, generic, cultural, or historical. Through boundary crossing, his works often problematize the official ethnic division of the Taiwanese and the mainlanders. At the same time, one boundary remains unabashedly unquestioned: gender hierarchy. Because of this unquestioned and perhaps unquestionable hierarchy, as well as the director's ethnicity-driven personal journey, deconstruction of the ethnic division in his films remains limited.

First, partly due to Hou's own anti-intellectual agenda, mainland culture in his films is frequently associated with writing, which is closely related to death, whereas the local culture is associated with oral performance, which represents life. Although the Taiwanese, the "numerical majorities," initially held the position of "social minorities,"[21] they have gained much more power in recent years due to political and economic developments. As a result, Hou's journey from the culture of the former "social majorities," the mainlanders, to that of the former "social minorities," the Taiwanese, is not as subversive as it might appear at first sight, since the numerical majorities have also gradually gained the position of social majorities. Furthermore, as in the case of many ethnic divisions, the line between the mainlanders and the Taiwanese has been artificially created and maintained, mainly to serve the political interests of various dominant groups at different historical moments. Hou's films, instead of questioning the foundation of this division, inadvertently reinforce it by preserving the distance between the two "ethnic" groups, for this distance is the raison d'être of his journey. Thus, despite its limited subversive role, this journey offers a reversed, mirror image of the official division between the mainlanders and the Taiwanese.

Second, in Hou's search for a Taiwan identity, women play only passive and subordinate roles, as either instruments or voices of their male counterparts. For this Taiwan director, the identity for which he has been searching first and foremost is a patriarchal one. This may explain why his search is exclusive, but not inclusive – despite changes in father figures – because it only shifts from one patriarchal system to another, without undermining the fundamentally divisive ethnic polarization. Not surprisingly, his journey from mainland culture to the local culture takes on the form of searching for a father figure. Consequently, the local culture into which he has integrated is the father's culture par excellence, whereas the mainland culture, which he has gradually rejected, has become feminized through its association with writing, as well as the absence of a powerful father figure.

Nevertheless, Hou's films, especially *City of Sadness,* are among the first to examine the consequences of this ethnic polarization, in the name of which the Taiwanese were oppressed as "social minorities" for decades. Furthermore, partly thanks to their emphasis on personal history, his films are often tinged with a lyricism, counterbalanced with a touch of humor – even in the case of life-and-death situations. As a result, his works may be emotionally intense yet maintain a low-key personal style. From time to time, this relatively carefree personal style, combined with emotional intensity, results in beautifully made movies, such as those studied in this chapter.

4

MELODRAMA OF THE CITY

EDWARD YANG: *TAIPEI STORY; THE TERRORIZERS; CONFUCIUS'S CONFUSION*

In his book *The Philosophy of Money,*[1] Georg Simmel, a German sociologist, explains changes brought about by the money economy to traditional Western society at the turn of the twentieth century.

First, the more advanced a money system is, the wider is the range of objects potentially available to be quantified by money. Since many more objects are available to monetary acquisition in a money economy than in a traditional barter economy, and since the value of an object for the desiring subject largely originates from its resistance to his desire, the resistance encountered by human desires in modern society inheres more in the quantity of money one may acquire than in the qualities of objects.[2] As the ultimate resistance to the desiring subject, money has gradually been transformed from a means to the ultimate value. Simmel – with a tinge of blasphemy – compares the value of money in an industrial society to that of God, "as the absolute means and thus as the unifying point of innumerable sequences of purposes."[3]

Second, Simmel believes that the money economy creates a degree of independence for an individual in his relationship with the rest of society, since as the abstract measurement of an increasingly divided laboring force, money has transformed a great number of interpersonal relationships, often based on mutual dependence in a barter economy, into various impersonal functions. "The modern division of labor permits the number of dependencies to increase just as it causes personalities to disappear behind their functions, because only one side of them operates, at the expense of all those others whose composition would make up a personality."[4] In other words, social contacts are objectified to the point that people in contact are reduced to various professional titles devoid of personality.

Third, since the movable property, money, has gradually replaced the immovable property, land, as the most important form of ownership in an industrialized society, the money economy also detaches people from traditional communities.[5] On the one hand, the larger the social circle, and the more freely a currency is circulating, the more easily an individual is displaced, along with his monetary possession. As a result, the community is enlarged by monetary circulation. On the other hand, due to this greater mobility, home loses its traditional meaning as the location for an eternal return. This sense of homelessness also disrupts traditional ties among members of the same family, clan, or community, since these ties are no longer rooted in solid ground – the land. Furthermore, because people, detached from their land, have lost their traditional sense of belonging, their interests in the collective cause have also declined accordingly.

Georg Simmel published his book in Germany at the dawn of the twentieth century, while capitalism was at a stage very different from that of today's world and stayed mainly limited to the Western sphere. The money economy in his book is portrayed in a relatively positive light as a "modern" system, as opposed to the "primitive" barter economy – that is, Western capitalism versus the rest of the world. Following this logic, the more advanced the stage of capitalism is, the more predominant money economy has become in a society. However, his analysis of the money economy also dialectically draws a rather gloomy picture of the "independent modern individual" in this system, cut off from his traditional ties and isolated from the rest of society, despite his relative freedom. This image touches the roots of many problems faced by late capitalist society at the start of the twenty-first century. Pushing Simmel's logic to its extreme, even if the individual in question belonged to the limited successful circle of the rich in the money economy, he would not be able truly to enjoy himself: Money, despite its materiality, is after all a means and a symbol, which cannot provide satisfaction in itself. In spite of its shortcoming, Simmel used the extent of money economy in a society to measure its degree of modernity. Following this logic, the modernization process in a non-Western society unavoidably brings with it the worship of the "absolute means" or "God" of capitalist society, which further disrupts the non-Western cultural value system.

By the late twentieth century, in the information age, the money economy had developed to a much more advanced stage. Its characteristics, as described by Simmel in his *Philosophy of Money,* have taken on much more pronounced features. The global economy has extended and reinforced the kingdom of money worshiping by making its abstract nature even more explicit – as the universal god in consumer society. In financial institutions as well as in everyday life, money no longer needs any physical presence in its paperless and cyberspace transactions. Further technological developments reinforce the abstract nature of social contacts. These contacts are deprived not only of personality but also of humanity *tout court* through means such as answering machines, remote controls, voicemail, and computer screens. At the same time, multinational corporations have broken national boundaries, and investments seek homes only in the most profitable locations in a global economy. In addition, our age has witnessed the rapid development of the most movable asset, intellectual property in cyberspace. As a result, the traditional sense of belonging to any community has become even less significant. Simmel's independent modern individual would have been stunned by these rapid developments. However, few would have been able to witness all these changes in one lifetime – except perhaps for those living outside the Western sphere in a postcolonial economy, such as in Taiwan, during the second half of the century.

In 1964, for the first time in Taiwan history, industrial production surpassed agricultural production. In the same year, the Nationalist government encouraged the trend of industrialization by launching the following slogan: "In the near future, let's change the nature of our economic structure from an agricultural to an industrial society."[6] By the end of the 1980s, Taiwan had not only reached this goal but also achieved a miracle as the fastest-growing economy in the world during this period. Taiwan has been transformed, first from a traditional agricultural society to a labor-intensive, export-oriented, industrial society in the 1970s, then to a high-tech-based consumer society in the 1980s. The long process of industrialization, which has lasted for centuries in the West, was condensed into an amazingly short period. In 1950, one year after the Nationalist government's move to Taiwan from the mainland, the per capita income was US$50. By the end of 1987, it had multiplied a hundredfold to $5,000 – partly thanks to Taiwan's stock market and real-estate boom. In other words, at the beginning of the 1950s, as an agricultural society Taiwan was still at an earlier stage of industrialization than Simmel's Germany had been in the 1900s. Three decades later, the two societies seemed to reach approximately the same stage as other high-tech-based, consumer-oriented economies. If Simmel's modern individual would have been shocked by today's Western world, one can imagine how shocking these developments actually have been for the population of this small Asian island, with its several centuries of colonial history.

Beneath the dazzling prosperity, Taiwan's economic miracle came at a high price. In its effort to modernize Taiwan economy, the Nationalist government has heavily relied on American support and Western investments. Furthermore, in Taiwan as in many other third-world countries, modernization, partly because of its intimate connections with technology, in many aspects is equivalent to westernization, depending on which part of Western culture is taken as a model. Moreover, due to Taiwan's geopolitical location, its initial reliance on Western investments, and its dependence on American military support, westernization plays an even greater role in its economic and social transition. As has occurred in other postcolonial societies, modernization in Taiwan means not only a transition from agricultural to consumer society but also a radical transformation or re-formation of traditional culture – namely, the family-oriented Confucian value system. This situation has further been complicated by the Nationalist government's effort to preserve the Confucian tradition as one of the most important ideological bases in Taiwan. In addition, since this transformation has never operated as a one-way street in any part of the world, modernization in Taiwan unavoidably takes on regional features. Stuart Hall states, "the law of value, operating on a global as opposed to a merely domestic scale, operates through and *because* of the culturally specific character of labor power, rather than – as the classical theory would have us believe – by systematically eroding those distinctions as an inevitable part of a worldwide, epochal historical tendency."[7] Taiwan New Cinema was born in the early 1980s, in the heart of this turbulent transitional period. As a product of its particular historical, political, economic, and social context, and thanks to its commitment to Taiwan culture, New Cinema serves as a mirror of this regionalized transition. Among Taiwan New Cinema directors, Edward Yang (Yang Dechang), through his urban films, most effectively captures the impact of the rapid modernization process in its specific cultural and sociohistorical context.

The two internationally recognized Taiwan directors seemingly are poles apart: If Hou Xiaoxian's works are focused more on changes that occurred in traditional family structure, especially in rural areas, Edward Yang is mainly interested in the impact of rapid industrialization on the city – the primary locus of modernization. This difference can partially be explained by their emphasizing two different groups of people. Despite his mainland origin, Hou is more concerned with the life experiences of the Taiwanese (*bensheng ren*), whereas Yang's works reflect more on those of mainlanders (*waisheng ren*). Because the mainlanders moved to Taiwan after the Second World War, their ties to the land are much looser than those of the Taiwanese, whose ancestors immigrated to Taiwan much earlier. The latter are more likely to own land and properties, whereas the former arguably fit better the profile of Simmel's description of the "modern" individual – homeless and also, to an extent, without origin. As their officially assigned origin on the mainland was for a long period unreachable and is still difficult to reach due to political segregation, this origin remains symbolic, if not fictional. Understandably, instead of concentrating on a tentative identity based on a hybrid combination of Chinese tradition and local culture, as in Hou's case, Yang's films are more interested in the alienation in the city, where each citizen is essentially portrayed as homeless in a vast and impersonal ocean of modern technology.

One of the dominant themes in Yang's films is how money, god of consumer society, has undermined and disrupted traditional Asian family structure – although the structure disrupted is shown in his films not to have much merit. If the modernization process has caused confusion among citizens in Taipei, returning to the past is definitively portrayed as not only impossible but also undesirable. Consequently, in Yang's films Taipei often appears as a society cut off from its past but at the same time without a viable future. In this chapter, I study the relations between tradition and modernity, money and people, technology and life, and between men and women in three of Edward Yang's city films: *Taipei Story* (*Qingmei zhuma*, 1985), *The Terrorizers* (*Kongbu fenzi*, 1986), and *Confucius's Confusion* (*Duli shidai*, 1994).

TAIPEI STORY

TRADITION AND MODERN LIFE

Taipei Story (*Qingmei zhuma*), a film directed by Yang in 1985, describes the life of a former baseball player, Along, whose team won the world junior championship in 1969. The Chinese title differs greatly from the English: Its literal translation is "Green Plum and Bamboo Horse" – a Chinese proverb originating in a poem written by a famous poet of the Tang dynasty, Li Bo.[8] This proverb refers to the childhood games of a young couple who have been playmates since they were toddlers. As time goes by, unknowingly, their innocent friendship has turned to romance. In the meantime, they are engaged to each other by their families. Soon after the wedding, the husband travels to a distant place. The wife, left alone at home, speaks of eternal love for him in Li Bo's narrative poem. Thanks to this famous poem, the phrase "green plum and bamboo horse" is used to describe romance based on the innocent friendship of childhood. Such a romantic title is unmistakably ironic for Yang's film, given his usually unsentimental approach. However, without irony the English translation directly reveals the true nature of the relationship. In any of Yang's movies, the city Taipei has been revealed as impersonal, cold, and indifferent to human emotions. Since the story is about Taipei, any love – not to mention the innocent and everlasting romance described in classical Chinese poetry – is necessarily illusory. In fact, this story is mainly about how a couple who build their relationship on their childhood friendship drift apart in the westernized city, despite their effort to cling to childhood memories.

The protagonist, Along, was a member of the national junior baseball team of the Republic of China that won the world championship in the 1960s. In his adult life, Along seems still to live in his past glory. He sticks to the traditional value system, that is, privileging family ties and friendship instead of material profits. Due to his old-fashioned code of honor, rooted in traditional Chinese patriarchy, Along appears at odds with most people living in the modern city, although the fame to which he identifies in the rest of his life originated in his participation as a youth in a Western game. By contrast, his girlfriend Azhen, who has known him since they were children, is eager to live a westernized life-style as a financially successful yuppie. Furthermore, Azhen wants to emigrate to America with Along, whose brother-in-law is a rich businessman in Los Angeles. His brother-in-law promises to help Along's emigration, with the condition that he bring with him a substantial amount of money. Without Azhen's agreement, Along lends part of his money to her father to help him pay a debt. (Azhen deeply resents her father for lacking financial responsibility and mistreating her mother and herself.) Furthermore, Along also has an intimate relationship with Ajuan, the daughter of his former baseball coach, who has just divorced her Japanese husband. His inappropriate (but family-oriented) generosity toward Azhen's father and his visit to Ajuan in Tokyo on his return to Taipei from the United States separate the two lovers. Meanwhile, Along's Americanized brother-in-law embezzles his money. At the same time, Azhen has a casual affair with one of her younger sister's idle friends, a teenager, who afterward follows her around on a motorcycle. Frightened, Azhen asks Along for help. In a lonely street late at night, Along starts a fight with the teenager in order to teach him a lesson, but the boy stealthily stabs him. Along bleeds to death amid a pile of garbage.

Unlike most mainland movies, whose English titles are usually literal translations of the Chinese, many works of the New Cinema in Taiwan have two very different titles, the Chinese and the English.[9] Such is the case with Yang's *Taipei Story:* The literal Chinese title, "Green Plum and Bamboo Horse," refers to a classical Chinese tradition overwhelmed by the modernization process. The English title indicates the outcome of the same process: The titular *Taipei Story* – like the story of any modernized big city in the world, such as Tokyo in Ozu's *Tokyo Story* – is of how the worship of money has gradually replaced traditional family ties as the central value in Asian culture.[10] With few exceptions, such as *Confucius's Confusion*, English titles for Taiwan new-wave films often address a certain commonality between Taiwan society and other international communities, whereas their Chinese titles, often close to structures of the classical language, are directly or indirectly connected to a vanishing tradition, with a nostalgic undertone.

In the opening long shot, Along stands inside the glass door of Azhen's new yuppie apartment, with his back to the audience. Then, Azhen enters the frame, and also turns away from the audience. Both face the modern city from different angles through the large glass doors. In the prologue, Azhen tells Along that she wants to equip the apartment with television, hi-fi, and VCR; Along voices his concern for the cost of all this. Azhen constantly moves around in order carefully to inspect the empty apartment, whereas Along stays on the same spot, indifferently positioning himself as though ready to hit a home run. However, he only *performs* the role of baseball player, and no longer *plays* as one [Fig. 8]. Like his childhood, his supposedly superb baseball skill belongs to a distant past. As an adult, he merely records baseball games from American or Japanese TV, vicariously playing by watching [Fig. 9]. Ironically, when Azhen's younger sister happens to see his videotapes, she skips all the baseball scenes and watches only Japanese commercials. For his girlfriend Azhen, these tapes have no significance except to prove Along's infidelity, since they reveal his visit to his former lover, Ajuan, in Tokyo. Although his treasured past – like these audiovisual images, seemingly without any spatial or temporary reality – does not interest anyone else, it nevertheless remains the only support for his identity in a world of alienation. As Ajuan explains to him, "You live in your own constructed world." Along's life is necessarily tragic, since he can measure the world only according to his idiosyncratic and traditional values, incomprehensible to other people and incommensurable with the common denominator of all the value systems in modern Taipei – namely, money.

Apparently, this bygone world is defined by a code of honor, which Along preserves for himself amid an indifferent, modern Taipei.[11] In traditional Chinese society, personal honor is supposedly valued higher by Confucian gentlemen than material gains. This honor in many cases is mainly involved with a face-saving (*mianzi*) effort. However, Along's loyalty to the traditional value system, like the bygone knightly code of Don Quixote, causes him endless trouble. The only place where Along feels comfortable in modern society seems to be the couch in front of the television. (Even his fantasy while dying is projected onto the screen of an old TV set abandoned amid garbage.)

His relationship with the modern world is exemplified by that with his girlfriend Azhen. Along and Azhen grew up together – the only element that fits the romantic image implied by the title "Green Plum and Bamboo Horse" – but different life-styles in adulthood increasingly drive apart the two childhood friends. Seemingly, Azhen's interest in her childhood sweetheart is tightly connected to her desire to emigrate to the United States with Along, thanks to the promises of his brother-in-law. At the same time, although Azhen is Taiwanese herself, she expresses through her preference for Mandarin a desire to create a world separate from that of her childhood in order to fit into the modern city of Taipei. Her attachment to Along, however, expresses her latent attachment to a traditional

8. Along positions himself for a home run in Azhen's apartment in *Taipei Story*, directed by Edward Yang (1985). COURTESY OF THE MUSEUM OF MODERN ART.

9. Along watches a baseball game on television in *Taipei Story,* directed by Edward Yang (1985). COURTESY OF THE MUSEUM OF MODERN ART.

value system, which partially hinders her from transforming herself into a successful modern career woman.

In this film, another character, Ms. Mei, for whom Azhen works as a personal secretary at the beginning and the end of the film, represents a type of masculinized aggressive woman who coldly threatens the traditional value system much more than does her male counterparts. In almost each of Yang's films, the excess of modernization is often represented by such a woman. Apparently, in his films the price for a woman's success in modern life is to become heartless, whether she is a businesswoman, as is Lin Xiaoyan in *That Day, on the Beach* (*Haitan de yitian,* 1983); a prostitute, like the half-breed girl in *The Terrorizers;* or a high-school student, like Xiaohua in *A Brighter Summer Day* (*Gulingjie shaonian sharen shijian*). In Yang's works, a woman who successfully functions in modern society as an independent entity usually must become more "masculine" than men to prevail in power struggles, to the point that she loses her gender identity. Because women lose their preconceived gender "differences" in the process, men are in a sense feminized. Generally speaking, masculinization of women in Yang's films is similar to technologization of human relations: In both instances, a process of denaturalization is at stake.

Ms. Mei is one of these new women par excellence. As a successful entrepreneur, she remains cool even while losing her construction company. After her first defeat, she is shrewd enough to move a branch of an American computer company to Taipei at the right moment. Despite Azhen's admiration for Mei, however, she is unable to imitate her boss. She remains passive after Mei's construction company goes bankrupt, so much so that even Mei suggests that she look for another job. Because Azhen lacks the same kind of drive, her identification with Ms. Mei has never been truly realized. Her dark glasses and fashionable dress do not hide her traditional side, which implicitly identifies her with her mother, who is her selfish father's concubine – traditionally, a "second wife" with implied lower status than the official wife – and is constantly victimized by him. In a sense, Azhen's attachment to Along is symptomatic of her failure to identify with her role model, since his nostalgia for a bygone world makes him an imaginary protector against her own fear of the unknown in a changing world. After all, "Along looks more and more like my father," as she once sadly comments to her mother. This apparently negatively comment is rather ambiguous, since familiarity can also create a certain sense of safety. She prefers Along because he represents the past, the reliable, and support, despite their fundamental differences. Moreover, she acts possessive in terms of his money, and jealous in terms of his affection, exactly like a traditional wife – except without a marriage certificate. Furthermore, as vague as it might be, the hope of emigrating to the United States with the help of her boyfriend's relatives seems much less demanding for Azhen than the task of moving a computer company to her homeland, as Mei does.

Before her departure from Mei's former company, Azhen is frequently shown standing in front of the revolving door, even in the middle of her conversation with her potential new boss. The repeated image suggests that wherever she may go, she always returns to the same point. Just as she prefers the safety of her long-term relationship with Along, professionally she always returns to the same boss, Ms. Mei. In other words, despite her ability to handle high-tech business, her relationship to her boss is still based on a sense of traditional loyalty. At least in one aspect, however, Azhen is much more "modern" than Along – namely, in her attitude toward money.

Slavoj Žižek points out:

What one should bear in mind here is that "fetishism" is a *religious* term for (previous) "false" idolatry as opposed to (present) true belief: for the Jews, the fetish is the Golden Calf; for a partisan of pure spirituality, fetishism designates "primitive" superstition, the fear of ghosts and other spectral apparitions, and so forth. And the point of Marx is that the commodity universe provides the necessary fetishistic supplement to "official" spirituality: it may well be that the "official" ideology of our society is Christian spirituality, but its actual foundation is none the less the idolatry of the Golden Calf: money.[12]

To a large extent, modernization of a non-Western society and third-world economy is equivalent to the process of westernization. In this context, modernity is necessarily associated with two sides of the same coin in the West: "official spirituality," that is, humanism, and its fetishistic supplement, the idolatry of the Golden Calf. In the process of rapid changes, humanism often plays an oppositional role to traditional culture – as in the May Fourth movement – due to its complicated roots in Western culture. As a result, the idolatry of the Golden Calf that characterizes capitalist society has much more impact on developing countries, because of rapid changes in socioeconomic infrastructure. Often, the place vacated by traditional ethics is even more conspicuously occupied by this idolatry. Yang chooses this phenomenon as a dominant theme in all his films. *Taipei Story* succeeds in dissecting these gradual but profound changes brought about by the rapid industrialization and commercialization of a previously agricultural society. Machines replace human beings while traditional family ties are overshadowed by the worship of money.

According to Along's narration, his brother-in-law literally got away with murder in America because he was rich and his victim was a poor black man. Apparently, Along does not condemn this. He even tries to identify with his brother-in-law by implicitly expressing his desire to follow in his footsteps. The U.S. racial–economic hierarchy, in Along's mind, is similar to traditional patriarchy. However, two different hierarchies, respectively justified by two different value systems in Taipei – one westernized, and the other traditionally Chinese – cannot easily integrate with each other. His traditional family-oriented value system prevents Along from successfully identifying with his brother-in-law. The brother-in-law, later on, even embezzles Along's money because – as Along sadly admits to Azhen during their last meeting – he "is no different from anybody else."

Success in a consumer society can often be achieved to the detriment of family ties, which are central to Along's traditional value system. Georg Simmel points out: "Within the money economy, as these phenomena illustrate, the specificity and individuality of objects becomes more and more indifferent, insubstantial and interchangeable to us, while the actual function of the whole class of objects becomes more important and makes us increasingly dependent upon it."[13] Like commodified objects, people in an increasingly consumer-oriented society become less bound by their family ties than by the universal common denominator of money. As a result, their relationships to each other are much more interchangeable than in a family-oriented traditional Chinese society.

Azhen seems much better adapted than her boyfriend to the westernized value system, although she appears to feel safer in Along's fantasy world of traditional Chinese family-oriented values. In Azhen's relationship with her parents, money also replaces feelings. Her closer tie to her oppressed concubine mother is expressed by the ten thousand yuan the daughter gives her. At the same time, she is so busy that she does not have time to explain to her mother how to take the bus home: An unknown girl student patiently explains the route to Azhen's disoriented mother and accompanies her to the bus station after the daughter hurriedly departs. Ironically, this stranger seems much more daughterly than the daughter herself. In fact, Azhen hastily leaves her mother only in order to join her yuppie friends in a Western-style bar whose walls are papered with American dollars, Japanese yen, and other currencies. Azhen's friendship with these people is exemplified by this image of the modern universal: money. In the bar, Along, who comes later to join his girlfriend, appears as a complete outsider to Azhen's yuppie world. Feeling uncomfortable, he tries to leave. He is forced to stay, however, because he loses a bet on a dart-throwing game. Symbolically, Along's defeat prolongs his stay in a society to which he does not belong. Furthermore, one of Azhen's friends laughs at Along's defeat by referring to his adolescent victories in baseball, and Along starts a fight with this joker.

Like Along's nostalgia for his past glory, Azhen's relationship with Along is based on a fantasy, one directed not to the future or present but to the past. This fantasy of living in a secure past is precisely why she cannot fulfill her dream of living successfully in the modern world, although otherwise Azhen seems to embrace the values of a consumer society unreservedly. Her fundamental misunderstanding of the nature of their relationship results from her belief in Along's ability to materialize her American dream through emigration. In reality, her relationship with him stands between her and her integration into contemporary society dominated by money economy. At the end of the film, Along explains to her that neither marriage nor emigration to the United States will be the "magic elixir" (*wanling dan*) to resolve the differences between them. As a matter of fact, his traditional family-oriented value system, interpreted as a sign of safety and reliability in Azhen's eyes, unavoidably weakens him, and makes him unable to support Azhen's dream of safety in the changing world.

DON QUIXOTE IN TAIPEI

Since his heroic image as a junior baseball player on the world championship team has become unsubstantial for others in his society, Along's appeal to Azhen mainly results from his connection to America. This twist gives the Chinese title a particularly ironic flavor. At the same time, neither a prospective emigration nor their childhood attachment have anything to do with their present life: One represents a wishful future, and the other a bygone past. When Azhen loses her job, she returns late to her home. Azhen seeks comfort from her estranged lover by asking him to talk about his impression of America. According to Along, by paying all cash to the seller, his brother-in-law bought a house in a wealthy residential area in San Marino County, which is otherwise exclusively reserved for whites. If Azhen's fascination with the United States can be explained by her admiration of what is considered "modern," Along certainly does not wholeheartedly embrace the value system of modernity or the West. By contrast, America represents for him the land of opportunity – not for those who are able competitors but for those who have enough money to buy the identity of honorary white

– like his brother-in-law. However, Along's money is not based on his own merit; it would come not from the textile shop he owns but only from the heritage of his late father's house, which will allow him to take profit amid Taiwan's real-estate boom. His last hope of repeating his childhood glory depends on the possibility, however remote, of emigrating with his father's money and his brother-in-law's help. Thus, his longing for the United States, a country of which he has only perfunctory knowledge, is vaguely connected to his nostalgic dream of past glory. To a certain degree, this vague dream, from two different angles, remains the tie between Along and Azhen. Their relationship then becomes hopeless when Along loses both his money and his emigration opportunity to his brother-in-law's embezzlement. In the final analysis, his brother-in-law does not necessarily treat him any better than he treated the poor black man he murdered.

To Along, identifying with white masters in a distant, hierarchical country (sufficiently reminiscent of traditional patriarchy), by means of his family ties, also affords an opportunity to preserve his traditional code of honor. However, the same forces that have made family ties so impersonal have also fragmented patriarchal power, and his code of honor requires the preservation of the traditional gender hierarchy. Both his vicarious racist imagination and his real sexist action attest to the failure of Along's traditional code of honor.

Aqing, his former teammate and now a taxi driver, is married to a woman who has become a compulsive gambler. Along, who cannot stand the idea that a man can lose control over his wife, publicly humiliates his friend's disobedient wife by dragging her out of the gambling house and beating her in public. He wants this to be an example to his former teammate of "how to act as a manly man." His allegedly heroic action to defend patriarchal honor for his friend leads to Aqing's wife's departure. Left alone with three young children, Aqing no longer has the strength even to stand up. In other words, Along's attempt to maintain traditional patriarchal order in this family only breaks it apart. His desire to make his friend a manly man (*nanzi han*) according to traditional Chinese standards only makes Aqing lose everything he can lose, including any remaining faith in life.

The tragedy of Along's attempt to conform with the traditional code is that the patriarchal ground has been shaken and shrunken. In this changing world, his belief appears illusory. No one will truly listen to him anymore, including women – perhaps especially women. Along, however, tries to preserve his identity as a man of honor by desperately sticking to a bygone code. At the same time, the loss of honor also leads to symbolic impotence, as in the case of Aqing. To a certain extent, Aqing's impotence is the only element making Along feel powerful and worthy. However, this powerful self-image ultimately is also illusory, because Along differs from Aqing not qualitatively but quantitatively. Along too is impotent, only to a different degree. He becomes poorer and poorer, even losing his precious red Mercedes-Benz through gambling. His sexual life is not successful either. As Ajuan comments, he has no courage to "love anybody" ex-

cept in "playing the role of a savior." In other words, Ajuan – his sometime
lover – perceptively points out that Along's superfluous code of honor is only
a cover for his inadequacy, or impotence.

Along's traditional code of honor from a bygone patriarchal era privileges
face-saving efforts among Confucian gentlemen. In contemporary Taipei, however, such old-fashioned masculinity has become an object of mockery. One of
Azhen's yuppie friends – who soon after has a fight with Along – asks his companions in the bar, male and female alike, to find an answer to a riddle: "The Chinese have it but a little shorter; Michael Jackson has it but a little longer; the Pope
also has it but never uses it." Along looks irritated by his obvious reference to a
penis. Asked by his female companions to explain, the joker says "last name"
in English, which refers to the Chinese word *xing,* as a pun for sex. Then he ac-
cuses his companions of ignorance, since he claims that they cannot understand
his heavily accented English expression. In this riddle, the manhood of Michael
Jackson – then the superstar of American popular culture – has become a masculine icon against which Chinese men must quite literally measure themselves.

America, the Western power that has had the greatest impact on Taiwan society, has always been a powerful symbol in Edward Yang's films, where it has
been represented mainly through its popular culture: the Michael Jackson reference in the bar and the portrait of Marilyn Monroe on Azhen's bedroom wall in
Taipei Story; the popular songs "Smoke Gets in Your Eyes" in *The Terrorizers*
and "Bright Summer Day" in *A Brighter Summer Day.* America, represented by
its popular culture, provides a romantic space in the impersonal modern city of
Taipei – romantic precisely because the geographic distance allows Taiwan characters to project their fantasy on a relatively unknown land. However, such contact with the United States on a day-to-day basis often has a chilling effect in the
films. In the final analysis Americanization is an important part of Taipei's modernization package, which Yang's films usually deem as responsible for the impersonal and alienating nature of city life. For example, the Eurasian girl in *The
Terrorizers* kills people at random and indifferently. Her behavior can largely be
considered a price paid for the short-lived pleasure provided by her mother to an
American soldier. As if seeking revenge for her abandonment by her unreachable American father, she steals from, or occasionally even kills, any man who
has sex with her.

In general, the attitude toward America portrayed in Yang's films reveals a
colonial complex: admiration mixed with resentment, partly because the reliance
of the Nationalist government on American support, especially at the beginning
of its power in Taiwan, to a degree granted America colonial power without colonial institution. In *Taipei Story,* Along loses his money to his brother-in-law in
America mainly because the latter rejects the traditional family-oriented Chinese
code of honor, in which you either stick together with your family members or
lose face. Instead, the Americanized brother-in-law adopts the impersonal code
of profit. Although Along admires his in-law's ability to become an honorary

white in a land of opportunity thanks to the power of money, the would-be emigrant has been treated by his relative much like the black man his brother-in-law shot – only Along is killed not literally but symbolically, by financial manipulation.

Because of the contradiction between the United States of popular imagination and the actual country, the only way to preserve its beauty as a fantasy space is to forget America as reality. After Along reveals his brother-in-law's treachery to Azhen, she does not comment on it. Instead, she also narrates a story, one about their childhood, in order to communicate to Along how eagerly as a little girl she was waiting for the return of the hero of her heart, Along as a player on the national junior baseball team. This apparently disconnected topic converges with Along's narration about America, since both create fantasy spaces either in a distant past or in a distant place. In another sequence, Along compares his hand to that of a Caucasian ballet dancer carrying a blond ballerina's body in a poster on the wall of Azhen's bedroom. To his disappointment, his own hand appears obviously too small. This picture, like Marilyn Monroe's portrait in the same room, also reveals a dream of his girlfriend Azhen – wanting to become the ballerina, beautiful and fragile, abandoning herself in the powerfully masculine arms of a man. (As Western women, these icons also suggest "modern femininity," with which Azhen would love to identify.) However, the man in question, Along, cannot fulfill this function despite his knightly desire to "become the savior," because he belongs to a different time frame and cultural space.

Ajuan, the daughter of his onetime coach, tells Along: "You are living in your fairy-tale world of compassion. As if no one could be saved except by your compassion. The world is no longer the same as in the days you were on your baseball team. Everything has changed since then, you are the only exception. I believe that even Azhen must also have drifted away from you." Like Don Quixote, the last knight in Spain, Along finds his compassion is often not only wasted but also ill-fated. When he lends money to Azhen's father to repay a debt, she is angry not only because the loan would jeopardize their plan to emigrate, but also because she deeply resents her selfish father, who has mistreated her mother and herself since her childhood. Apparently, the reason Along lends him the money is his belief that family ties are more important than material interest. As he explains to Azhen: "If I don't help him, who will? He is, after all, your father." Unfortunately, these family ties, which he is so eager to preserve, are no longer truly meaningful for Azhen. Moreover, her ability to rebel against filial piety, the central value of traditional Chinese ethics, puts Along's code of honor in jeopardy, since a daughter's rebellion shakes the basis of that code, the father's power. In a way, Along's pride in his baseball championship is not substantially different from Azhen's father's bragging about his past sexual conquests. Both men still live in their fantasy world as outsiders to contemporary Taipei; both live in accordance with a traditional patriarchal code, deeply rooted in Chinese tradition and further reinforced by the half-century of Japanese colonial influences, especially in the father's case. The only difference is that one is a giver, believing his generosity to be his raison d'être, and the other is a taker, believing that as a father – the representative of the supreme value in a patriarchy – he can take anything from anyone with impunity. Aware of this affinity between her selfish father and her apparently selfless boyfriend, Azhen sadly tells her mother, "Along looks more and more like my father." Her statement not only groups the two men of the two generations in the same category, but also joins her mother and herself in a different category, that of victims of traditional patriarchy.

The dissolution of family ties also diminishes differentiation among individuals. Like the impersonal buildings in the Taipei streets, individuals increasingly lose their distinctive identities. Right after the news of the buyout of Ms. Mei's company has spread around, an extreme long shot shows two small shadows who seem to be imprinted on the glass wall of the ultramodern high-tech building: Azhen and her occasional lover, Xiao Ke, an architect. While a tracking shot rapidly shows a series of seemingly endless nearby and distant buildings, Xiao Ke states: "All these buildings look the same, whether I designed them or not. It is insignificant to have or not to have my input." Not only do these buildings look strikingly similar, but in fact repetition and boredom seem the only two components in Xiao Ke's mediocre life. The only food he seems to eat is "pork liver noodles" (*zhugan mian*) – in anyone's company, whether that of his mistress or his wife. The only suggestion that he makes to Azhen is invariably, "Would you like to have a beer?" – regardless of any circumstance, even if he intends to talk about getting a divorce. In his lack of differentiation, Xiao Ke himself personifies the impersonal big city.

In this impersonal society, the only way for Along to enjoy the illusion of preserving his honor is in saving other people who appear to be in more distress than himself. He even stands in for Aqing, to "teach his gambling wife a lesson" through physical violence, as if he represented the masculine power that is lacking in his friend. In a sense, Azhen's situation is like Aqing's: Her trouble is also indirectly caused by Along's benevolent actions – toward her father as well as toward his former girlfriend, Ajuan. He disappointment in Along causes her to seek consolation among idle youngsters, despite the warning of the public sign: "Danger: Vacant Building. Do Not Enter." Indeed, located in an unlawfully occupied space, her pleasure-seeking activities lead to serious consequences.

A teenage boy has become infatuated with Azhen. In the film, we never hear him pronounce a single word – he represents a voiceless generation. His conversation with Azhen in the bar is completely inaudible, buried under the loud rock 'n' roll music and dancing crowd. This generation lives atop the city of Taipei – as Azhen's sister describes it, "I have the impression that I could see everyone, but no one could see me." They are distant spectators of Taipei, uninvolved and indifferent. In fact, what the sister observes is not human beings but cars moving on streets: Humans are submerged by the ocean of automobiles. Through these idle youngsters, the film paints a gloomy picture of the future of modern Taipei.

Interestingly, Along is later killed by one of these teenagers, representatives of the dark future of the impersonal city.

In many respects, Along is as violent as his younger eventual killer. Unlike the boy, however, he has the illusion that he is fighting for his honor, an honor so difficult to define that it has become idiosyncratic. As Along explains to Azhen (after his fight with her yuppie friend in the bar), he believes that fighting is for a kind of "spirit" (*yiko qi*) or a "sense of righteousness" (*zhengyi gan*). When the teenager stalks Azhen, Along beats him mercilessly after lecturing him. The boy does not seem to deserve such a punishment; moreover, Along's attachment to his girlfriend is not strong enough to justify such a jealous outburst. To this extent, Along's violence is not so different from his killer's, despite his own belief in a justifiable cause. The boy, however, responds by attacking him with a knife from behind, instead of fighting with Along face to face as required by the traditional code of honor and its face-saving ethics. Then he flees on his motorcycle and leaves Along bleeding to death on a street corner amid a pile of garbage, including an old television set. In the deserted Taipei street, mortally wounded by a dishonorable act, Along is completely abandoned by the world. His final futile attempt to wave for a taxi is ignored by the driver, who is probably afraid of getting himself in trouble with a wounded passenger. Ironically, Along finally finds his place among garbage, piled up with all kinds of useless articles that have already been consumed by the city. Like the TV set and other city trash wrapped in plastic bags, he is the useless leftover of another age.

On the empty screen of the abandoned TV, Along hallucinates watching the news of his baseball team's victory approximately twenty years ago. On their return from their world championship, Along and his teammates are called the darlings and sweethearts of Taiwan, the glory of China's sons and daughters. Along laughs bitterly at this fantasized announcement. As Aqing had commented earlier, pretty clothes are more important than excellent skills for the current junior baseball team in Taipei, because appearance is more significant than substance in contemporary society. The pursuit of national glory becomes meaningless in a commercialized modern city. His very honor also belongs to this trash heap, forsaken in the heart of the modern city.

In the following shot, the camera cuts to Azhen, who casually sleeps on a chair in her apartment. Her former boss, Ms. Mei, phones and offers her a job, and the two meet in a newly constructed office building. The huge, empty, and faintly lighted hall, where the only distinctive sound is Azhen's high-heel shoes knocking at the floor, echoes the beginning scene of her visit to the new apartment with Along. The only difference is that her partner is no longer a man, her childhood sweetheart, but a woman, her boss and business mentor. Not only in terms of gender but also in many other aspects, Ms. Mei is just the opposite of Along. As in the past she again demonstrates her ability to remain on top of the modern world by moving a branch of an American high-tech company to Taiwan when information technology is on the verge of becoming the leader in the world economy.

Azhen looks down from the huge glass window, silently listening to her boss describing the future of the newly born computer company. Another cut gives the illusion of directing her eyes to the sidewalk covered by Along's blood near a pile of garbage. In Yang's usual style, the camera does not show the body, merely suggesting its presence by a prodigious amount of blood. A doctor behind an ambulance, after signing Along's death certificate, blithely exchanges cigarettes with the policemen and seemingly does some idle chatting, as if celebrating a certain happy event. In fact, Along's death does not seem to deprive the city of anything. On the contrary, it liberates Azhen further from the burden of traditional family-oriented ethics, allowing her to begin a life associated with potential professional success.

The camera returns to Azhen: In response to Ms. Mei's inquiry as to the possibility of her emigrating to America with Along, Azhen tersely replies, "Probably not" – a conclusion of their childhood romance, although she has not yet learned of his death.

Along's death is also the death of the traditional code of honor. The modern code of honor is expressed in Taipei mainly by financial power; traditional honor always gets in the way of the pursuit of money. The preservation of traditional masculine identity or sense of honor in this money-worshiping world of the modern city reveals itself as derisory, worthy of the scrap heap. The glory of the past, which has its last reflection on the old television screen abandoned on the street corner, has also died with its final defender, whose imagination was its last refuge. In the modern world, it was already dead a long time ago – or, more precisely, it has existed only retrospectively in a fantasized reconstruction of tradition.

THE TERRORIZERS

TECHNOLOGY AND TERROR

The world of *The Terrorizers* (*Kongbu fenzi,* 1986) is a world devoid of any passion, compassion, or even hatred, except for an insurmountable boredom that seemingly dominates everyone's life; only boredom motivates each one's (terrorizing) action, which occasionally disrupts someone else's boring routine. At the same time, the sense of boredom and indifference also ties together the different story lines of three otherwise barely related groups of people. The first consists of upper-middle-class adolescents: a teenage boy from a rich family, an amateur photographer, and his girlfriend, a bookish student. The second group is focused on the milieu of underground criminals: A Eurasian girl, after running away from her ever-angry single mother, lives on the street by means of thievery, prostitution, and occasionally murder; she is often associated with her underworld friends in various illegal activities. The third group comprises middle-aged professionals: Zhou Yufen, a writer, who constantly suffers writer's block; Li Lizhong, her husband who works as a lab technician in a hospital; Xiao Shen, an entrepreneur and her former lover in college, with whom she later renews the relationship; and the police chief, Li Lizhong's childhood friend. The three groups are loosely connected by the activities of the Eurasian girl. Locked in her mother's apartment, she randomly chooses Li's phone number from a directory and calls, pretending to Zhou Yufen to be her husband's mistress. These phone calls cause the breakdown of Zhou's already shaky marriage. The young shutterbug, infatuated with the Eurasian girl, briefly lives with her in her old apartment. When accidentally he learns of Zhou's broken marriage (through her award-winning fiction), he realizes his ex-lover's role in this family tragedy and reports what he knows to Li Lizhong, who then tries unsuccessfully to get his wife back. The film leaves us with three possible endings. In the first two endings, Li either shoots everyone who supposedly played a role in his professional and personal failures – his boss, wife, and her lover – or commits suicide pitifully, in the same way as he lived his life. The third ending suggests that everything happens only in one of Zhou's long-lasting nightmares.

Although the characters activities tend to be relatively isolated from each other, a pattern of crosscutting scenes mismatched with sounds from previous locations suggests certain connections among them. For example, when the Eurasian girl's mother, a woman apparently abandoned by her American lover, listens to the hit recording from the late 1950s of the American song "Smoke Gets in Your Eyes," the camera cuts to the photographer's empty apartment, where his girlfriend stands in front of his farewell note and enlarged prints of herself. In a sense, the past situation of the Eurasian girl's mother, abandoned by her American lover, is not unlike the current situation of the girlfriend, abandoned by the photographer infatuated with the Eurasian girl at this moment. Both women are attached to men who apparently do not feel particularly responsible for the consequences of their sexual drives.

The same kind of analogy between the Eurasian girl and another character is also established through crosscutting. When the Eurasian girl, confined by her mother in her small apartment, makes phone calls to various people, known or unknown, a shot of the barred window creates a prisonlike atmosphere. The following shot cuts to Zhou's prisonlike study, where she sits lonely and bored, struggling against her writer's block. These parallel shots suggest a strong analogy between the two women. On different occasions, the activities of criminals in the film border on those of allegedly normal people, who often appear to be on the verge of overstepping the line into criminality. In a sense, the Eurasian girl's anonymous phone calls are not fundamentally different from Zhou Yufen's attempt to write fiction, nor, for that matter, from activities of any other characters. To a degree, they all attempt to overcome boredom, often to the detriment of others. Since their "victims," if not necessarily unknown to them, are usually chosen at random, these activities can all be considered terrorist in a broad sense.[14]

In a brief dialogue between the photographer and the Eurasian girl, the boy asks: "You play these practical jokes by phone, is this really fun?" Instead of answering him, the girl returns the question: "You take pictures at random without other people's consent, is this really fun?" Each character in this film, despite differences in social status, profession, and age, seems to fight his or her loneliness by means of various actions – photography, fiction writing, lies, anonymous phone calls, denouncement of a friend, flirtation, adultery, prostitution, and murder. Each of these activities is directly, indirectly, or potentially harmful to other people. In this sense, almost every character in the film can be taken as a terrorizer.[15] Furthermore, if other people's lives are disturbed by these various actions, it is mainly because in their lives the terror has already been deeply rooted. Technology in the film reduces life to dependence on its media, such as telephones, cameras, cars, and guns. This overwhelming sense of dependence on technology carries the seeds of crisis in any interpersonal relationship by objectifying them, since these media through a mimetic model also replace human ties. To this extent, it is not an exaggeration to perceive technology, surrogate of human bonds, as the major terrorizer – one that participates directly or indirectly in each "terrorist attack" in the film, both as the cause of boredom in a dehumanized and dehumanizing society and as the means of executing such an action.

The opening shot in *The Terrorizers* of a patrol car, accompanied by the high-pitched sound of sirens, creates a frightening atmosphere in the streets of Taipei at daybreak. The car drives through the city to a gunfight location to arrest gang members. The extreme long shot captures the modern city with its high rises, which seem to sleep restlessly in a prolonged nightmare. The intersection where fast-moving cars briefly encounter one another in the prologue can serve as a prelude to the human relations portrayed in the rest of this film. As cars meet in this impersonal, dark, and somehow ominous corner of the city, human beings encounter each other in an equally arbitrary, unpredictable, and unstable manner in the filmic world.

After leaving his jealous girlfriend behind, the young photographer is wandering around. A long take of a pedestrian bridge, apparently following his changing camera angle, captures flows of pedestrians coming and going, indifferently encountering each other for a brief moment. This scene of casual encounters on the walkway is followed by another scene of a Taipei intersection, where a flow of cars passes monotonously. Both scenes are captured by the boy's moving camera. By paralleling human relations with those between technological devices, the film depicts an effect of the commodification of human ties: The relationship between things, especially machines, replaces the relationship between people to such an extent that the position of human beings and the instruments of which they are supposedly masters has been reversed. Society emphasizes technological development so much that it forces human beings to model their behaviors toward their peers on the relationships among technological devices. As a result, technology becomes the true master of the modern city, and people are its slaves.

One can also say that the two sequences suggest that personal relationships in Taipei are "technologized," and that ties between people amount to casual encounters, like cars in an intersection. Sometimes human beings encounter cars, unrelated to one another. The Eurasian girl, for example, is repeatedly shown standing on sidewalks, just about to cross a street. Once, she even faints in the middle of a street crossing, while numerous cars pass by her body without even slowing down.

This parallel between human society and technology depicts a general situation in a commercial society. Whether cars as means of transportation, telephones as means of communication, cameras as means of visual recording, or police guns as means of law enforcement, all technological products often have the opposite of their intended effect of making life easier for people. Sometimes they destroy human beings instead of serving and protecting them. The film records the technological invasion of life coldly, in a desperately precise and clean fashion. In this sense, the film camera is similar to the boy's expensive picture-taking tool. Despite his claimed passion for the Eurasian girl, the boy still takes time to photograph her carefully several minutes after her fall in a street crowded with fast-moving cars, despite the imminent danger to her life. Like all his other pictures, the one of the fainting girl in the middle of the street appears impersonal and emotionless. Similarly, the filmmaker's camera catches its characters at their most vulnerable moments, indifferently and impassively. Paradoxically, the most melodramatic moments are often shot with a precision suggesting an impeccable objectivity.[16] In other words, the dramatization of a careful *mise-en-scène* is complemented and enhanced by a skillful and emotionless technological manipulation of camera apparatus. This may explain why Edward Yang's *The Terrorizers* has gained the reputation, among a number of film critics, as one of the coldest films ever seen.[17]

Despite the comfort provided by the money of his unseen father, the boy with the camera is attracted by the underworld, exemplified by the Eurasian girl. The Eurasian girl's life experiences are, for the boy, approachable only as subjects of photographs, taken by himself, or as fiction, written by the writer, who later summarizes the story in a TV interview. In short, the boy seems attracted more to the girl's image than to her real person. Furthermore, the size of a woman's picture seems to be the only measurement of his emotional attachment to her. His girlfriend leaves a note to him before her failed suicide attempt: "You are the person who cares about me the most in this world." Her offscreen voice is associated with her enlarged portraits, which are obviously her former lover's works, as if the pictures were the only mark of his past affection for her. The same logic is applicable to his relation with the Eurasian girl. He has stealthily taken her picture during her escape from the police. In order to develop the photos of her, he exchanges two of his expensive cameras for an oversized enlarger. The size of the prints, which apparently measures the boy's emotional tie with a girl, symbolizes the objectification of human relations in the modern city. This measurement not only creates larger-than-life pictures of the two girls but also dehumanizes and objectifies them, because they look more like the billboard advertisements in Taipei than portraits of "real" people. If the girlfriend appears traditional and bookish, the Eurasian girl, by contrast, is half-American in blood and a tough survivor in Taipei's dangerous streets. After his separation from his girlfriend, the photographer moves into the Eurasian girl's old apartment. Oversized black-and-white pictures of the Eurasian girl, similar to the photos in his former girl-friend's place, only much larger, function as the insignia of the boy's living space and dominate this tiny apartment.

When the Eurasian girl, in a feverish state, returns to her former apartment, currently occupied by the camera buff, she encounters her own larger-than-life portrait in dim light. This nightmarish apparition frightens her so much that she faints before her own image. On the one hand, she is a fugitive who tries to hide her face from her mother as well as from the rest of society. On the other hand, her picture overexposes her, not simply as a real person who has a (criminal) his-tory but rather as an objectified Other even in her own eyes – in a darkroom im-permeable to daylight. Later on, the Eurasian girl steals the boy's camera and abandons the self-titled artist for her former boyfriend, a street-smart pimp on a motorcycle who just got out from the prison. Then the forsaken lover, in his des-peration, opens the curtains for the first time in the film. For the first time, the Eurasian's oversized portrait is fully exposed to the daylight. At the same time, a powerful wind blows at the small squares pieced together to form the larger-than-life picture, revealing fragments of the white wall beneath these squares. As a result, the fragmented portrait looks surrealistic, as if the picture in question were objectified to the extent that it had nothing to do with the runaway girl on the back of the pimp's motorcycle. Between the subject of his photography and the object of longing, a wall (which may be invisible to the outside world, hid-den behind fragments of the enlarged photography) always remains. The subject of his photography is an exotic beauty whose image is confined in his darkroom, whereas the object of his longing is beyond this wall, running around with crim-inals and committing all kinds of crimes. In this case, technological means allow the boy to retain the image of his dreamed beauty, while keeping him from any physical contact with her except in a room where they could not tell day from night. Ironically, for the Eurasian girl coming from the "real world," the rich boy's technological toy is meaningful only for the money she could get for it from a black-market dealer. In other words, technological devices used as "sup-plements"[18] to personal feelings in the boy's case also replace these feelings in the girl's case to the extent that "thingness" dominates human relations.

If an ordinarily insignificant action, such as an anonymous phone call from the Eurasian girl, may cause the collapse of a marriage, this is because the mar-riage has a shaky foundation. According to the writer herself, Zhou Yufen mar-ried her husband for a "clean start," wanted a child for another "clean start," be-gan to write fiction for another "clean start," and leaves her obedient but obtuse husband for another "clean start." The phone call provides Zhou with an excuse for her adultery with her former lover, Xiao Shen – another "clean start" she has desperately sought. The urge for constant renewal can be perceived as symptomatic of modernity. On the one hand, feelings are mediated by technology, which gradually reduces private space. On the other, feelings also take after their medium, technology, in its need to renew itself ceaselessly. To this extent, technology becomes the predominant mimetic model of city life. In this reversed instrumentality between people and machines, traditional bonds between lovers, husband and wife, mother and daughter, father and son, friends, overwhelmed by their mimetic model, have virtually disappeared. The indifference makes their relationships with each other extremely fragile. People are tied together like various parts of a gigantic worn-out machine – mechanically and contingently. The fragility of human ties creates an atmosphere of terror, as if life might collapse at any moment. This sense of terror legitimizes the characters' potential acts as terrorizers allegedly for the sake of self-protection. To this extent, everyone in the film is a terrorizer, both implementing terror in others' lives, and subject to terror in his or her own life.[19]

To reinforce this sense of isolation, some conventions used in classic narrative films to depict human communications are replaced by a less personal way of editing. Shot–reverse shots, traditionally used in narrative films for conversations, are often replaced by long takes. In comparison with the use of long takes for conversation in Hou Xiaoxian's films,[20] apparently similar long takes in Yang's film are usually much less subjective. These shots often expose the indifference and the lack of communication between two conversational partners. For example, Zhou Yufen, the writer, repeatedly asks both her husband and her lover on various occasions: "You do understand me, don't you?" The husband remains speechless, wrapped in his misperception of her, whereas the lover ingeniously steers the conversation in a different direction. At the same time, the woman who so eagerly seeks understanding from her sexual partners doesn't appear to make an effort to understand either of them. Everyone seems in need of understanding and affection, including the Eurasian girl, but no one is ready to provide these to another human being. In the same vein, the camera-wielding boy tells the Eurasian girl to wait for him during his military service. His apparently passionate speech does not provoke a single response, either verbal or emotional, from the girl. Yang's long takes often make various conversations look more like monologues, despite the simultaneous presence of the two speakers on the screen, since nobody seems interested in listening to others. In another scene, the Eurasian girl, locked in her mother's apartment, repeatedly dials the number of an electronic voice that mechanically reports the time at each second. Communication between people is replaced by the voice of a machine, senseless, indifferent, and undisturbed by any human emotion. Again, human relationships are modeled on a technological instrument, and human voices become analogous to the mechanical voice of an answering machine through monotonous repetition.

INTERNAL AND EXTERNAL TERRORS

Generally speaking, *The Terrorizers* portrays two kinds of terror: first, external and physical terror, which appears illegitimate in public, such as theft, conspiracy, and murder; and second, internal and psychological terror caused by solitude or emotional and verbal abuse, which apparently is not a threat to public safety. Nevertheless, these two kinds of terror are interrelated, often serve as expressions for one another, and complement each other. External terror, such as robbery and murder, may appear temporarily exciting for someone like the shutterbug and the writer. That's partly why the young photographer is drawn from his bookish girlfriend's bed to the murderer's apartment, and also why Zhou finally obtains her national award by basing her story on the Eurasian girl's illegitimate acts. Internal terror, by contrast, apparently results from boredom, or lack of any excitement. This terror is often caused by a double-bind situation: an implicitly frustrated emotional need for others combined with the impossibility of establishing an emotional tie with them in this modern city saturated with high-rise buildings, high-tech equipment, and high-speed vehicles. As a result, the film portrays loneliness as an unavoidable price of modernization. At a deeper level, the two kinds of terror converge – as the two sides of the same coin. If the Eurasian and her underworld friends commit crimes, this is partly because, like most ordinary people in the city, they suffer the same kind of internal terror, loneliness and boredom. The difference is that they externalize them much more blatantly. At the same time, internal terror makes each "normal" person a potential criminal, as in the case of the initially harmless lab technician who later becomes a cold-blooded murderer in one of three endings vacillating between fantasy and reality. The line of demarcation between a normal citizen and a criminal remains blurred, if not invisible. Furthermore, the excitement caused by external terror in the long run appears as boring as internal terror, as a close-up of Li Lizhong's friend, the police chief, shows at the beginning of the film. He accedes to an irresistible urge to yawn in the middle of a homicide investigation. The shot of his enlarged yawning face is crosscut with that of a dead body lying on the street as a result of a gunfight.

In this impersonal city, life seems cheap and fragile, and personal ties are changeable. The only element that remains consistent is an insurmountable sense of boredom, which looms in the air of the city. The monotonous and impersonal city life is exemplified by the huge (and controversial) spherical gas tank surrounded by ugly tubes and situated in the heart of the city. Three large characters inscribed on this tank – "Big Taipei" (*da Taibei*) – suggest that this technological device has become the perfect emblem of Taipei, the westernized Asian city. Be it in the office, hospital, family house, shop, or apartment building, in every corner of the city, the same kind of grayish and impersonal atmosphere prevails. Often, a certain technological device is the only distinguishable feature in a scene, as in the case of this monstrous ball surrounded by various tubes. Otherwise, not only does each scene resemble all the others, but also people are not truly distinguishable from each other in their commonly shared sense of boredom, be they gangsters, writers, upper-middle-class kids, lab technicians, prostitutes, or murderers.

Terror reigns in life, on the street, at home, in the office, in the apartment building, in any kind of human relationship, in the film or even in the process of filmmaking. We should not be surprised that the Eurasian girl shocks us by her coldness toward the world either in her anonymous phone calls, her murdering, or her prostitution, since what she is doing is merely returning what the world has given to her. In her former apartment, currently occupied by the photographer, to which she returns in a semiconscious feverish state with her keys, she encounters her own enlarged portrait in a dim light. In the same vein, she also returns the world its own image reflected in her actions. Nobody seems ever to care about her. Her American father abandoned her after a probably casual relationship with her forever depressed mother. The mother frequently vents her anger on her daughter, since she considers the girl the product of the father's sin. People and cars pass by her unconscious body in the middle of a busy intersection. The aspiring lover, the photographer, is interested in her more as an object to be captured by his camera than as a person in need of affection. The Eurasian girl pointedly asks the boy what the difference is between her harmful practical jokes and the boy's apparently innocent picture taking. In both cases, the two youngsters act out of boredom, without any regard to other people's desire, interests, or well-being. The boy from the well-to-do family differs from the street girl in that he does not need to murder in order to survive, nor make anonymous phone calls to overcome the boredom of confinement: His father's money provides him with enough freedom, and less dangerous means, to entertain himself.

Nevertheless, when the boy finds out that the Eurasian girl's anonymous phone calls destroyed the marriage of the writer Zhou Yufen, he is completely overwhelmed by a sense of terror. He keeps repeating to his girlfriend, with whom he recently renewed the relationship: "It's too frightening, truly too frightening." At the same time, he seems to have forgotten that his recent infatuation with the agent of this terror, the Eurasian girl, almost cost the life of his girlfriend, who failed in her suicide attempt. In this sense, external terror, which is acted out in public, shocks decorum by violating certain societal rules or conventions, whereas internal terror is hardly noticeable, although the consequences may be just as severe. *The Terrorizers* levels the two kinds of terror – that caused by indifference and lack of compassion, even in a close private circle, and that caused by random violence, often in a public sphere. If the two are not on an equal footing, at least violence in society is shown to be an extension of loneliness and indifference in a private circle, to the point that the two almost become indistinguishable.

In the same vein, Zhou Yufen is no less a terrorizer. She is demanding emotionally, feeling eternally misunderstood by her sexual partners, but at the same time refuses to make an effort to understand them. As a result, she can harm others less intentionally, and without a sense of self-knowledge. After receiving anonymous phone calls from the Eurasian girl, she never asks her husband whether the accusations are true or not, because the most important factor is her "unclean feeling" – as she explains to her lover. This unclean feeling may very well be a desire to leave an unattractive husband with an honorable excuse – an easy way out of the unfruitful marriage – in order to have another "clean start." In this sense, the anonymous caller mainly allows the writer to act out her hidden desire. In other words, the Eurasian girl's phone calls do not cause the collapse of the marriage but rather are only a catalyst for already existing problems in the marriage: Zhou Yufen's narcissism and Li Lizhong's obtuseness. As two of the three conflicting endings suggest, the husband's repressed personality later leads him down a much more dangerous path: He may either become a senseless and dangerous terrorizer, armed with his friend's police gun and enraged by a need for revenge; or a self-destructive loser, who kills himself with the same gun in his friend's sloppy Japanese-style bathroom. Furthermore, even prior to this moment, Li Lizhong has already earned the title of terrorizer in his own right. In order to become the chief technician of the lab group, he does not hesitate a moment in wrongly accusing his friend and colleague, Xiao Jin, whose only fault is competing with him for the same promotional opportunity. To this extent, the various possible endings reveal how fragile the line of demarcation between law-abiding citizens and criminals is in a modern city like Taipei – since a person as obscure as Li Lizhong can be equally victim and perpetrator of violence, depending on which way the wind blows.

The terror, which each character is both a subject of and subject to, permeates Taipei, the modern city. The film's three alternative endings are all terror-laden. In one, armed with the police gun he stole from his inspector friend, Li Lizhong murders his boss, seriously wounds his wife's lover, and drives Zhou Yufen herself temporarily insane with an intentionally missed gunshot. He finds the Eurasian girl who prostitutes herself on the street in order to squeeze money from her customers through either murder or blackmail. The sequence when he, as a potential customer, follows her to a hotel room is itself open-ended, since it is impossible to figure out whose blood is splashing on the locked door of the room in this final encounter of the two equally dangerous murderers. In the second possible ending, horrified, the police chief discovers Li Lizhong's dead body bleeding silently in his sloppy bathroom. The third possible ending shows the writer waking up, nauseated beside her lover, as if everything happened only in her nightmare. However, the three alternative endings do not necessarily diminish the weight of terror in the film. These sequences, neatly shot with remarkable precision, remind us of details in numerous previous scenes, such as the impersonal setting of the hotel room, the Eurasian girl's gesture of grasping the knife hidden in her jeans, and Li Lizhong's obsessive hand washing. The clean and elegant precision as well as the cold but obsessive repetition provide these night-marish endings with an inescapable sense of reality. As a result, the variant end-ings become more restraining than a conventional single conclusion, because even the possibility of escaping in fantasy from the overwhelming sense of terror appears nullified. The terror permeates the modern city so irresistibly that the worst nightmare is at any moment realizable and realistic, because reality and nightmare in the final analysis become indistinguishable. At any moment, life may turn into a nightmare and a normally law-abiding citizen may commit an unimaginable crime.

In an interview, Edward Yang describes his *The Terrorizers* as an "intellectu-al game" (*yizhi youxi*).[21] As a result, any sentimental element is eliminated from this game. Be it a nightmare or a game, this film presents the modern city as a gigantic prison where each individual lives in his or her isolated cell. At the same time, one can also perceive Yang's modernist work as a strange elegy for tra-ditional society, in which tradition is conspicuously absent. The present is un-livable, whereas the past is irretrievable. Even the film's visual precision and elegance contribute to depicting modern life as a suffocating dead-end in its cin-ematic closure. However, this notion of dead-end is also applicable to his own filmmaking. Following *The Terrorizers*, Yang has never again used the same im-peccable precision to portray a perfectly unsentimental and impersonal world. Partly due to market pressure, Yang's later films are much more narrative than his earlier ones (in this respect, similar to those of his mainland colleagues, but to a lesser degree). They are either nostalgic (*A Brighter Summer Day* [*Guling-jie shaonian sharen shijian*], 1990), satirical (*Confucius's Confusion* [*Duli shi-dai*], 1994), or even slightly sentimental (*Mahjong* [*Majiang*], 1995). Despite stylistic changes, two factors remain consistent in his films. First, they all con-tinue to question the process of filmmaking as well as its matrix, technology. Second, in almost all of them a woman character represents one of the worst as-pects of modernity – like the Eurasian girl in *The Terrorizers*. Women in Yang's films represent not only technology – just as in Friz Lang's modernist work *Me-tropolis* – but also the West, partly because the West and technology often play interchangeable roles in the process of modernization in Taiwan.

CONFUCIUS'S CONFUSION

SENTIMENT AND INVESTMENT

Hence, once again, pastiche: in a world in which stylistic innovation is no longer pos-sible, all that is left is to imitate dead styles, to speak through the masks and with the voices of the styles in the imaginary museum. But this means that contemporary or postmodernist art is going to be about art itself in a new kind of way; even more, it means that one of its essential messages will involve the necessary failure of art and the aesthetic, the failure of the new, the imprisonment in the past.[22] – Fredric Jameson

Edward Yang's *Confucius's Confusion* (*Duli shidai*) is a satire of the artistic milieu in the schizophrenic Taiwan society torn between "sentiment" or "affection" (*qing*), a value allegedly central to a Confucian tradition, and money, the idol of a consumer society. In the film there are four young couples, whose relationships can at best be called strange. Having fallen in love with each other during their high-school years, Xiaoming and Qiqi are considered a perfect couple. Molly and Aqin are engaged because their rich families want to combine their wealth by means of marriage. Xiaofeng, a former actress, is the mistress of Larry, a married man, who is also Aqin's confidant and business adviser. Molly's sister, a talk-show hostess, is separated from her writer husband, whom she married for love during her college years despite her family's opposition. In addition, the drama director Birdie is a former classmate of Qiqi, Molly, and Xiaoming; he circulates among these couples as a clown. At the same time, Qiqi, who works for Molly's advertising agency, is also the best friend of her boss, whereas Xiaoming and Liren, one of his coworkers in the governmental office, are buddies. To a great extent, these couple's same-sex friendships often appear more important than their marital engagements. By the end of the film, the dynamics of the relationships have changed: The perfect couple decides to separate, the family-arranged engagement is broken off, bosses lose their employees, and friends are no longer speaking to each other. All these changes occur with a lighthearted playfulness, which reminds us of one of Woody Allen's films, *Bullets over Broadway*.[23] Both Yang's and Allen's films are satires of the artistic milieu.

However, unlike in *Bullets over Broadway*, in *Confucius's Confusion* performance is more important in life than onstage. Everyone performs in order to fill the gap between the traditional notion of sentiment/affection (*qing*), which supposedly plays the central role in the traditional Confucian relationships (*lun*), and money, the prime value of a consumer society. Often, the more that characters are motivated by their material interests, the more they are eager to disguise this motivation in the name of *qing;* and the harder they try, the more nakedly selfish their motivation appears. Although most people in the film make a living in connection with the performing arts, the film emphasizes the role of performance in life to the extent that the line of demarcation between life and the stage is blurred. Interestingly, the play within the film, *Ah*, can be seen as a flea market of commodified artifacts – acrobats dressed in classical Chinese clothes dancing to cheesy Western-style music. After its rehearsal, Birdie, the so-called great master and director of *Ah*, anxiously asks a young woman, his simpleminded admirer and assistant: "Do you think this show is good? Will it sell?" In other words, marketable value becomes the only measurement of artistic excellence. As the pastiche of performing arts within the performing world, *Ah* doubly emphasizes the function of money as the ultimate goal of performance either in life or onstage. In the prologue, running around the stage on a pair of skates, Birdie compares politicians with performing artists, since both depend on "tickets" (*piao*), whether "votes" (*xuanpiao*) or "box office" (*piaofang*).

In Yang's first satirical comedy, life becomes a degraded imitation of the past. People quote or misquote Confucian sayings, traditional proverbs, or each other's words to hide the sense of emptiness in their lives; yet these quotations of a distant or not-so-distant past, rather than filling the void, are themselves filled with the same void. They become meaningless and laughable. People also speak about life from a vantage point of the arts either as artists (Xiaofeng) or as arts commentators (Larry), to illustrate similarities between life and the arts in their commonly shared performative nature. Art in this case becomes synonymous with the commercialization of tradition, especially a vaguely defined Confucian tradition in its allegedly central value of sentiment/affection (*qing*). The emphasis on sentiment supposedly comes from an indirect interpretation of family-centered "five relationships" (*wulun*)[24] in the Confucian tradition. In other words, "sentiment" in the name of the arts is not truly distant from what, in a more straightforward context, we would call hypocrisy: People use the word *qing* when they try to get what they want by pretending to be altruistic. The film starts with a quotation from Confucius's *Analects* in order to prove that his distant descendants are doing exactly the opposite of what their ancient sage told them thousands of years ago. Although the master said that wealth should enhance education and civility, Yang suggests in his film that Taiwan's wealth makes people culturally deprived. The once-popular novelist, Molly's former brother-in-law, now a misanthrope, compares himself to Confucius. Instead of quoting from the master, however, he attributes all the elements in his own life to the ancient sage, as if he were the modern model of Confucius, rather than Confucius being his role model. Instead of remaining an authority figure, then, Confucius has become a metaphor for a common Chinese man, caught between his traditional beliefs and modernity.

Despite Yang's use of pastiche, his film still differs from Jameson's definition of a postmodern film, in which "the very possibility of any linguistic norm in terms of which one could ridicule private languages and idiosyncratic styles would vanish, and we would have nothing but stylistic diversity and heterogeneity."[25] By contrast, his film serves as a transition to postmodern works, such as *Vive l'amour* (*Aiqing wansui*), a film made in 1994 by Cai Mingliang, a Taiwan director of the younger generation. Cai's film is about the accidental encounters of three young people in a newly built, and still unoccupied, luxury apartment. All three of them are merchants: a salesman of funeral urns, a male peddler of illegally imported clothes, and a female real estate agent. The urn salesman obtains his keys to this house by stealing them from the keyhole, where a real estate agent must have forgotten them. The real estate agent comes here to sleep with the peddler, who followed her from a cafeteria to the streets. Afterward, the peddler also steals the apartment keys from her. In the course of the film, the urn salesman never faces the real estate agent: He only peeps at her or listens to her sexual intercourse with the peddler, who becomes acquainted with him by illegally sharing the apartment. The concluding sequence of *Vive l'amour* shows the young woman walking endlessly through a muddy construction field. During her long walk, her high heels monotonously hammer at the viewers' nerves. She finally reaches a large empty stadium and sits on a bench. Then, wordlessly and desperately, she starts crying. An old man reading a newspaper on a nearby bench does not even raise his eyes. The film ends in an extreme long take of the woman's overexposed weeping face.

The satirical nature of *Confucius's Confusion* implies a certain judgment from the perspective of an absent moralistic reference point, which is vaguely (or "confusedly" – as suggested by the title) connected to the Confucian tradition. In Cai's *Vive l'amour,* by contrast, any imaginable reference is lost, since individuals are portrayed as unrelated atoms in their occasional encounters (which become the only possible kind of human encounter in the film). In Yang's film, a "linguistic norm," or the distinction between truth and falsity, still exists despite (or because of) its negation, whereas in Cai's film any linguistic norm, such as truthfulness, is simply no longer an issue. Since none of these individuals in *Vive l'amour* is truly interested in communicating with another, any constative reference point also becomes unnecessary. The woman talks to her customers but only in order to *perform* her function of real estate agent. However, she never says a single word to her lover. The only time she speaks to him is on her cellular phone, because she mistakes him for a customer. When she finds out who he is, she immediately hangs up. In other words, language is only a business tool, useless in personal relations. By contrast, in *Confucius's Confusion* people still talk, even occasionally appear too talkative – often to fake certain feelings. In other words, lies exist as a mirror image of a truthful language with which communication can be relatively sincere – as in the final conversation between Xiaoming and Qiqi. Due to the ironic touch in his film, Yang remains a modernist filmmaker, unlike Cai Mingliang, in whose film moral judgment is virtually absent. In this respect, Yang is similar to his Fifth Generation counterparts, whereas Cai is much closer to the newer generation of mainland filmmakers, arguably named the Sixth Generation.

Although at different levels the word *qing* (sentiment/love/affection) recurs in the film, in almost all circumstances its usage is always ironic. Qiqi – "Whoever sees her loves her, because she pays special attention to sentiment," as Larry comments – mentions this word for the first time in the prologue. In the opening shot, Qiqi and her male colleague on the verge of leaving Molly's advertising agency, are situated in the same frame. They seldom look each other in the eye. The narrow corridor in front of the elevators serves as an important stage for various actions. During Qiqi's conversation with her colleague, people constantly pass by them in order to use the elevators, sometimes even walking between them. Through open windows in the background, one can vaguely see a group of high rises in the streets of Taipei – a reminder of impersonal life in the city. Qiqi implores her colleague to stay in the name of "sentiment" (*qing*). He replies that sentiment is no longer a valid word in contemporary society, since "everything could be a performance. For example, your elegance, kindness, innocence, and loveliness could also be the result of an excellent performance." Qiqi remains speechless, left alone in the hallway among indifferent passersby and background images of Taipei streets. As an echo of the words of her departed colleague, the background also underscores the inadequacy of the word "sentiment" to which Qiqi refers.

As an ironic voice, the screen titles constantly anticipate the keywords in the ensuing scene. The following screen title registers a quotation from Larry's conversation with Molly: "The Chinese pay great attention to 'sentiment' [*qing*]." Larry, as the financial adviser to her fiancé, Aqin, talks to Molly about the relationship between sentiment and performance in the subsequent scene. Without any ceremony, Larry puts the two concepts on an equal footing. He takes Qiqi as an example of a "perfect cultural product – elegant, kind, and pretty. Whoever sees her loves her, because she pays special attention to sentiment." As cultural product, sentiment must be "cultivated" and has little to do with genuine feelings. Like artistic and cultural products, sentiment is highly marketable, "exactly as in the case of any high-risk and high-efficiency investment," as Larry says. In other words, sentiment has nothing spontaneous or personal, since it is both faked – as "performance" – and utilitarian – as "investment."

Interestingly, the film often uses large pieces of glass as important props: We might see actors through a car window – Molly and one of her interlocutors sitting in the front seats of her expensive Porsche – or a view of the city through large glass windows, as in this scene. The glass rooms cast an ironical light on the repeatedly emphasized notion of sentiment. On the one hand, the glass reinforces the impression of isolation – as if an invisible wall were separating people from each other. For example, couples – Xiaoming and Qiqi, Xiaofeng and Larry – often see each other through the huge glass windows of the bar Friday's. On the other hand, by dint of endless mutual reflections in gigantic pieces of glass, the film also creates an impression of similarity among different settings, be it a bar, an office, a bordello, or Molly's luxury house. Objects, houses, human beings, and emotions look strangely alike, as if they were deformed but indistinguishable copies of each other.

Considered the favorite object of male desire and female friendship, Qiqi occupies the center of "sentiment" in the world of this film. Larry, as we've seen, attributes her success as a "cultural product" to her emphasis on "sentiment." She dresses like a doll and is always posed in a perfect position to be seen. The glossy slow motion in her TV advertisement underlines her artificiality. When Qiqi explains her hairdo to her fiancée's stepmother – "They arranged my hair for the advertisement" – this ironically summarizes her life. Like *qing* that she supposedly personifies, Qiqi is indeed a cultural product, arranged to perfection by "them" in order to compete for a better price in a market economy. At Molly's request Qiqi visits the writer, Molly's brother-in-law, to convince him to release the copyright of his previous work to her agency so that Birdie would be free of the charge of plagiarism made by some journalists. The writer angrily responds, "In order to convince me, they have even sent a lovelier one [in comparison to Xiaofeng, who had visited him previously] to reach their goal." In other words, Qiqi represents *qing* both subjectively, due to her special attention paid to human ties, and objectively, as the most desirable woman. At the same time, the writer's comment also suggests that working women's success is measured by their to-be-looked-at-ness. The more beautiful they appear, the more valuable they must be for their jobs. However, there is an inherent contradiction between the Hollywood model of female glamour and the Chinese virtue of traditional female modesty. Qiqi's secret of success is in combining these two apparently incompatible qualities, being looked at while remaining apparently indifferent to (or modest about) her own to-be-looked-at-ness. This combination gives her leverage, allowing her to be seductive without appearing intentional or utilitarian, thanks to her emphasis on "affection" (*qing*). Paradoxically, most characters in the film perceive this combination both as exemplary of women's highest achievement in their workplace, and as faked, since it cannot be anything else but the result of a performance.

Due to the highly performative nature and investment value of sentiment, sexual relations between men and women are understandably portrayed in a humorous light. The film includes two bedroom scenes: One is in Xiaofeng's apartment with Larry; the other is in a Japanese-style hotel room – Molly with Xiaoming. In Xiaofeng's bedroom, Larry stands outside the bathroom in his flowery underwear, looking pitiful and ridiculous. While he swears to Xiaofeng that nothing has happened between him and Molly, Xiaofeng, locked in the bathroom, describes step by step how Molly would have treated him in such a virtual affair. Since Xiaofeng's imaginative description corresponds exactly to what has indeed transpired, Larry stands by the closed door, pathetically astounded. When she comes out, she suggests to him how to teach Molly a lesson through his relationship to Aqin, her fiancé. Her suggestion is obviously motivated by her desire to take revenge on Molly, her whimsical ex-boss, who fired her for no apparent reason. Blissfully unaware of her true motivation, Larry listens to her admiringly. When the light goes off and Xiaofeng's affectionate voice requests a hug, the screen title mockingly concludes this first bedroom scene as follows: "Affection becomes a cheap excuse, a faked feeling is more convincing than a true one."

The prelude to this scene is no less ridiculous. On the one hand, in a strange date, Molly just rejected Larry and dumped him in a gas station after having tortured him verbally in her fashionable sports car. On the other hand, Xiaofeng would have slept with Xiaoming had she not happened to spot Larry before the two men saw each other. The three successive scenes of this strange couple with their respective potential or real lovers suggest that their relationship is not only based on fake and cheap feelings but is also accidental and interchangeable.

The prelude to the second bedroom scene is even more absurd: After a quarrel with Qiqi, Molly looks for her everywhere and ends up in front of Xiaoming's mother's house, although Xiaoming knows nothing of his fiancée's whereabouts, because he too had just argued with Qiqi. A violent quarrel between these two perceived rivals, both attracted to Qiqi, leads to a physical fight in the narrow, dark lane. Accidentally, this violence makes them fall into each other's arms, in part because of their shared frustration over Qiqi's absence. The camera cuts to a Japanese-style hotel room, where Molly asks Xiaoming if he loves her, obviously after lovemaking. When Xiaoming refuses to give the requested answer, she angrily leaves the room, claiming that her engagement with Aqin is perfectly normal. Left alone, Xiaoming murmurs to himself: "It's normal. Everything is normal: Boxers, the Cultural Revolution, Tian'anmen Square, and unification of China, everything is normal." In other words, Xiaoming is confused by sexual relationships as much as by modern historical traumas in mainland China. Like these historical traumas, the changing dynamics of sexual relationships is part of the modernization process imposed upon Chinese men like Xiaoming. This process destabilizes traditional Confucian culture and makes his own confusion "normal" – as Molly claims – in the "Independence Era" (a literal translation of the film's Chinese title). To this extent, the film's Chinese and English titles converge, since it is the "Independence Era" that leads to *Confucius's Confusion* – a perfect description of Xiaoming's current situation.

WOMEN'S INDEPENDENCE AND MEN'S CONFUSION

Each of three young women in this film is associated with a technological prop. Qiqi is constantly shown with her cellular phone. When she forgets her phone, she seems also to lose her usual self-control: Despite her carefulness, when she sees Xiaoming through the windows of Friday's, she hastily runs out and accidentally drops her phone. The following scene shows their quarrel concerning dinner arrangements with his father and stepmother. The usually soft-spoken Qiqi is shouting at her angry fiancé. She forgets her phone only once, in the writer's tiny apartment. When she later returns to fetch it, the writer believes it is an opportunity for him to start a romantic relationship with Qiqi – as if the phone spoke for her feelings. Furthermore, Molly perceives Qiqi's dead phone battery, which prevents her from calling Qiqi, as a sign of the latter's indifference toward her. In short, for others as well as for Qiqi, the cellular phone serves as the filter, if not the expression, of her feelings, to the point that it has become an extension of her body.

Molly is often associated with her fancy black Porsche, which indicates her financial situation and social status. She usually stages intimate talks with her partners in this car, which provides her with an aura of superiority. Sitting in the driver's seat, she is the owner and the master. In other settings – when she talks to Larry in her office, to Xiaoming in the restaurant, on the street, and in the bedroom, or to Qiqi under the night sky – she appears much more vulnerable. In other words, her apparent independence largely depends on her car, a technological product that symbolizes her family wealth.

Xiaofeng, for her part, seems eternally in the process of looking for her contact lenses. In Friday's, she searches for them. When Xiaoming encounters her outside the bar, she appears to wipe her eyes. When Xiaoming asks, she claims to have lost her contacts again; but later, she has no trouble spotting Larry before the two men have a chance to see each other. Her lenses, essentially invisible to anyone besides herself, thus conveniently serve her deceptive nature, as if their loss prevents her potential sexual partner from seeing through her. At any moment, she can pretend to lose them in order to hide her feelings. They even foster a sense of her innocence: During her job interview with Birdie, the director of *Ah* and the so-called great master, he compares her to a lovely little girl lost in a big city, when she loses her lenses.

In all three cases, the female protagonists need their respective technological devices to establish their individualities, or their "independence" (as the literally translated title "Independence Era" suggests). Women's independence not only needs to meet the self-contradictory requirement of successful femininity in the workplace, as in Qiqi's case, but also depends on products of technology – the marker of the modern world. As a result, this independence to a great degree looks artificial. However, the dilemma of working women does not necessarily make their male counterparts fare better in modern society. Men are utterly confused – like the writer, the self-proclaimed modern reincarnation of their sage ancestor, Confucius, puzzled by an ever-changing postindustrial world and by "independent" women armed with their technological devices.

The relationships of these three young women with men are problematic: Xiaofeng goes out with a married man, Larry, to advance her career. Molly is engaged to Aqin under the pressure of their two rich families to marry and consolidate their wealth. At the end of the film, Aqin breaks their engagement, believing he finally and truly tastes love with Birdie's assistant, whose simple-mindedness is a good match for Aqin's own. Qiqi and Xiaoming are engaged and considered a "perfect couple" (*jintong yunü*) by most people; yet both are involved in triangular relationships, and the two have never ceased quarreling. In fact, Molly believes that the prospect of her loveless arranged marriage with Aqin is better than the outlook for her friend Qiqi with Xiaoming. Not surprisingly, at the end of the film the perfect couple also decides to separate. To a great extent, the failure of (hetero)sexual relationships in *Confucius's Confusion* creates a double-edged irony, whittling away at women's apparent independence and men's derisory efforts to preserve their masculinity. On the one hand, the women's independence is mainly based on their looks, which enable them to become "artworks." On the other, the film's male viewing subjects can have little security concerning their own masculinity, as the boy seemingly can never get the girl.

Curiously, the most important relationships of infidelity for both Qiqi and Xiaoming are not heterosexual but homoerotic attachments.[26] Although these ties are not exactly sexual, they appear much more solid than their engagement. Qiqi is attached to Molly despite her constant complaints about her boss/friend to her fiancé. Liren is Xiaoming's buddy, although Xiaoming inadvertently traps him, manipulated by their boss and other officemates. Molly's relationship with Qiqi has been a constant subject of quarrels between the couple. Xiaoming not only beats Molly but also gives Qiqi an ultimatum, asking her to choose between him and her friend. In a sense, his fiancée makes her choice by leaving him. At the same time, although Xiaoming has never told Qiqi that he loves (*ai*) her, he does use this word to describe his feelings toward Liren: When Molly asks Xiaoming, after their one-night stand, if he loves her, Xiaoming responds that love does not mean much, since he was responsible for Liren's dismissal although he loves (*ai*) him. In the Chinese language, people seldom use the word *ai* to describe the relationship between two adults (except for certain intergenerational close relatives), since in these circumstances the word has a passionate and often sexual undertone. As a result, although the film does not deal explicitly with the subject of homoeroticism, the only possible love in this film seems to be between people of the same sex, since both women and men respectively do not need to perform their femininity (as images of beauty) or masculinity (as images of power) for their same-sex peers but must do so for their heterosexual partners. To this extent, same-sex affection has strangely become an oasis for all these individuals exhausted by their daily (emotional) performances. Even the stable traditional family needs performance to maintain itself in a constantly changing postindustrial world.

Kaja Silverman points out, while analyzing Ulrike Ottinger's film *Bildnis einer Trinkerin* (*Ticket of No Return*):

In other words, it is a signifier of the impasse at the heart of traditional femininity: the impossibility of approximating the images in relation to which one is constantly and inflexibly judged. In this fantasy sequence, as in those which precede it, *Bildnis* suggests that if the specular domain figures more centrally in conventional female subjectivity than it does in its masculine counterpart, that is not because woman is the image, but because – more than man – she is *supposed* to be.[27]

Qiqi represents the perfect image of femininity in the eyes of most people, so perfect that it scares her. One dark night, she and Molly sit in front of a wall, chatting. Molly puts her hands around her friend's shoulders. Qiqi explains that she is saddened by her own loveliness, since people suspect that she is faking. In other words, a double-bind message is passed to women. On the one hand, everyone needs to fit the perfect image, like Qiqi, as Larry suggests to Molly in their first conversation; those who do are rewarded. On the other hand, since fitting this ideal image perfectly is in reality impossible, those who come close to perfection, like Qiqi, are also punished because of their supposed falsity. Following this paradoxical logic, most people, especially of the opposite sex, see Qiqi as feminine perfection: The distance between the imaginary and the symbolic is seemingly abolished in her case. At the same time, this external identification also makes her an image of perfect hypocrisy, not because of her actions but rather because of the inherent flaw in the required image of femininity. A good performer like Qiqi creates a sense of reality, since "nobody can even find anything wrong with her," as Xiaofeng suggests. At the same time, because performance is a copy of reality, one should maintain a certain distinction between the original and the copy in order to remain truthful to reality. Precisely because of her truthful performance, Qiqi is considered hypocritical, since her performance reveals that truth is a copy in itself – a copy of a higher quality. In other words, goodness itself becomes performative in its essence.

Every man in the film seems to have preconceived images about not only Qiqi but women in general. After Qiqi escapes from the embrace of the writer, she shouts at him: "You are like all these men, you assume you know what I think." Larry also assumes that he knows Molly's thoughts, since as a rich heiress who does not have much life experience she is supposedly simpleminded. Ironically, Molly sees through him and pitilessly laughs at his lies, then dumps him from her fancy Porsche at a lonely gas station. In this sense, women's independence can be understood as their differences from men's preconceived image of them, although they also pretend to fit this image when it is to their own advantage. Their relationship to the image, then, is that of masquerade, as Mary Ann Doane writes in her well-known essay.[28]

If this image burdens women in their relationships to men, men are also burdened because they seem surprised by the fact that these women are not simply images. Moreover, men have to fit the image of the rational, the powerful, and the enlightened in their relations to the opposite sex. This image of ideal masculinity is usually represented by westerners, often Americans. To this extent, cultural or racial difference feminizes Chinese men in their relations to women, because they are expected to fit images of masculinity suggested by the visual presence of American men. The conflicting value systems of modern westernized and traditional China further reinforce the inherently self-contradictory nature in the respective images of both genders. In the final analysis, no one, man or woman, can truly fit these images. At the same time, women's differences from their male partners' preconceptions even further shake the latter's confidence in their own self-images, partly because men in a patriarchal society rely on the marginality of the opposite sex to define their own central position.

In Yang's films, women are usually portrayed as more the beneficiaries of modernity, since they have become relatively independent – financially as well as emotionally – in the process of modernization. Women's relative independence makes Yang's male characters extremely uneasy, for it undermines the image of masculinity based on a gender division in traditional China: Women took care of the household, whereas men were the only providers. However, unlike in Hou

Xiaoxian's films, where women are still mostly relinquished to the spaces around the kitchen, Yang is keenly aware of changes in gender situation, which his films generally portray as unavoidable and irreversible – as part of the modernization and westernization process. At the same time, his films also express a deeply rooted uneasiness toward these changes by portraying "modern" women either as evil or as unhappy. In other words, the negative effect of modernization is closely related with changing gender situations or changing women. By contrast, men in his films are often portrayed as victim of these changes. In general, men prefer to remain stable; thus, they also seem more reliable than their opposite sex in the changing world. Occasionally, at risk of their personal interests, men remain anchored to the traditional value system – stay "Confucian gentlemen" in the modern era – partly because of their uneasiness with the westernized concept of masculinity redefined by changing images of gender relations.

From time to time, in the form of male bonding, men share their nostalgia for a safer past where they did not need to fulfill a new standard of masculinity. For example, Xiaoming talks to Liren in a nightclub to ask him to help a contractor, who claimed to be on the verge of bankruptcy because he missed a deadline. Meanwhile, behind their backs, a gigantic television screen shows an NBA game. The TV camera constantly moves, following fast-running athletes and shifting back and forth from extreme long shots to close-ups. Larger-than-life images of fast-moving American basketball stars form a striking contrast to the two motionless Taiwan office clerks. Their small figures before the immense screen look so inadequate in this supermodern technological era, of which America is the perfect representation. Furthermore, basketball, a sport dominated by Americans, also symbolizes the very concept of modernized masculinity on this occasion. At this moment, Liren laughs at Xiaoming's compassion – "You still behave like a mandarin in the Qing dynasty" – although he is persuaded by his friend to help this contractor at the risk of his own career. Unlike Along in *Taipei Story,* who disappointedly compares his own much smaller hands with those of a Caucasian ballet dancer in his girlfriend's poster, the two speakers are not disturbed by, nor even aware of, the contrast between their own resemblance to Qing mandarins and the images of modern masculinity incarnated by American basketball superstars. Instead, they stick to their old-fashioned morality and, contrary to their own interest, help the allegedly distressed contractor by changing the deadline after the fact. As a result, they fall into the trap of their director and other colleagues, who use this trick to force Liren to resign – due to his "unlawful" behavior. Thus their "altruism," dictated by traditional ethics of Confucian gentlemen, backfires on them, as does that of Along in *Taipei Story.* Because Xiaoming is less interested in a preconceived image of what a man should be in the modern era, he can get along with his male friend much better than with his fiancée. With Liren, Xiaoming as a Confucian gentleman can remain indifferent to, or at least much less "confused" by, the image of a relatively new notion of masculinity, with which he is constantly asked to identify in relations with the opposite sex. At the same time, this comfort is in the final analysis illusory, since it cannot withstand a reality check. As a result, under the pressure of the "real" world, Xiaoming and Liren lose both their mutual friendship and their jobs due to their Confucian gentlemanly benevolence. This quality represents the residual notion of traditional masculinity, with which the two male friends, like most male characters in Yang's films, feel relatively comfortable.

In all three of Yang's films discussed here, the city – Taipei – is portrayed as the source of danger, contradiction, conflict, anxiety, and confusion. At the same time, city life is also fascinating, due to its complexity, perversity, changeability, fast pace, and indeterminacy. The city, which has almost been endowed with a multilayered personality in Yang's works, constantly offers surprises through its close relations with technology, industrialization, and modernization. One can never predict what is going to happen next in the city, since it is changing rapidly beyond any rational comprehension. In Yang's films, the city is a melodramatic "body" par excellence – "seized by meanings."[29] However, these meanings appear meaningless to Yang's characters, who live inside this body. Since they can neither predict changes or grasp their inner logic, his characters are often bored, confused, frustrated, if not terrified. Because everyone is constantly taken by surprise, nobody is truly the hero in this drama besides the city itself. That may explain why Yang's films usually do not have any individual hero in a traditional sense, except for Along, who loses his battle against the changing city in *Taipei Story*. The other two films offer fragmentary images of lives of various groups who occasionally interact with each other in a casual manner.

In most cases, women are portrayed as somewhat more comfortable in dealing with new situations due to their recently acquired economic independence in the modern era. Often, the association of femininity with the changing city makes men even more confused, because it further disrupts the firm ground in which traditional patriarchy can take root, namely, traditional gender hierarchy. Men, however, appear much less open to changes and, thus, much more frustrated by changing situations than their sexual counterparts. Usually, men are also forced to fit images of ideal (westernized) masculinity, mostly derived from American culture. Interestingly, their masculine models are drawn along a distinct racial line. Blacks, such as Michael Jackson and Michael Jordan, represent ideal masculinity in a physical (or sexual) sense, as in the case of Azhen's yuppie friend's crude joke involving penis size in *Taipei Story* and the background large-screen images of NBA players in *Confucius's Confusion*. Often, the comparison between Chinese men and these images of black icons of American popular culture suggests an insurmountable difference between them.

The only successful case of a Chinese man's identification with Americans in Yang's three films is that of Along's brother-in-law in *Taipei Story*. According to Along's account, his brother-in-law "bought" his identity as a honorary white American with his cash payment for a house in a wealthy Los Angeles residential area. This new identity, unlike black-based physical models of ideal but alien masculinity, is uniquely based on an economic factor and strictly limited to rich whites. In fact, if we can believe Along's account, the brother-in-law – to reassert his (honorary) white identity – gunned down a poor black with impunity in his own courtyard. At the same time, this potential identity is vaguely associated with Along's own nostalgic dream of recovering a bygone patriarchal order, exemplified by his idiosyncratic traditional code of honor.

In short, formation of a different concept of masculinity in Yang's films vacillates between physical differentiation from blacks and economic identification with whites. This vacillation reveals a certain similarity between the traditional Chinese patriarchy and the American racial hierarchy – despite the apparently conflicting value systems of the ancient East and the modern West. In cases of both black and white Americans, however, different images of masculine models problematize Chinese male subjectivity bound to traditional ethics to the extent that Chinese men often appear confused facing a brave new world. In *Confucius's Confusion,* the ancient Chinese sage becomes a metaphor for the confused Chinese man in the modern era: Even the revived sage in person would not be able to restore the glory of his ideology, which prevailed in traditional China for thousands of years. All he could do is be puzzled – as puzzled as his descendants facing the rapid modernization process. Following the same logic, Confucianism has never served as a truly positive value in any of Yang's films. On the contrary, it appears to be an oppressive part of a patriarchal family structure. The Confucian tradition is depicted to represent the irretrievable loss of a distant past, which now plays only the role of counterpart to the value system of the contemporary consumer society in Taipei.

Despite the critical edge of Yang's modernist approach, the somewhat simplistic division between the ancient East (Taiwan and China) and modern West (often represented by the United States) falls into the trap of cultural hierarchy inherent in the discourse of modernity. The past portrayed in Yang's films has never existed as a historical entity, except as a fantasized space reconstructed on the basis of an orientalist imagination. Yang uses this imaginary past as a referential point to express anxiety facing rapid economic, gender, axiological, and social changes that occurred in contemporary Taipei.

Arif Dirlik rightly points out:

The EuroAmerican assault on imperial China both provoked the emergence of Chinese nationalism and, ironically, provided it with images of the Chinese past that could be incorporated in a new national identity. While different political strands in Chinese nationalism focused on different aspects of the past, and evaluated this historical legacy differently, metonymic reductionism has been apparent in the identification of China among liberals and conservatives with Confucianism, despotism, bureaucratism, familism, or even racial characteristics, all of them traceable to Orientalist representations, or an unchanging "feudal" or "Asiatic" society, in a Marxist version of Orientalism. What was common to all was a contemporary consciousness of which "Western" ideas, including the "imaginative geography" of Orientalism, were an integral component.[30]

According to this orientalist imagination (adopted by Orientals themselves), China (or the Orient) remains frozen in a fantasized past. In the final analysis, the dichotomy between the ancient East and the modern West leads to an unavoidable conclusion: Despite all its shortcomings, the West is the only true master of the modern world. Regardless of how reluctantly non-Western people may undergo westernization, those who live in today's world are either westerners or westernized, since any change that occurs to Orientals necessarily makes them unfaithful to their tradition, which is supposedly the main source of their cultural identity. Following the same logic, strictly speaking, an Oriental culture does not have a history of its own, because it has been identified with an unchanged and unchangeable tradition (Confucianism in this case). Therefore, any historical change in such a society can be explained in spatial terms, as the consequence of a geographical displacement – namely, westernization.

Part III

THE THIRD-WORLD
INTELLECTUAL IN THE ERA
OF GLOBALIZATION

5

THE ZHANG YIMOU MODEL

RAISE THE RED LANTERN

The paradox of phallocentrism in all its manifestations is that it depends on the image of the castrated woman to give order and meaning to its world. An idea of woman stands as a linchpin to the system: it is her lack that produces the phallus as a symbolic presence, it is her desire to make good the lack that the phallus signifies.

– Laura Mulvey[1]

During the 1980s and 1990s, Chinese cinema has become relatively popular among Western filmgoers, especially critics. Chinese films won various prestigious awards at international festivals. At the same time, the so-called Chinese cinema includes three regional cinemas that are fairly independent from one another: mainland Chinese, Taiwanese, and Hong Kong cinemas. The most internationally recognized filmmakers, those of the Fifth Generation, emerged on the mainland with the two films *One and Eight* (*Yige he bage*), directed by Zhang Junzhao, and its better-known close follower, *Yellow Earth* (*Huang tudi*), by Chen Kaige.[2] Both films, released in 1984, stunned audiences with their ambitious experimentations. The young directors grouped under the ambiguous label Fifth Generation[3] were born in the 1950s and were mostly graduates from the first post–Cultural Revolution class at Beijing Film Institute.

One may divide their development roughly into two major steps. The first step can be characterized as experimental. During the early 1980s, China started opening up economically, culturally, and also to an extent politically. At the same time, since studios were still owned by the government, filmmakers did not need to worry much about box office. Enjoying a brief moment of the best of two worlds, the Fifth Generation directors made a significant number of highly experimental and artistically refreshing, even shocking, films, such as *On the Hunting Ground* (*Liechang zasa*, 1985) and *King of the Children* (*Haizi wang*, 1987).[4] The second step can be called the period of the Zhang Yimou model.[5] I should first emphasize that films following this model have never been mainstream in the Chinese market despite their emphasis on commercial success. In fact, they represent only a very small number of the films made in China. However, this model has been predominant in the international market to the extent that one can say that most Chinese films imported to the United States followed this model to some degree during the early 1990s. In other words, their audiences were more global than local. Moreover, a number of well-known Fifth Generation filmmakers, such as Chen Kaige, Li Shaohong, Huang Jianxin, and Zhou Xiaowen, followed this model during the late 1980s and early1990s in one or more films. In this sense, one can say that the Zhang Yimou model brought the end of formal experiment among Fifth Generation directors.

Since China's economy has increasingly become market-oriented, box office has understandably become a predominant concern for any filmmaker. At the same time, due to the Tian'anmen incident in 1989, censorship in film production also has intensified. Some internationally established mainland directors, such as Zhang Yimou and Chen Kaige, obtained financial support from multinational corporations. Although in this way they can avoid state censorship in China, these filmmakers are then enslaved by the box-office demand of an international market, due to their financial responsibility toward their multinational investors. Furthermore, a multinational corporation, selecting a project to sponsor, would more likely base its selection on a film's conformation to conventionally accepted rules than on any formal innovation. Thus in order to obtain a multinational's support, a filmmaker in most cases must comply with its rather conventional taste. In this sense, the need for investments from multinational corporations is a different form of censorship, one not directly political but mainly commercial.

Among these directors, Zhang Yimou is the most successful in reaching global audiences, partly thanks to his unusually keen marketing sensibility. Based on the international success of his first film, *Red Sorghum* (*Hong gaoliang,* 1987, winner of a Golden Bear Award in Berlin), Zhang developed and perfected a model in his two following movies: *Judou* (1990) and *Raise the Red Lantern* (*Da hong denglong gaogao gua,* 1991, nominated for an Oscar in 1992). His third film, *Raise the Red Lantern,* can be considered the most telling example. Later, many mainland and even Taiwan filmmakers followed this model; but although some other filmmakers still do so, Zhang later shifted his attention to the Chinese market. His urban film *Keep Cool* (*Youhua haohao shuo,* 1997), which focuses on alienation in the modern city, was an instant hit in China. Ironically, unlike his previous rural films, which are much less popular in his native land, this film has barely been mentioned by Western critics.

RAISE THE RED LANTERN

WHO PLAYS THE ROLE OF A HOLLYWOOD SHOWGIRL?

In order to examine how the mechanism works in this model, it will be helpful to begin by analyzing *Raise the Red Lantern.* However, before a close examination of the film itself, I would like to look at some of its differences from Su

Tong's popular novella *Wives and Concubines* (*Qiqie chengqun*), on which the film was based. The most important additions are ritualistic practices, such as foot massage, ordering dishes at the family dining table, and raising lanterns – this last practice giving the film its name. All these bizarre rituals are privileges reserved to the woman with whom the master has chosen to spend the night. As a result, they all have sexual implications – as contingent on the master's sexual favor. These rituals are portrayed as originating in the "ancestors' rules," although they are just as exotic for Chinese audiences as for Western ones, having been invented in the film from scratch. Other changes mainly aim to create visual effects. The third wife, for example, decorates her bedroom with gigantic colorful masks of Peking Opera characters – supposedly because of her former profession as an opera singer. As a matter of fact, these masks are nonexistent not only in Su Tong's story but also in China of the 1930s. Even in contemporary China, the only place to find them is an expensive souvenir store reserved for foreign tourists.

The rest of the film somewhat follows the story line of Su Tong's work. A rich man in his late fifties lives with his four concubine-wives. Among them, the newly acquired fourth wife, Songlian (Gong Li), and the third wife, a Chinese opera singer (He Caifei), are particularly attractive. The film is about the conflicts among these wives, who compete for the master's sexual favor. At the beginning, Songlian, as the youngest and newest, has monopolized the master's favor, until she seriously offends him because of her temperamental behavior. In order to secure her position, she pretends to be pregnant [Fig. 10]. Not surprisingly, the master discovers the truth, and Songlian loses his favor for good. In an intoxicated state she also reveals the third wife's affair with the family doctor. At the end of the film, Songlian by chance witnesses the execution of the third wife and as a result loses her sanity.

The luxurious but prisonlike mansion, shot from a bird's-eye view, serves as the most important setting of the film. Ever since Songlian walks into this courtyard as a newlywed at the very beginning of the film, not a single shot is staged outside it. As a product of strictly traditional Chinese aesthetics, and because of its overwhelming majority of female inhabitants, this setting represents China as an exotic and feminized other in its restrictions, oppression, and closure. Through this filmic metaphor, China is doubly feminized, because its oppression is exclusively registered on the female body. This body, which represents lack not only in terms of gender but also in terms of nation, exemplifies cultural and sexual difference. This double lack provides an empty signifier to the phallus – in terms that Mulvey stated in her essay[6] – but in this case a culturally specified Western phallus. In fact, the phallus, in this context, functions more as a cultural symbol than as a gendered one, taking into account that the sexuality of the Chinese male protagonist in this film is expressed only in an abstract and voyeuristic, if not gender-neutral, form. At the same time, this signifier is beautified by the surrounding rituals, such as lanterns and foot massage, and by huge masks indicative of Chinese opera. In order to make difference more striking, all these rituals, as already noted, are invented from scratch – as signifiers of Chineseness for an international audience. Precisely because they have no reference point whatsoever in Chinese culture, the rituals function even more effectively as visual signs of pure difference – without any understandable logic that may diminish the clear-cut Otherness.

Mulvey states succinctly:

Traditionally, the woman displayed has functioned on two levels: as erotic object for the characters within the screen story, and as erotic object for the spectator within the auditorium, with a shifting tension between the looks on either side of the screen. For instance, the device of the showgirl allows the two looks to be unified technically without any apparent break in the diegesis. A woman performs within the narrative; the gaze of the spectator and that of the male characters in the film are neatly combined without breaking narrative verisimilitude. For a moment the sexual impact of the performing woman takes the film into a no man's land outside its own time and space.[7]

At first glance, the two young wives of the male protagonist in *Raise the Red Lantern* are the only ones fulfilling these two functions of a showgirl in a Hollywood movie. The third wife constantly sings Chinese opera while performing traditional dances, whereas thanks to her commodified image within an international market, Gong Li as the fourth wife alone constitutes already quite a spectacle simply through her close-ups, a trademark of all Zhang's early films. To a large extent, the two erotic objects – one for the character, namely, the Chinese male protagonist himself, and the other for the spectators – are fused together, since the protagonist plays only an abstract role. During the entire film, the audiences never sees his face. Even his voice sounds disembodied and abstract. The shots of his back, usually in soft-focus, bring the audiences inside the screen and allow our gaze to concentrate exclusively on the object of visual pleasure: the female protagonist. The gazing protagonist no longer poses as a mediator between the camera eye and the object. As a result, the looks onscreen and off become virtually identical – not only at the moment that a woman performs, since she is forever a spectacle – even for her diegetic sexual partner.

Moreover, the protagonist's presence in his wives' courtyards is always symbolized in highly striking visual rituals – red lanterns as shining symbols of his presence and foot massage as an erotic symbol of his masculine power. The protagonist no longer occupies the subject position onscreen with which a spectator can identify, since he himself becomes simply one of the spectators for the visual symbols of his own sexual activities. These symbols lend the film an exhibitionist dimension, one both contrary to Chinese tradition, in which sexuality has never been publicly celebrated, and unlike the original book. (In Su Tong's novella, the female protagonist never fakes pregnancy: She is banished mainly because, while intoxicated, she kisses her master publicly in the course of his birthday ban-

10. Songlian fakes pregnancy in *Raise the Red Lantern,* directed by Zhang Yimou (1991).
COURTESY OF THE MUSEUM OF MODERN ART.

quet. In other words, she is punished due to her "indecent" or openly sexually
behavior.) The faceless male protagonist keeps asking the heroine to show herself to him – under the light, in the mirror, or on the bed. At his request, Songlian turns to the camera and poses for her typical close-ups – not for him, but
directly for the audience, since his gaze is forever absent from the screen. Because his sexuality is reduced to visual symbols that he himself watches as his
only act of participation onscreen, anyone offscreen who watches these symbols
– red lanterns, foot massage, close-ups of Songlian, or Chinese opera scenes –
is already participating in his sexuality. In the final analysis, the male Chinese
protagonist is also feminized or emptied to give way to the free play of fantasy
of the audience, whose members are gendered as male and cultured as non-
Chinese – more specifically, as westerners. Consequently, the interplay of an
objectified difference and a virtually unmediated identification allows an inter-

national audience to enjoy almost unlimited sexual fantasy without feeling threatened by a potential return to the real, the traumatic moment, or the castration complex.[8]

Partly thanks to the seemingly unchallenged confinement and isolation provided by the exotic Chinese courtyard, the world in the film – regardless of how much one can enjoy the male's fantasy – turns into an eternal "no-man's land."[9] In other words, audiences can fully possess in their fantasy these oppressed Chinese female bodies in visual terms, taking into consideration that in this film the sexual is equivalent to the visual. At the same time, since these erotic objects are marked by irreducible cultural differences, signaled by the exotic rituals, Western audiences do not need to feel threatened by their sameness. They will never be contaminated by the lack of these completely alien objects, no matter how attracted they are by their female beauty. As Songlian says to the opera singer in the film: "In this courtyard, human beings look like dogs, cats, or pigs, but never like human beings." On the one hand, this statement reinforces the objectified position of the characters, since their only field of action in the film is the courtyard. On the other, by changing the subject of the original sentence in Su Tong's novella, "women" (nüren),[10] to the gender-neutral "human beings" (ren), the film also indirectly pays homage to the Western tradition of humanism. The new term reassures Songlian's multinational audiences of her irreducible difference – her difference from a human being living in the democratic West. For Western audiences, she is safer than the visual spectacle of a Hollywood showgirl, since as a Chinese woman she is doubly feminized.

Furthermore, Songlian and the other concubines are not the only showgirls in this endless ritualistic performance. To an extent that the male protagonist is endowed with a ritualized femininity, represented by foot massage and red lanterns, one can say that metaphorically he too is a Hollywood showgirl. In the final analysis, rituals also replace his much less attractive physical presence on-screen. In this context, the invention of rituals kills two birds with one stone: On the one hand, it makes the Chinese male protagonist less present or real, and thus less threatening to the audience, since he can no longer remind them of their own lack through his potential similarity to them. On the other hand, his appearance, replaced by glamorously exotic and ritualistic activities, is greatly embellished; it gains a showy quality metonymically. These activities ultimately endow him with the qualifications of a showgirl's Hollywood. Furthermore, even his servant, who lights lanterns every night, performs a stage walk each time he appears on the screen, accompanied by music of the traditional Chinese opera.

While commenting on the field of Chinese studies, Rey Chow insightfully states:

A look at Chinese literary history would suggest that these traditionalists are, literally, right: *Chinese history has been a history of men who want to become women.* In the past, male authors adopted women's voices and wrote in "feminine" styles, in the modern period, male authors are fascinated by women as a new kind of literary as well as social "content." We may therefore argue that it is in the sense of men preempting women's place as the minor (vis-à-vis both tradition and the West) and claiming that place for themselves that "the Chinese woman," to use Mao Zedong's words to André Malraux, "doesn't yet exist." Chinese women are, in terms of the structure of discourse, a kind of minor of the minor, the other to the woman that is Chinese man.[11]

As "the minor of the minor," the Chinese woman is to a large extent an empty signifier, one that can be used as male authors' alter ego, to express their frustration regarding their own social conditions. In certain types of classical Chinese poetry, for example, male poets took the voice of a woman in lamentation.[12] This signifier also can voice their iconoclastic ideological stance against the evils of traditional society, as in May Fourth and later socialist realism.[13] Furthermore, it can also stand for the progress made in the new society, as in some socialist realist films during the 1960s and 1970s where the female protagonist often takes the most progressive and revolutionary stance. In all these literary and artistic practices, we apparently hear women's voices; in reality, we hear men's voices speaking and also acting as those of women. Therefore, Chinese male authors have a tradition of taking women's places often to gain advantages for themselves. However, to feminize Chinese men for the sake of financial gain in a global market is no doubt new with the Zhang Yimou model, although its predecessors' tradition of taking the position of minor vis-à-vis the West has certainly facilitated this invention. Since traditionally Chinese male authors have been accustomed to using a woman's voice for some lofty goals, it seems rather logical that occasionally they can also, with resignation, accept the position of the opposite sex for a goal far less lofty. In this case, they seduce their global audiences, and thus their multinational bosses, with their (sexual or cultural?) appeal by staging their own Otherness.

THE SUBJECT PRESUMED TO ENJOY AND THE SUBJECT PRESUMED TO SUFFER

The first shot in the film consists of a close-up of Songlian's suffering face. According to her conversation with her stepmother's voice-over, after three days and nights of persuasion, Songlian has finally accepted her stepmother's proposal to become the concubine of a rich old man. Her father has just committed suicide due to financial hardship. This long take ends in her face bathed in tears. Similarly, one of the most voyeuristic later scenes also ends in Songlian's tear-stained face – reflected in a mirror. Ordered by her master during the wedding night, she lifts a red lantern to show her face directly to the audience (although apparently to the unseen master). In the middle of the same night, he has to abandon Songlian in order to visit the third wife, the former opera singer, who is claiming to be seriously ill. Left alone in her wedding room, Songlian repeats the same gesture, previously ordered by her master, in front of a mirror. Under the red lantern, her beautiful face is again covered with tears. In both cases, Songlian's showy quality is closely associated with her suffering, which is often of a sexual nature.

The seemingly luxurious household is also full of sadness. Servants are located at the bottom of the hierarchy in this mansion. A servant's transgression of one of the rules set by unspecified "ancestors" may lead to a deadly punishment, as in the case of Yan'er, Songlian's jealous maid. The fates of the four wives, reduced to competing for the sexual favors of one aged master, appear no less pathetic than those of their servants. They are bound to be sexually and emotionally frustrated one way or another. However, the more beautiful a woman is, the more tragic her fate will be. At the end of the film, the talented opera singer is brutally murdered and beautiful Songlian is driven mad. Yan'er suffers a tragic ending in part because she is supposedly the most beautiful servant, the one with whom the master has chosen to have an affair. Furthermore, each character seems to acquire his or her showy quality at the price of happiness. Yan'er loses her life precisely because she illicitly repeats Songlian's showy gesture from her wedding night, stealthily raising the red lantern in her own corner. This transgression of one of the ancestors' rules leads to a showy punishment in accordance with another pseudorule: Yan'er must kneel on the snowy ground overnight – accompanied by dramatic Peking Opera music. Even the master himself cannot avoid following the same logic. Since his so-called sexuality is completely composed of visual elements – the red lantern, foot massage, and the showing off of his concubine's beauty to offscreen audiences, he himself is portrayed as sexually unfulfilled. Despite the number of women apparently at his disposal, his only function consists of running from one to another of his wives' corners, almost as an invisible shadow of the camera's eye, in order to bring visual pleasure to his audience. To this extent, visual pleasure for audiences in this film largely results from characters' endless sufferings, which often have a sexual nature. One can say that the realm of pleasure belongs only to the offscreen world, beyond the gigantic prisonlike courtyard. This courtyard, shot repeatedly from an oppressive bird's-eye view, is also a metaphor for Chinese society – like Lu Xun's well-known metaphor of the iron house from early in the century. In other words, the realms of pleasure and suffering are divided not only spatially – onscreen and off – but also culturally – Chinese and Western.

Within the world of *Raise the Red Lantern*, gender difference, or for that matter any difference, tends to become less significant, overwhelmed by the various characters' commonalties, that is, exoticism, femininity, and lack. All these common denominators contribute to creating the image of a backward China, responsible for a commonly shared victimization, facing the condescending gaze of a progressive West. Therefore, one can say that China as a cultural icon also has been staged as a Hollywood showgirl, representing cultural lack. Her showiness is closely associated with suffering, which offers visual pleasure to audiences supposedly outside the confinement of its courtyard, the metaphoric prison of traditional Chinese culture. As a result, the film creates an illusion that suffering is an exclusive property of the Chinese subject in his or her confinement, a subject presumed to suffer par excellence, since suffering originates from the deficiency of his or her backward cultural environment. By contrast, the Western subject occupies the position of the subject presumed to enjoy, through a refraction of the admiring gaze of the cultural other.

Žižek explains:

His [the subject presumed to enjoy] role is fundamental in obsessional neurosis: for the obsessional neurotic the traumatic point is the supposed existence, in the other, of an insupportable, limitless, horrifying *jouissance;* the stake of all his frantic activity is to protect, to save the Other from his *jouissance,* even at the price of destroying him or her (saving the woman from her corruption, for example). Again, this subject does not have to exist effectively: to produce his effects, it is enough for others to presume that he exists. This supposed *jouissance* is one of the key components of racism: the Other (Jew, Arab, Negro) is always presumed to have access to some specific enjoyment, and that is what really bothers us.[14]

To a great extent, the image of the unrepressed westerner with his unlimited sexual power in the imaginary of Chinese modern intellectuals is also "one of the key components of racism" in China. This image suggests a fantasized difference, which has become the implied basis of an imaginary cultural hierarchy. In Chinese history, any ethnic group different from the Han Chinese has been considered "barbarian" (*fan* or *hu*). Since the Song dynasty, under the influence of Zhu Xi's neo-Confucianism, the term "barbarian" has taken on an increasingly negative tone in a clear-cut division between "us" and "the Other." Initially, westerners were also mainly perceived as barbarians by the Qing government, forced to kneel before the emperor of the Middle Kingdom. However, China's defeat in the two Opium Wars as well as other conflicts with Western powers during the nineteenth century provided a proof that these "barbarians" were different, due to their superior military, technological, scientific, and economic power. Western military and economic superiority has endowed their fantasized difference of unlimited sexual power with new meanings: It signifies no longer only primitivism – as in the case of other "barbarians," who had previously encountered Chinese civilization – but rather their cultural excellence. Although primitivism or barbarianism has always been there as an implied subtext, this image is also associated with another fantasized difference: Like its unrestricted individuals, Western society is free, democratic, and rational in opposition to the oppressive, repressive, and totalitarian China. In other words, sexual freedom is not simply symptomatic of lack of civilization but to a certain extent it is a product of a freer and more rational civilization. At the same time, the implied subtext of barbarianism in this image has never been completely absent, since in the final analysis sexual freedom cannot escape an implicit or explicit association with moral decadence, despite its liberating association with individualism. However, unlike the westerner facing the inferior cultural Other as his subject who is presumed to enjoy, the Chinese weakened by his civilization cannot claim to be able to save his Western Other, presumed to enjoy, from his *jouissance,* since this *jouissance* has been rationalized by a scientific and democratic social order. Following this logic, this order makes Western civilization more powerful, regardless of how "primitive" it might be to start with. Instead, the Chinese needs to learn from the westerner's *jouissance,* since it has become the access to Western cultural treasures, such as individualism, democracy, and freedom.

In short, free love in the West, for its Chinese admirers, reveals the rational social order of the West, of which China is deprived. In other words, sexual repression becomes symptomatic of China's lack of Western democracy and rational social order. As a result, a Chinese subject is presumed to suffer in his deprivation, victimization, or minor position. Ingeniously, Zhang Yimou turned this imaginary position of the Chinese subject presumed to suffer into a commodified object of the Western gaze. The interchange of imaginary gazes between the Chinese subject presumed to suffer onscreen and the Western subject presumed to enjoy offscreen allows the latter to achieve a cultural suture. Naturally, this cultural suture cannot be accomplished without the discourse of modernity in China according to which the westerner occupies an imaginary subject position – free of oppression, repression, and discontent.

THE ZHANG YIMOU MODEL

As we can see from this analysis, not only striking visual effects but also an artificially maintained distance between Chinese characters and their potential Western audiences contribute to the international success of *Raise the Red Lantern.* This difference becomes a trademark of the Zhang Yimou model. One can say that Zhang developed his model by reinforcing this difference throughout his first two movies, *Red Sorghum* and *Judou,* reaching perfection in his third film, *Raise the Red Lantern.* During the early 1990s, films made in accordance with the Zhang Yimou model generally use three similar strategies:

First, the protagonist(s) must be a young woman (or several women). Just like Songlian in *Raise the Red Lantern,* this young beauty is badly oppressed by some strange tradition of feudal China. Her oppression is often of a sexual nature, and she is involved in some kind of undesirable, if not unwanted, sexual relations. She may be a concubine or a wife of an impotent husband, who is usually much older (like the master in *Raise the Red Lantern* and the protagonist's husband in *Judou*), a prostitute (as in Gu Rong's *Red Dust* [*Hongchen*] and Li Shaohong's *Blush* [*Hongfen*]), a widow (Huang Jianxin's *Wukui*), a child bride (in Xie Fei's *A Girl from Hunan* [*Xiangnü Xiaoxiao*]), or destined to celibacy for her family's sake (in He Ping's *Red Firecracker, Green Firecracker* [*Paoda shuangdeng*]). In short, she is sexually deprived, physically abused, and spatially confined. Additionally, the more a woman is oppressed, the more beautiful and desirable she looks. Even in her death or in the middle of a horrible torture, the beautiful heroine always looks as if she had just returned from a high-class beauty salon.

Second, there is a tendency to invent numerous pseudotraditional Chinese rituals – a factor that is particularly striking in *Raise the Red Lantern*. Almost all the films in this model tend to create their own "traditional rituals," competing with each other in the exotic nature of their creations. In most cases, these rituals are associated with women and sexuality. Some may be visually enticing or intriguing, like lantern raising in *Raise the Red Lantern,* the firecracker competition in *Red Firecracker, Green Firecracker,* and the supposedly traditional wedding ceremony in *Wukui* in which a male servant carries his master's bride on his shoulders through a dangerous desert. Some may even be sadistic, as in the case of the third wife's execution after the discovery of her adultery in *Raise the Red Lantern*. In *Wukui,* for example, the female protagonist is crippled, according to the "ancestors' rules" against unchaste women, simply because the young widow flirted with *Wukui,* a servant. Sometimes, these rituals can be both visually striking and physically shocking. In *Red Firecracker, Green Firecracker,* the male protagonist is genitally mutilated in a firecracker competition – a ritual according to which he may win the hand of his lover, the sole heiress of the firecracker production family. Supposedly, the unfortunate suitor fires powerful firecrackers between his legs – as required at the highest stage of the competition.

The third strategy involves the famous metaphor, in which Lu Xun, a prominent May Fourth writer, eight decades ago wrote of China as an iron house without any windows or doors. In this house, people are sleeping and awaiting death by suffocation in their dreams. In *Raise the Red Lantern,* the courtyard in which the master's four wives and their numerous servants are confined creates the same kind of prisonlike atmosphere. As Songlian succinctly points out, people living in this courtyard are like cats, dogs, and pigs, but not at all like human beings. Thus the traditional courtyard in the Zhang Yimou model functions like Lu Xun's iron house, as a metaphor for China, since it traps and confines the female protagonist. This courtyard may be used as a wine workshop (*Red Sorghum*), a dyehouse (*Judou*), or, more often, a luxurious mansion (*Raise the Red Lantern, Wukui, Red Firecracker, Green Firecracker,* and Chen Kaige's *Temptress Moon* [*Fengyue*]). Whatever this courtyard may be, the female protagonist, despite her efforts, cannot truly escape from this confining space, except at the cost of her life.

WOMEN'S OPPRESSION

Among these three elements, women's oppression plays a pivotal role, partly because it can also provide visual pleasure while signifying the oppressive nature of Chinese society. As a matter of fact, there is nothing new about this theme. The problem of women's oppression has held center stage from the very beginning of the Chinese film industry. In the course of history, images of women as the oppressed and the deprived have changed in accordance with different ideological needs. During the May Fourth period, women were portrayed by left-wing filmmakers as powerless and often speechless objects on whose bodies the evils of traditional society are registered, despite – or because of – their physical and moral beauty. A case in point is the self-sacrificial mother who tries to provide her son with an education through prostitution in Wu Yonggang's *The Goddess (Shennü,* 1935). The socialist realist tradition during the 1950s and 1960s inherited the images of oppressed women from the May Fourth tradition. However, the previously speechless victim could now shout revolutionary slogans against her oppressor – namely, traditional China – under the strict guidance of her communist patriarchal savior. *The White-Haired Girl (Baimao nü,* 1950), directed by Wang Bin and Shui Hua, serves as a perfect icon of this salvation process. Raped by the landlord, the heroine escapes to the mountains in order to survive. Due to malnutrition, her hair turns white and she looks like a ghost. At the end, her fiancé returns as a communist soldier with the revolutionary army and rescues her from class oppression. During the 1980s and 1990s, the images of women's oppression, made over by the financial and technical support of multinational corporations, have become a salable symbol of China's evil tradition in a global market, as in the Zhang Yimou model.

Nevertheless, women's oppression, as one of the most powerful symbols of the discourse of modernity in China, no longer speaks for a radical change at an ideological level to Chinese audiences, as it did for previous generations. Turned into commodified images in a global market, women's oppression has become the symbol of China's Otherness. Ironically, this transfer from the ideological to the commercial domain in the Zhang Yimou model has been successful in the West not because of cultural differences – as suggested by this model – but rather because of the similarly patriarchal nature of Western society. On the one hand, located in a conventional system of visual pleasure predominant in Hollywood movies, the oppressed Chinese woman first of all functions as the object of a (Western) male gaze.[15] Because oppression in this context becomes exotic – as belonging to the other culture – oppression itself almost has a decorative dimension in relation to female beauty. Since the cause of suffering can be attributed to cultural difference, one can look at the oppressive act from a mainly aesthetic point of view – without emotional involvement or identification. This may partly explain why in this model the more a woman is oppressed, the more beautiful she looks. On the other hand, if these commodified cultural products easily find their audiences in the West, this is partly because the discourse of modernity in China also repeats certain clichés of orientalism in the West. In this model, the Oriental sees his own culture as a refraction of an imaginary gaze of his superior Western counterpart. Chen Kaige in his *Temptress Moon,* for example, often borrows and reappropriates Bertolucci's perspective in *The Last Emperor,* an orientalist vision par excellence.[16]

The May Fourth movement at the beginning of the century, socialist realism in the middle, and the Zhang Yimou model at the end, all have used women's oppression to express modern stances. However, in the first two cases, since the goal is straightforwardly ideological and the value system is idealized at an abstract level, as the product of a radical imagination, the idealized value system need not be tested by social reality in the West. In the last case, because the main concern is commercial, the West becomes much more tangible, embedded by the financial support of multinational corporations and the fascinated gaze of global audiences. Consequently, it goes without saying that in the Zhang Yimou model, women's oppression needs to have a much more attractive look than in ideological manifestations or political propaganda. Using advanced technology provided by multinational bosses and internationally recognized stars, especially female stars, these films succeeded to different degrees in making the old revolutionary theme an attractive commodity for global audiences.

TOWARD A GLOBAL MARKET ECONOMY

Žižek describes the situation in his native Sarajevo:

The unbearable is not the difference. The unbearable is the fact that in a sense there *is no difference:* there are no exotic bloodthirsty "Balkanians" in Sarajevo, just normal citizens like us. The moment we take full note of this fact, the frontier that separates "us" from "them" is exposed in all its arbitrariness, and we are forced to renounce the safe distance of external observers: as in a Moebius band, the part and the whole coincide, so that it is no longer possible to draw a clear and unambiguous line of separation between us who live in a "true" peace and the residents of Sarajevo who pretend as far as possible that they are living in peace – we are forced to admit that in a sense we also imitate peace, live in the fiction of peace.[17]

During the 1990s, China has increasingly moved toward global market economy. The West is no longer an unreachable symbol for Chinese intellectuals but part of their daily life because of MTV, Hollywood movies, high-tech products, luxury goods, and branches of multinational corporations in China. The flow of capital and the labor force makes China part of daily life in the global market – even the existence of the Zhang Yimou model attests to it. This global context makes China somewhat unfit for the role of a mysterious Other. China's exported goods have filled a global market. By means of shoes, toys, clothes, gifts, all labeled "made in China," China has also become part of everyday life in the West. Although on the surface modern intellectuals' dream of China's modernization has never appeared so close to realization – just as the visit of a real dragon scared to death Master She, who had passionately spent all his life painting fake dragons – this dream also increasingly appears, to the previous passionate promoters of modernization, like a frightening nightmare. The proximity of the two worlds makes any further idealization of the West and mystification of China unsustainable. Precisely because the foundation of the cultural hierarchy has become increasingly shaky, the Zhang Yimou model, which reifies the fantasized difference, has become a highly marketable commodity among global audiences. By making believe that there is indeed such a difference, this model contributes to making "what is unbearable"[18] – lack of hierarchical differentiation between the two cultures – much more bearable to audiences familiar with the orientalist perception of China, at least for the time being.

Since 1991, *Raise the Red Lantern* has won prestigious international awards in Venice, Rome, New York, London, and other Western cities, including an Oscar nomination. The global success of Zhang Yimou's films, especially that of *Raise the Red Lantern,* has attracted many multinational investors to mainland China. In 1991, only six films made in mainland China, including those directed by Taiwan, Hong Kong, and European directors, had multinational investments. In the following years, this number doubled. In 1993, about forty films on the mainland were entirely or partially sponsored by multinational corporations.[19] Moreover, these corporations no longer limited their investments to the works of a handful of well-known mainland directors. A number of less-known directors, such as He Ping, the director of *Red Firecracker, Green Firecracker,* also obtained funds from the multinationals. Nevertheless, in most cases these corporations invested only in two kinds of movie: kung fu movies, addressing Hong Kong and other Asian audiences, and films that follow the Zhang Yimou model, catering to the taste of Western audiences. A large percentage of the films mentioned in this essay were entirely or partially sponsored by multinational firms, such as *Judou* (1990), *Raise the Red Lantern* (1991), *Farewell My Concubine* (Chen Kaige, 1993), *Red Firecracker, Green Firecracker* (1993), *Wukui* (1993), and *Temptress Moon* (1996). A number of them obtained prestigious international awards.

During the First Opium War in 1839–42, China had its first experience of the military superiority of the West over the Middle Kingdom. Unlike in the past with nomadic invaders, the West not only enjoyed military superiority but had its own complicated social, institutional, political, ideological, and cultural structures. These structures, supported by their science and technology, have implicitly or explicitly been interpreted by various generations of Chinese intellectuals – including my own generation – as expressions of cultural excellence following a social Darwinist logic. Consequently, from this point on, modern intellectuals have constantly viewed their own people, culture, and nation from a perspective mediated by their knowledge of the West. In other words, their images of their own people are like a distorted mirror image: The viewers themselves are included in the reflection, framed by a westernized and modernized gaze. This gaze grants the viewers active roles and subjective positions. In order to secure this vantage point, they need to identify their perspective with the powerful West. As a result, the process of analyzing Chinese culture has become a constant task of Othering the self – from the perspective of an imaginary or real West. It goes without saying that under this kind of scrutiny, China has always been presented as an Other in the eyes of its own intellectuals, although this Other often includes the viewing intellectuals themselves.[20]

For example, Lu Xun, the prominent May Fourth radical writer, in his preface to *Call for Arms* (*Nahan*, lit. "Cry Out," 1922), considered himself and a few other comrades the only ones awake among a sleeping nation confined within a suffocating iron house. In this case, although he is a member of the sleeping crowd, his gaze is identical with that of an awakened westerner, living outside the iron house of China. Interestingly, at the end of the century, this relationship between China as the object of the gaze and the Chinese intellectual as the gazing subject, whose perspective is mediated by the West, has turned into a marketable commodity in the global market of cultural production through the Zhang Yimou model.

Immanuel Wallerstein rightly points out:

The capitalist world-economy is a system built on the endless accumulation of capital. One of the prime mechanisms that makes this possible is the commodification of everything. These commodities flow in a world market in the form of goods, of capital and of labor-power. Presumably, the freer the flow, the greater the degree of commodification. Consequently, anything that restrains the flow is hypothetically counter-indicated.[21]

The Zhang Yimou model is a product of the free flow of goods, capital, and labor power in an increasingly globalized Chinese economy. Like in other economic sectors, as cultural production the film industry has also been globalized. Since Chinese labor is still much cheaper than in developed countries, the cost of filmmaking in China is much lower. Usually, a Zhang Yimou movie, which is far more costly than a normal Chinese film, costs about one million dollars – only 1 or 2 percent of a typical Hollywood budget. With a relatively limited amount of money, a talented Chinese director like Zhang would be able to refine his filmmaking in China. As shoes or toys designed by American brands and fabricated in China would be more competitive in a global market in terms of price, Chinese movies following the Zhang Yimou model are also internationally competitive in their own right. They do not need to be as successful as Hollywood movies in terms of box office in order to make the initial investments of multinational corporations pay off. Similar to the Japan described in Tanizaki's *Some Prefer Nettles*, pseudotraditional China portrayed in the Zhang Yimou model proves how far China has moved toward the global market economy. Frederic Buell comments on the insightful Japanese novelist: "The result was a novel that reveals that 'return to Japan' was actually, au fond, a stronger form of Japanese internalization of external material than was the cosmopolitan, consumerist absorption of the West Tanizaki suggests in *Naomi*. At the same time, recovery of

'Japanese tradition' was, in many ways, a more powerful form of westerniza-tion."[22] In fact, the Zhang Yimou model, which reinvents Chinese tradition for a Western gaze, represents a radical step toward westernization, namely, the com-modification of cultural products in the global market economy. This reinven-tion of a tradition is indispensable in a world that increasingly erases cultural and national boundaries by means of the free flow of goods, capital, and labor power in a capitalist global economy. Paradoxically, this reinvention of an apparently irreducible cultural difference also increases the capacity of the free flow in the global cultural market through the commodification of imaginary differences. Submerged by this free flow, Fifth Generation directors ended their era of for-mal experiment with the Zhang Yimou model.

6

CULTURE AND VIOLENCE

LI SHAOHONG: *BLOODY DAWN*

M ost well-known experimental films made by the Fifth Generation directors, especially in their early careers, focused on China's past, be it Confucian or communist. Although some directors, such as Huang Jianxin and Zhou Xiao-wen, were from the very beginning more interested in contemporary topics, their films usually have urban settings. *Bloody Dawn* (*Xuese qingchen,* 1990) by Li Shaohong, a woman director of the Fifth Generation, broke away from the pattern of nostalgic portrayal of the countryside. Li's film focuses on problems existing in contemporary China in the process of moving toward a market economy. In most Fifth Generation films, both Confucian and communist traditions are portrayed as obstacles to individual freedom, whereas Li's film shows that the ideological vacuum in postsocialist China does not make individuals freer. What governs the village is no longer written law, traditional or modern, but a "community nightly law"[1] – to borrow Slavoj Žižek's words. This nightly law implicitly binds villagers against an Other by encouraging its members to transgress the written law – as in the case of the teacher's murder in the film – in order to reinforce its group identity. This murder also shows how insignificant the role of culture or education (in Chinese, words so much more closely related than in English that they are interchangeable in most circumstances) is in post–Cultural Revolution China. For several decades, the Communist Party has invented a minority discourse, which allows it to speak from the position of a minor in order to justify its power position. In other words, since the party represents the oppressed, it needs more power to protect these "minors." Among other themes, women's emancipation is an important component of the party's minority discourse. As a woman director caught between the predominant party's discourse of women's liberation and the daily reality of women's oppression, Li Shaohong in this film chose to portray gender oppression visually but not verbally – partly to avoid using a language similar to the minority discourse of the party.

Without any previous knowledge, it is difficult to imagine that this story about a remote Chinese village is based on a Colombian novel. Xiao Mao, a playwright, along with the director herself, adapted Gabriel García Márquez's novel *Chron-*

icle of a Death Foretold (*Crónica de una muerte anunciada*)[2] as the basis of the film script. The basic plot in the film remains roughly similar to that in the novel. During the wedding night, after discovering that his bride is not a virgin, the groom sends her back to her mother's house. Her two brothers, Pingwa and Gou-wa, cannot stand the idea of losing their family honor and decide to murder the man responsible. Beaten violently by her family, the dishonored bride is forced to provide the alleged perpetrator's name; but the one she gives is likely not that of her actual lover, possibly due to lingering attachment. Taking her confession at face value, the two brothers publicize their murderous intent – secretly hoping that the publicity of their plan will provide enough time for others to stop it, so that they would be able to save face without risking their own lives. However, since no one seriously does try to stop them, they end up brutally murdering their victim in front of a great number of witnesses.

Despite these roughly similar plots, the Chinese film has a subplot in which Pingwa, one of the brothers of the bride, Hongxing, simultaneously marries Xiu-qin, the sister of Qiangguo, her future husband, as marriage exchange between the two families. Since Xiuqin is slightly handicapped, she was unable to find a husband until in her thirties. However, for Pingwa, who was reduced to celibacy by poverty until thirty-five years of age, the "discounted" bride still remains a good match, especially taking into consideration that the "most important sin against filial piety is not having descendants" in the Confucian tradition. This added detail has changed the focus from a question of lost honor in the Colombian novel to that of lost propriety in the Chinese film, since a wife in this circumstance is primarily valued as a commodity. After Qiangguo, the rich carpenter, discovers that his bride is not a virgin, both brides in the film are now perceived as handicapped, one physically, the other morally. The difference is that economically this makes the balance unequal, since Qiangguo should not accept any discount because of his wealth, whereas his sister's discount has been already written in the contract due to Pingwa's poverty. Because the discovery of Hongxing's loss of virginity makes her no longer a worthy bride in the eyes of her husband, and the two marriages are based on the same contract, her elder brother, Pingwa, logically loses his property. Qiangguo returns the bride to her family, while taking away his own sister from the brother of his returned bride. Given that the poverty-stricken family cannot afford to find a bride on its own for either of the two brothers, Pingwa's economic loss appears even more severe. As a result, the brothers' anger appears more plausible in contemporary Chinese society.

One other aspect shared by the novel and the film is that in both cases the murder victim has been alienated from his community. Santiago Nasar, as an Arab, is racially alien to the townspeople of the novel, whereas Li Mingguang, the only one who can read and write properly in the village, is culturally alien to the film's villagers. Thus, for different reasons, they are regarded as strangers by their own communities: Santiago Nasar for his racial and cultural background, Li Ming-guang for his education (the supposed heritage from an "educated youth" [*zhishi qingnian*] with whom Mingguang spent a considerable amount of time during his childhood). Partly due to their alienation, their lives are locally perceived as less valuable than those of other community members. The townspeople in Márquez's novel repeat several times that Arabs are capable of anything, and villagers in the film accuse Mingguang of being obscene merely because of his subscription to a film journal widely circulated in most Chinese urban areas. In both cases, the status of outsider amounts to an implicit proof of the person's obscene nature: Outsiders enjoy filthy pleasures forbidden to the rest of the honorable community. Partly for this reason Santiago's maid in the novel refuses to warn her master about the murder plan because "in the depth of her heart she wanted them to kill him";[3] similarly, some villagers (the teacher's future father-in-law and the murderers' coworker, for example) in the film believe that the loss of a teacher's life is not as significant as the premature loss of virginity of a rich man's bride. Furthermore, the victims in both cases are fatherless.

The men to whom the two girls were briefly married are also different from the rest of the community, but in ways perceived as much more favorable. Bayardo San Roman is a rich descendent of a prominent military family, and Zhang Qiangguo is a carpenter who earn a considerable amount of money in the city. Thus, unlike the Colombian and the Chinese murder victims, both the Colombian and Chinese grooms impress their communities by their wealth or/and social status. However, in the Colombian novel, both Nasar and San Roman are from communities different from their current one, whereas in the Chinese film both Mingguang and Qiangguo were born in the same community. In this sense, the latter are insiders affected by outside influences, either culturally or financially. If villagers look down on education as represented by the teacher, like the rest of the country they worship the power of money, represented by the carpenter. In this sense, the village is subject to the influence of an increasingly commodified contemporary culture. During 1984–90, various Fifth Generation films, such as *On the Hunting Ground (Liechang zasa), Yellow Earth (Huang tudi), Big Parade (Da yuebing), King of the Children (Haizi wang), Judou, Red Sorghum (Hong gaoliang),* and Zhang Junzhao's *Arc Light (Huguang),* can be considered products of an intellectual anticultural trend that criticizes traditional and communist cultures for their restrictions on individual freedom. However, the criticism in these films of the past culture often carries a nostalgic overtone, as if the past were the only subject worthy portraying, even if in a negative light.[4] At the same time, these films often classified communist ideology as a continuation of the Confucian tradition despite its prima facie antitraditional stance. Li's film can be taken as an attempt to break away from the nostalgic pattern prevailing among "art films" made by her well-known classmates during the 1980s. Instead of criticizing a past, the film draws a rather negative picture of the current society. In this society, unlike in most nostalgic movies, culture no longer functions as a burden on individual freedom. By contrast, the lack of culture (in the sense of education) seemingly makes individual freedom no longer possible, due to the tyranny of the unwritten nightly community law.[5] Furthermore, in most early art films made by her famous classmates during the 1980s, tradition is condemned as part of the cultural package. In her film, by contrast, tradition is pitted against culture – or more precisely, education.

At the same time, both her classmates and herself are descended from their May Fourth forefathers, whose notion of culture is often associated with that of "new culture" or "modern culture." Chen Kaige and Tian Zhuangzhuang appear radically nihilistic in their portrayal of culture partly because they are more interested in the destructive effect of communist ideology, which is already a rebellious culture against the Confucian tradition. Li Shaohong portrays culture more positively in her film partly because she shifts her attention to post–Cultural Revolution China, in which communist ideology no longer plays a dominant role, overshadowed as it is by the value system of a market economy. Her notion of culture, however, is mainly "modern" culture, which is to an extent westernized, defined in opposition to the local culture of the backward Chinese village.

TRIAL OF THE MURDERERS OR THE MURDER VICTIM?

Bloody Dawn begins with a close-up of a ringing bell. Since it is the bell for the Buddhist temple, which is currently used by the school, the huge bell in the prologue represents both traditional China and modern education for the future generation. Nevertheless, the two functions do not exist simultaneously. In this sense, the bell captures the conflict between education and tradition – a conflict that occupies a significant place in the rest of the film. Then, a tracking shot follows the back of a boy hastily climbing the stairs of the former temple and current school. A reverse shot briefly focuses on the boy's face. In a high-angle extreme long shot, a group of children happily play in the temple around the huge statue of the Buddha. The little boy's voice breaks the state of the cheerful anarchy: "Bad news: Our teacher is murdered." After a brief moment of silence, all the children start running away from the temple as quickly as they can. Children's chaotic movements, in reaction to this news, indicates that in their confusion they vaguely understand the connection between the teacher's death and their own situation: His death marks the end of their education – at least for a considerable period, since he is the only one available to teach all elementary-school-aged children in this village. By the concluding sequence, the empty temple, used in the prologue to educate the future generation, has become a museum, commemorating a distant past.

The opening sequence is construed around the teacher's dead body. By contrast with the panic reaction of his students in the prologue, adults in the village treat Mingguang's death with marked indifference. A series of low-angle shots of gray, tall, stern, motionless, worn-out old buildings forms a striking contrast with the opening high-angle extreme long shots of active children dressed in colorful clothes. At the end of this sequence, the camera cuts from the isolated shots of vertical buildings to a high-angle shot of a narrow lane paved with stones and bordered by two stern stone walls. The tracking shot stops at a corner of a paved road, stained with blood and littered with several books. Then the camera cuts to a corpse that, covered with a piece of shabby cloth, lies in the deserted lane near the stone wall. Two dogs smell the corpse and indifferently run away. At the same time, the voice-over matter-of-factly announces the dead person's identity: "The victim is Li Mingguang, masculine, 24 years old, the teacher of the elementary school sponsored by the Village of the Great Water Pond [*Da shuikeng*]."

In the following sequence, a close-up shows the hands of an invisible pathologist, holding a pair of scissors and cutting off Mingguang's pullover soaked in blood. Then, the sizes of his wounds are measured and reported matter-of-factly to the investigator. With no facial expression, the investigator mechanically takes notes on comments made by the coroner. At the same time, the film crosscuts to a group of spectators, trying to enter the room despite the guards' efforts to prevent them. Their facial expressions show curiosity and indifference, as if they were eager to see a free show. Although many of these indifferent bystanders are parents of Mingguang's students, their reactions show that they do not consider important the death of the only teacher and thus the loss of educational opportunity for their children.

From this point on, the film is structured around the investigation of the teacher's murder. Often in this process, a witness's speech tends to accuse Mingguang for his alleged affair, whereas flashback images, supposedly based on a speaker's reminiscence, often undermine his or her verbal accusation. In general, these images favor the victim more than the witnesses' speeches do. For example, Mingguang's only defender, his uncle, hesitates to defend his morality verbally. In contrast to his accusers' assertiveness, the uncle expresses his opinion only through a somewhat timid negation: "I have not yet seen him [Mingguang] making trouble." The following flashback brings us to his classroom, where he alone teaches the classes for three different grades. Although the flashback is introduced by the uncle's words, the images are not limited by his perspective. The sequence shows how Mingguang even carries the baby brother of one of his girl students in order to provide students with a tolerable study environment. Hastily told by his own younger brother that their grandmother needs him to return immediately to take care of newborn piglets, Mingguang tells the students to work by themselves and then starts to walk away from the classroom with the girl's brother still on his back. When the girl timidly reminds him about her brother, the teacher hastily returns the baby to her. This flashback, which does not correspond exactly to the uncle's point of view, argues much more forcefully for Mingguang's morality than do the uncle's words. Despite his own responsibility at home (he is the only adult living with an aged grandmother and two underage brothers), Mingguang devotes his life wholeheartedly to his students' education in a difficult environment, with little support from either parents or the village administration. His devotion to his students in the past forms a striking contrast with the indifference to his death presently expressed by his students' parents.

Except for his uncle, the same witnesses who had failed to prevent his well-publicized murder now, after his death, implicitly condemn his behavior. As a result, the investigation of the murder is a moral lynching of the murder victim. At the same time, flashback images corresponding to accusers' speeches usually reveal flaws in their accounts of Mingguang's alleged indecency. For example, Manyi, a student, obtains an issue of his teacher's *Popular Cinema (Dazhong dianying)*, from which he cuts a picture of an actress in a swimming suit. This he sticks on the door of his home. The picture scandalizes his mother and Pensao, a middle-aged woman who owns a small restaurant in the village. To a large extent, this picture offers the only basis on which both women accuse Mingguang of being "indecent." In their minds, this accusation also serves as a proof for his alleged affair with Hongxing, supposedly the cause of her lost virginity. Ironically, *Popular Cinema,* which is perceived as outrageously indecent by villagers, is a popular film journal widely subscribed to by the film's predominantly urban viewers. As a result, the villagers' accusations only prove their own ignorance in the eyes of potential audiences. A short circuit between reality and interpretation cleverly introduces different value systems: legal evaluation represented by the investigator, community evaluation articulated by various witnesses within the village, and the evaluation of the director and her urban viewers through restructuring visual images. Often onscreen villagers and offscreen urban audiences have diametrically opposite opinions about the same events. Nevertheless, Mingguang's perspective as well as those of the urban viewers are portrayed in an ironical light through this trivial image of a fashionable, Western-style, half-naked movie star. As a matter of fact, these kinds of icon have prevailed in the cultural scene of contemporary Chinese urban area.

In the course of the investigation, the most important question is not about the two criminals but rather the murder victim: whether Mingguang was guilty of Hongxing's loss of virginity. In this trial, the murder victim is considered guilty not because of any concrete proof, but because of the commonly shared perception of him as a cultural outsider. In this sense, Mingguang serves as a scapegoat against whom members of the community attest to their solidarity. For this reason alone, he is doubly sentenced for a possibly imaginary affair: not only executed physically by the two brothers, but also condemned morally by the entire village after his gruesome death. The two brothers sentenced him to death for their family's lost honor, and the community judges him guilty mainly because of his difference. In other words, villagers believe in his guilt because they "believe in belief [of the others] itself."[6]

On various occasions, several villagers say that had they themselves been in the two brothers' positions, they would have had no other choice but to kill the teacher. Following the same logic, the murder is not only justified but also prescribed by the unwritten rule in the community. The community law might even have condemned the two brothers if they had failed to act against the teacher.

Moreover, the investigator, to a degree, implicitly accepts this logic. After Hongxing denies that she had any sexual relationship with Mingguang, the investigator's voice-over says: "In this case, the motivation for murder no longer exists" (*sharen chengyin bei tuifan le*). However, this motivation remains still valid – as the investigator adds immediately – since Hongxing's madness discredits her current testimony. Although Mingguang could not be condemned to death by the explicit written public law simply because of his alleged affair, this affair was enough for his death sentence according to the counterpart of the written law, "its obscene, superegoistical inverse" – to borrow one of Žižek's expressions:[7]

Superego emerges where the Law – the public Law, the Law articulated in the public discourse – fails; at this point of failure, the public Law is compelled to search for support in an *illegal enjoyment*. Superego is the obscene 'nightly' law that necessarily redoubles and accompanies, as its shadow, the 'public' Law. . . .

As numerous analyses from Bakhtin onwards have shown, periodic transgressions of the public law are inherent to the social order; they function as a condition of the latter's stability. (Bakhtin's mistake – or, rather, that of some of his followers – was to present an idealized image of these "transgressions," while passing in silence over lynching parties, and so on, as the crucial form of the "carnivalesque suspension of social hierarchy.") What "holds together" a community most deeply is not so much identification with the Law that regulates the community's "normal" everyday circuit, but rather *identification with a specific form of transgression of the Law, of the Law's suspension* (in psychoanalytic terms, with a specific form of *enjoyment*).[8]

In this remote village where people remain closely related to each other, villagers identify with the "nightly law," which binds the community together by encouraging transgression of the written public law and by implicitly supporting the elimination of an individual marked by his difference – namely, the teacher. This law is nightly because it can be never written nor spoken of publicly, due to its inherently unlawful nature – as judged by the public legal system. At the same time, this nightly nature is precisely the source of its power, thanks to its link to collective unconscious. The public written law cannot exist without its counterpart, the community nightly law, which represents the dark area of excess in a legal system. In other words, the legal system and the nightly law complement each other in order to keep a society functioning.

Despite the benefits of education, Mingguang's influences may be perceived as dangerous since education eventually encourages people to question the community's seemingly unchanged tradition. The two brothers who end up murdering Mingguang are torn between the written public law and the unarticulated nightly community law. On the one hand, according to the community nightly law, they have to kill Mingguang if they want to save their faces, or to remain respected members of the community, because he has "ruined" their sister's, and thus their family's, honor. On the other hand, according to the written public law, if they actually commit murder, they have to pay for their transgression with their lives.

The conflict between the written public law and the nightly community law has been one of the important subjects in contemporary Chinese films, because of the urgent need for a relatively responsible legal system in a market economy. Four years later, in 1994, the same subject is explored by *Master Shangang, the Defendant (Beigao Shangang ye)* directed by Fan Yuan, which was awarded a Huabiao Prize in China during the same year. In Fan's film, the written law is articulated by Shangang's grandson, a student at an elementary school. The grandson, who has gained some legal knowledge in one of his classes, writes an anonymous letter to accuse his grandfather, the village chief, of using unlawful and excessive means to control the village. The grandson does so in order to test whether his grandfather is beyond the written law as long as he serves the village's interests effectively – according to the commonly accepted rules in the community – as the village chief himself claimed. The result is that Shangang is arrested in accordance with the written law, despite the deep regret of everyone, including the judge who sentences the guilty man. As a result, the community nightly law is romanticized and glorified by its perfect incarnation, the idealized patriarch figure, Shangang, who is victimized by the inhuman nature of public written law. Ironically, Shangang is in reality a loyal defender of the interests of the party's legal system by wielding unlimited power in the party's place. In other words, he does what the party would truly like to do but cannot do openly, due to the limits of written law. Consequently, it does not surprise us that the worst punishment for him is not imprisonment but the potential loss of his party membership. This film inadvertently shows not only the apparent conflict but also a deep collaboration between the public written law and the community nightly law.

Though made four years before Fan Yuan's film, *Bloody Dawn* offers a much less romanticized view of community law. To a certain extent, the entire community is guilty in Mingguang's murder – due either to their indifference prior to the murder, or to their effort to justify implicitly the murder in the name of Mingguang's alleged affair with Hongxing. Mingguang's true crime is not his allegedly obscene life-style, but his difference as a cultural outsider. In this sense, the two brothers inadvertently execute the collective will of the community. However, torn between the two versions of law, the community cannot justify the two brothers' murder openly. Therefore, almost all the witnesses insist on Mingguang's illicit affair with Hongxing, although what they have witnessed (flashback images) does not confirm what they say (narrative voices). This choice of the "belief in the belief [of the others]"[9] puts them on the side of the community nightly law, according to which, Mingguang's true crime is occupying the position of an obscene outsider – that is, he is obscene precisely because he is an outsider.

As Žižek states:

We could also say that this nightly obscene law consists of *proton pseudos,* the primordial lie that founds a community. That is to say, identification with community is ultimately always based upon some shared guilt or, more precisely, upon the *fetishistic disavowal of this guilt*.[10]

Since the entire village, except for the potential victim, knew the murder plan, every villager – including Hongxing, who accused him; his fiancée, Yongfang, who locked him outside her door; and the village chief who treated the potential murderers so lightly – has partly contributed to his death. As a result, not surprisingly, the trial against his murderers has become a collective disavowal of their guilt – against an individual stigmatized by his difference.

AN INDIVIDUAL IN A COLLECTIVE TRAGEDY

Although the film uses medium and long shots extensively, the representation of Li Mingguang, the teacher and the murder victim, is an exception.

As the director herself explains:

A role of the teacher of the elementary school existed in *Bloody Dawn*. Who should play this role? I thought about this question thoroughly. I believed that this teacher must represent life and *civilization* [emphasis added] in the remote village. Although the part he acts is not really heavy, we should be able to show how precious his life is. His smile should have a radiant quality, which shows hope to audiences. Therefore, when the knife touches his body, audiences would feel great pain in their heart. They would feel that the ignorant brothers killed not only one person, but also the sole radiant life in this village.[11]

Li Shaohong adds that the actor Hu Yajie was selected to play the teacher for his "radiant" (*canlan*) smile and star quality. At the same time, the more distinguished Mingguang appears to audiences, situated in a cultural space distant from the community in the film, the more unavoidable his death will be, because what allows urban audiences to identify with him is precisely his alienation among his fellow villagers. His limited educational background, which is nevertheless unique in his surroundings, literally associates him with outsiders or "educated youth" (*zhishi qingnian*) – urban youngsters who spent their formative years in the village during the Cultural Revolution – or with "civilization," to use the director's own expression. In other words, villagers are lined up against "civilization." As an orphan, Li grew up among "educated youth" and received his education from them. Taking into consideration that Li Shaohong and her fellow students in the Film Academy belong to the same generation as the "educated youth," and that a great number of these filmmakers were indeed former *zhishi qingnian*, it should not surprise us that the directorial point of view often sides with the teacher against the villagers.

However, this shining moment of his radiance, so carefully staged according to Li Shaohong's explanation, is actually extremely brief. After the testimony of Mingguang's grandmother, a medium shot shows his last gaze at her retrospectively viewed from her perspective. He stands at the threshold and gradually turns his face toward her (and audiences) with the "radiant" smile. At the same time, his grandmother "knows nothing about her grandson" – as the investigator points out, her perspective is also necessarily that of ignorance, her parental love notwithstanding. As the grandmother explains before this shot, she attributes his death to her failure to interpret her dream correctly (a reminiscence of the dream of Santiago Nasar's mother prior to her son's death in *Chronicle of a Death Foretold*). From her perspective, his smile (or radiance), like the circumstances of his death, remains incomprehensible. To this extent, his radiant quality as an emblem of "civilization" is exclusively staged for viewers beyond the screen, since everyone onscreen, including his closest family members, is blissfully unaware of it. By contrast, a following scene shows how obscure his life appears within the community. A handicapped coworker of the two brothers tries to bribe the investigator with wine and cakes in order to persuade him to spare his former partners' lives. After realizing the failure of his attempt, the coworker asks a question rhetorically and contemptuously: "How could the two brothers end up paying their lives for the death of a teacher [*jiaoshu de*]?" He also tries to defend the brothers' murder by saying that he would have done the same thing had he been in their place. This "deviation" (*chaqu*), as the investigator's voice-off defines it, is intriguing. Precisely because his relationship as a coworker is rather distant from the two murderers, his gesture is more representative of public opinion among his fellow villagers than that of a close relative – such as Mingguang's uncle, his sole defender among the villagers. Furthermore, on various occasions the same opinion has been voiced repeatedly by other characters in the film. Li's careful choice of an actor with star quality forms a striking contrast to an equally carefully staged contempt for the teacher's life onscreen. This contrast further underlines the different points of view between the rural characters onscreen and the urban director and viewers offscreen.

After Mingguang's death, Manyi, his mischievous student, obviously without any understanding, reads the teacher's poem written on the wall: "What is left are the mountain, the river, the youth, and the beauty" (*liuxia shan, liuxia shui, liuxia qingchun, liuxia mei*). A moment later, in a series of high-angle shots, the poor kid is thoroughly beaten by a group of boys. The little boy's short-lived poetic pretension comically reflects the inadequacy of his teacher, whose youth and beauty, instead of remaining as mountains and river, disappear without a trace. The film portrays Mingguang's life as a brief poetic moment in this village with a somewhat condescending smile. Although he is closer to his urban viewers due to his (limited) education, in their eyes Mingguang is still one of the villagers, despite his difference. However, this difference has doomed his life from the very beginning.

In the penultimate scene, Mingguang's painful death is portrayed in slow motion. As in the scene of his last farewell to his grandmother, Mingguang slowly turns his head to the village chief and articulates painfully, "Uncle, they have killed, killed, killed me . . . ," before collapsing on the ground. Since the film mainly uses medium and long shots, nonprofessional actors, and fast-paced camera movements on most other occasions, the use of slow-motion and close-ups (in addition to the actor's star quality) distinguishes Mingguang from the rest of the community, despite his limited footage. This distinction singles him out as the representative of "civilization," as Li Shaohong put it. What did she mean by this word? As we can see, this civilization is definitely "modern," which is defined against the local culture of the Chinese village. In this sense, the directorial point of view implicitly identifies with the discourse of modernity inherited from the May Fourth movement by attributing (modern) civilization mainly to the West.

At one time, an interviewer asked Li: Why is there not a single close-up among eighteen shots of the sequence of the two brothers' arrest? She answered:

It was because I felt if I added a close-up at this moment, I might destroy the entire film. Just imagine, under the cloudy sky, a group of villagers stand at the entrance of the village, watching the two brothers brought to the patrol car by policemen. One of them shouts: "Mother, the money for fertilizers is under the straw mat. If it's not enough, borrow a little from neighbors." His voice is strong enough to be heard by everyone present in the film. If instead of this scene, I had used a close-up to emphasize the hand tightly grasping the stone gate or the mother's weeping face, it would not have had the same effect created by medium shot, since the audience would have taken this scene as a family tragedy. Medium and long shots suggest that everyone present is sharing the same tragic fate.[12]

Despite their brutal murder of the teacher, the two brothers reveal their gentler side in their attachment to their family members and especially in their own vulnerability. In this respect, they are victims of ignorance and poverty as much as is the elementary-school teacher. As Mingguang's kind-hearted grandmother sadly points out at the moment of their arrest: "Where are they (police) going to bring these kids? They are all (our) kids after all" (doushi haizi). In this collective tragedy, each participant is portrayed more as an object of the various converging social forces than as a subject of his or her actions. As the director states: "Because of ignorance, the entire village, the collectivity of villagers is the murderer."[13] Partly for this reason, she in most cases deliberately avoided melodramatic tension by eschewing close-ups. On the one hand, each member of the community contributes to Mingguang's death as his moral detractor. On the other, everyone is also a victim of the same tragedy, a victim of the collective ignorance. Since villagers participate in this murder mainly as passive spectators, they also implicate the film audiences in this collective tragedy by sharing their viewing experiences. Despite the spatial and ideological distance that separates villagers from their urban viewers, it is difficult, if not impossible, simply to condemn villagers for their share in this murder. Viewers are no longer in a position to judge them "objectively," since they are not simply the objects of a viewing experience but also viewers of the same tragedy, albeit from a different space.

Consequently, the collective tragedy in a fictional village based on a Colombian novel acquires an allegorical dimension for contemporary Chinese society. This theme can hardly be attributed to Li's innovation, however. Since the May Fourth movement, a tragedy caused by collective ignorance has been a favorite theme for modern Chinese intellectuals.

This impression of collective tragedy is further reinforced by another feature in this film: Various characters are often presented from behind. For example, the tracking shot early in the prologue is of the back of a little boy, who breaks the happy anarchy among his schoolmates by announcing the death of their teacher. Soon after, the boy becomes part of the crowd – faceless and nameless. Thus the fear revealed in his voice expresses collective emotion among his fellow schoolmates. On another occasion, a brief medium shot of Mingguang's mother, who after his father's death left her children in order to remarry in a different village, is followed by a long take of her from behind, disappearing gradually in the narrow lane, supported by some women. In this long shot, it is difficult to distinguish her from the rest of the crowd. As a result, the victim's mother near her son's corpse is blended into a collective anonymity as a symbol of motherhood. Another similar case can be made concerning Hongxing's suicide. From the gate where she and Yongfang had earlier had an intimate girl-talk, the camera in a high-angle long shot follows Hongxing's back before cutting to a crane shot of her body floating on the river. In the sequence that follows, the camera briefly shifts to several groups of women mourning her death. Because the last shot of Hongxing prior to her suicide focuses only on her back, the film creates an illusion that the victim might be one of these women in the crowd. As a result, an individual tragedy takes on a collective dimension shared by women in the village.

GENDER OPPRESSION AND MINORITY DISCOURSE[14]

In one interview, Li states:

My greatest wish is making a feminist film.

Strictly speaking, there isn't a single feminist film in China, although there are many women directors as well as films on women. When the representatives of a French feminist film festival came to China to choose films, they could not select a single one. A feminist film should be made from the women's perspective. Up to now, our films on women are made from an overall social perspective, but not gender perspective.

China only has limited understanding of women as a gender. For so many years in cinema, films portrayed women as resisting feudalism, husband's rights, ritual hierarchy, and demanding gender equality. But nobody has ever asked what women truly think about these problems. In either Red Detachment of Women [Hongse niangzi jun], Woman from a Good Family [Liangjia funü], or The Single Woman [Dushen nüren], images of women are portrayed in accordance with social demands. So far, this society has never had time to listen to women's voices. It is this entire situation that prompts me to make *Blush* [*Hongfen*].[15]

However, in 1995, after *Blush* had already been released, I asked her if she believed that she had indeed made a "feminist movie." Somewhat to my surprise, Li categorically denied that she had ever had such an intention.[16] This apparent self-contradictory stance reflects an ambiguity toward gender issues among women intellectuals in postsocialist China. On the one hand, like most of women writers and filmmakers in any culture, it is difficult, if not impossible, for them to remain indifferent to the problem of women's marginalization in their own society. On the other hand, the communist appropriation of minority discourse leaves little room to articulate their subject positions on this issue in their own terms. As Li rightly points out, this discourse mainly serves the party instead of representing women's voices. Still, the question remains: How can a woman gain her subjective voice within a space already saturated for several decades by the party's discourse on women's emancipation? Caught by this dilemma, Li's definition of "feminist film" or "women's film" (*nüxing dianying*) appears inherently self-contradictory. First, the so-called woman's perspective is defined by French feminists who rejected all Chinese movies as not feminist enough, but whose criteria are not necessarily valid in many respects in contemporary Chinese society. This is because some of their vocabulary had already been used repeatedly by the Communist Party in its minority discourse. In the course of history, it has invented and reinvented this discourse to speak for – and in the place of – the "minors" in terms of gender and class, thereby gaining and consolidating its power.[17] Women's emancipation is one major component of this minority discourse. Thanks to its position of spokesman of the powerless, the party can justify its unlimited power in the name of protecting the oppressed. At the same time, because of this deep resentment of the party's minority discourse, few Chinese women intellectuals of Li's generation have been particularly interested in studying feminist theory in depth: The less they understand feminist perspective, the more easily they accept the party's claim of spokesman for gender liberation. A better understanding of feminist theory, despite its superficial analogy to the party's minority discourse and its cultural limitation, can be quite helpful in calling into question the party's minority discourse by revealing its fundamentally patriarchal nature. Luce Irigaray, for example, has frequently criticized the patriarchal notion of gender equality, because to the detriment of sexual difference this "equality" is still measured by masculine standards, whose universality remains unquestioned in a patriarchal culture. In other words, women's differences make them appear inferior as they are treated like men, because in a patriarchal culture their sex still does not exist at various levels.[18] To a great extent, Irigaray's criticism succinctly explains why the party's women's-emancipation movement could not bring about fundamental changes. For the party, as for any patriarchal order, the female sex does not exist except as the object of its salvation.[19]

Li's attempt to borrow Western feminist discourse in order to criticize the party's gender policy – especially in a perfunctory manner – was bound to fail. At first glance, it is difficult even to distinguish the two discourses. For example, "social demands" criticized by the Chinese woman director, which include "resisting husband's rights, and ritual hierarchy," are not necessarily so distant from the feminist agenda in the West. Furthermore, "gender equality" is prima facie a feminist agenda. In order to maintain its subversive edge, Li's notion of women's perspective must first of all be able to distinguish itself from that of the communist discourse. Meanwhile, this means that she has to distance it from that of Western feminists as well, because in China feminism is often simplistically understood only as equivalent to a demand for gender equality. At the same time, the official appropriation of discourse on women's emancipation has not resolved the problem of gender oppression: On the contrary, the imposed salvation of the oppressed gender not only preserved a great deal of traditional gender hierarchy but also reinvented certain new forms of sexual oppression as part of the basic structure in a new patriarchy. Since it relinquishes any form of sexual oppression to traditional China, gender oppression supposedly does not exist discursively in contemporary China. In other words, gender oppression has become a code word in the official discourse to justify the replacement of traditional authority by communist power. Consequently, it is difficult to describe the prevailing sexual discrimination in contemporary China in an appropriate language, due to the ideologically loaded vocabulary of women's emancipation.

Caught between the discourse of the Communist Party and the misogynistic discourse prevailing in post–Cultural Revolution literature and arts,[20] women intellectuals in China understandably do not generally show their interests in gender issues publicly, and they have difficulty articulating their agenda – although the post–Cultural Revolution generation of women intellectuals are somewhat less reticent to pronounce their feminist agenda, partly thanks to the decreasing influence on them of the party's minority discourse. Li's film *Blush,* based on a Su Tong novella, is a case in point. This film focuses on the life of two prostitutes, Qiuyi and Xiao'e, who live on the threshold of the Communist Revolution. For different reasons, both prefer their previous life-style in the brothel to their new one, imposed by the communist government, as workers in a factory. On the one hand, the film succeeds in revealing the hypocritical nature of a new patriarchal order by ridiculing its minority discourse. On the other hand, the subversion of this discourse also falls into an old trap of sexist definition of women. Despite an avowed emphasis on women's individualities, the two prostitutes roughly follow Su's polarization of women into two familiar types.[21] Qiuyi is defined by her self-sacrificial motherly instinct, whereas Xiao'e belongs to the category of born prostitutes. When Qiuyi tells her former lover, on the verge of his execution, that his newborn son will be raised as his surrogate (at the end of the film she adopts him from his biological mother, Xiao'e, her former friend and current rival), she assumes a role of universal mother – unconditionally forgiving and loving. Xiao'e, by contrast, claims to be a prostitute by birth and tries to fulfill her sexual appetite, to the detriment of her wifely and motherly duties. As a result, the subversion of communist ideology in the film unwittingly speaks for a return to traditional gender hierarchy. These women's perspectives, despite their subversion of the official discourse, are in the final analysis not far from Su Tong's masculinist perceptions of women. As in his original novella, femininity in the film is portrayed as mainly determined by male desires. Furthermore, in many aspects, this film also follows the Zhang Yimou model, even in terms of exploitative representation of the female body. Thus it is perhaps not so surprising after all that, having finished *Blush,* Li categorically denied her initial intention to make a "feminist film" (*nüxing dianying*), since in no way may this film be classified as such, even according to the director's own equivocal standards.

However, although she has never explicitly claimed to pay special attention to women's issues in *Bloody Dawn,* Li did succeed in presenting gender inequality powerfully in that film. In the first place, the film focuses on the problem of virginity, which is symptomatic of gender oppression in contemporary China, especially taking into consideration several decades of the party's discourse on gender equality.[22] Second, Li's Chinese film tends to be more sympathetic to women than is Márquez's Colombian novel: The novel ends in the description of the rejected bride's everlasting unrequited love for her angry husband, whereas in the film Hongxing chooses suicide. The Chinese bride's death is a much more rebellious gesture than the Colombian bride's "magic" conversion. Third, in the film women are generally portrayed as more sympathetic toward the murder victim, partly because they themselves are constantly subject to violence. In fact, except for the penultimate scene of Mingguang's murder, violence among adults in the film has always been directed at women's bodies. Hongxing is severely beaten by her husband, Zhang Qiangguo, on their wedding night after he discovers the absence of blood on their bed. When he returns her to her family, her two brothers savagely beat her with heavy instruments and push her from the top of the stairs to force her to confess her lover's name. The mother stops this beating only by protecting her daughter with her own body, while desperately shouting to her two sons: "If you still want to beat her, why don't you beat me first?" In Márquez's novel, neither the husband nor the brothers beat the rejected bride: The mother alone punishes the daughter physically. By changing the mother's role from a perpetrator of violence to the only protector of the bride against the violence of three men, the film draws a clearly cut gender line in relation to violence. Later, the two brothers show that they are indeed also capable of violence against their own mother when she tries to stop them from murdering Mingguang. In fact, beside the ultimate violence, the murder itself, the film offers an exhaustive range of pictures of domestic violence against women as wife, sister, and mother.

Jia Leilei describes the portrayal of gender in this film:

Cinematographically, women are always oppressively framed by lanes and streets, door frames, arches, and half-ruined walls. Rarely there is blue sky on top of their heads. Even the two girlfriends' most intimate talk has to be framed by an oppressive stone gate. Sometimes, they are even in a reversed position, unable to stand up. Since they are categorically denied the right to be located in the same space with men, they are considered subhumans. . . . Thus, we can see the screen of *Bloody Dawn* is not merely a material and externalized space. It has become a spiritual and cultural space. It is both realistic and symbolic.[23]

A flashback of the episode that leads to Qiangguo's unfortunate marriage to Hongxing exemplifies this kind of gender division. A group of young men work for Qiangguo in the millhouse on top of the mountains. A group of girls, including Hongxing, climb the mountain road while happily chatting. Males and females are clearly segregated: The girls are at the foot of the mountain, the boys on top. The boys gaze at the girls boldly from the top, whereas the girls return their gaze stealthily from the bottom. Tricked by some other girls' practical joke, Hongxing enters the millhouse to look for her brother. By breaking the clearly cut gender line, she offers herself to the closer scrutiny of the male gaze, especially that of a rich man, Zhang Qiangguo. This moment decides her fate as the desirable beautiful trophy for the richest man in the village. To a certain extent, this sequence offers a sociopsychological picture of a strictly divided gender line – in terms of personal behaviors as well as spatial locations. The impression of discrepancy of power along the gender line is reinforced by the arrangement of the two marriages. In Hongxing's marriage with Qiangguo and her brother's marriage with Qiangguo's sister, none of the women, neither the brides-to-be nor the mothers of the engaged couples, has any say in the final decision. Men are discussing women's fates in the dining room, while women are working in the kitchen and eating men's leftovers in this scene of double engagement.

All these images of gender oppression would not have been unusual had they portrayed precommunist China. However, because they realistically picture the gender situation in current rural China after several decades of the party's discourse on women's emancipation, these images subvert that discourse by pointedly revealing its superficial nature. Within limits, the official discourse covers only the urgent need to change the gender situation in China, while occupying the spokesman of the oppressed gender. At the same time, this false analogy between communism and feminism has been used by the misogynistic discourse prevailing among Chinese intellectuals to silence women's voices. As the loss of virginity leads to the loss of the life of the only educator in Li's film, women's oppression is partly associated with the absence of education. At the same time, the emphasis on the value of virginity, a phenomenon that indeed prevails in today's China, shows how much the core of traditional gender hierarchy remains intact despite several decades of the party's antifeudal and antitraditional stance, which is in the final analysis utterly patriarchal. Many Chinese women intellectuals like Li Shaohong sense the need for change in this respect, since they are constantly not only witnesses but also subjects of gender discrimination. However, talking about women's emancipation risks identifying them with the party line. Furthermore, the party's minority discourse, which often serves a decorative function for its domination, makes the very notion of women's emancipation lose its critical edge, to the point that it becomes an empty signifier.

During a conference in Hong Kong in 1995, some participants asked why mainland Chinese women were in general skeptical about feminism. Li Shaohong's film to a degree indirectly answers their questions. If women still remain oppressed, as shown in the film, after several decades of the party-led women's-emancipation movement, it is understandably much more difficult to believe that the power of idealistic slogans will be strong enough to save women from their daily oppression, or to grant them the right to speak for themselves. As a result, regrettably, very few Chinese women from before the recent generation are willing to look at feminist discourse more closely. At the same time, despite the lack of a suitable discourse, the existence of women's oppression in contemporary Chinese society is an incontestable fact. However, the difficulty in forming a transindividual discourse makes it almost impossible for women to articulate a feminist standard against the patriarchal order, since this position has been preempted by the party, in the name of the oppressed women, as part of its modernization package – though for the sake of the newly established patriarchal order itself. As a woman director caught between the daily situation of gender oppression and the lack of an effective counterdiscourse, Li Shaohong made a film in which this oppression is visualized but not verbalized. This ambiguity also expresses the dilemma faced by a large number of women artists and intellectuals on the mainland. How can they articulate their positions toward gender hierarchy after the women's-liberation movement led by the party failed even to let women speak for themselves, despite an exhaustive use of minority discourse? The answer is not so difficult: If one can see through the patriarchal nature of this discourse, its analogy with a feminist stance will fade away. In this sense, the visual mockery of its hypocrisy in Li's film, which contributes to its deconstruction, is one of the first steps in the right direction.

Bloody Dawn seamlessly transforms a Colombian magical realist story into a film depicting current Chinese rural reality. By shifting the focus on racial tension in the original work to the problem of education or culture, the film addresses an urgent problem for contemporary Chinese society in the process of moving from a socialist regime to a market economy. In a sense, both Mingguang, the murder victim, and Qiangguo, the rich groom, are subject to outside influences, because the former acquired his education from "educated youth" – youngsters in the city who spent several years of their lives in the village during the Cultural Revolution – and the latter obtained his wealth from his urban employers. However, Mingguang's education earns him contempt, if not hatred, from villagers, despite his devotion to their children, whereas Qiangguo's money provokes respect and admiration among them. The differential treatment of outside influences in the forms of education and money reflect an attitude that prevails in contemporary Chinese society in the process of moving toward a market economy – an attitude of money worship, often to the detriment of education. Mingguang is the victim not only of the two brothers' murderous brutality but also of this collective contempt for education. Because his education made him an outsider, he is condemned by the nightly community law. Unwritten and unarticulated, this law nevertheless binds the community together against Mingguang – an imaginary Other because of his "obscene" life-style.

At the same time, the film raises another question about contemporary China: After several decades of the party's discourse on women's emancipation, what does actually happen in the lives of Chinese women? The images of gender situation in the film are not encouraging. The theme that loss of virginity leads to the loss of an innocent person's life already points to sexism inherent in the current society. Although the film fits the genre of the thriller, strictly speaking, there is no individual villain, since the tragedy is primarily collective. The perpetrator is also the victim – victim of his or her own ignorance, as in the case of the two murderers in this collective tragedy. In short, the film offers a rather gloomy portrait of contemporary Chinese society – allegorically and realistically represented by this fictional village, out of a Colombian novel. Interestingly, despite its origin, the film remains inherently "Chinese" in that it touches several of the most important social problems in contemporary China.

7

A POSTCOLONIAL REFLECTION

BUDDHA BLESS AMERICA

The Indian Aboriginal did not flourish in pre-British India. . . .There is something Eurocentric about assuming that imperialism began with Europe.
— Gayatri Chakravorty Spivak[1]

Both mainland China and Taiwan have experienced "belated modernity" in their own respective ways.[2] Unlike Greek culture, which is considered relatively peripheral to normative western European modernity despite its status as the cradle of Western civilization, these Chinese cultures are situated much further away from the West. However, as one of the four most ancient civilizations in the world, Chinese culture on the mainland and in Taiwan shares at least one aspect with Greek culture — an uneasy position between its own traditions and the processes of modernization. Since the May Fourth movement at the beginning of the century, Chinese "modernists" (a broadly defined expression, which includes a wide range of people of different ideological backgrounds, from radical intellectuals to humanists, from communists to individualists) have repeatedly used the term "modernization" interchangeably with "westernization" — the West is associated with the most important means of modernization: science and technology. In addition, the West also symbolizes revolution, democracy, or individual freedom, depending on the speaker's ideological beliefs. At the same time, these modernists have been ardent nationalists concerning their cultural identity. Although mainland China and Taiwan claim authenticity to Chinese cultural heritage in their own ways, both societies have changed considerably in the processes of modernization. Consequently, an "authentically" Chinese culture, which had never existed in a strict sense, has become more than ever a myth. Paradoxically, people on both sides of the Taiwan Strait claim more advanced modernity (or westernization), since modernity is associated with progress and tradition with backwardness in the "universal" language of the global civilization — especially for a third-world culture. These apparently self-contradictory statements reveal a reality in the era of globalization: If the dichotomy between the East and the West was an orientalist invention by the West to create its Other,[3] this division has become more than ever unsustainable. At the same time, this does not imply that the whole world can celebrate a happy universal entity. In the process of globalization, differences have not been reduced without the violence of the "hyperreal financialization" – to use Gayatri Spivak's expression.[4] Furthermore, this process may also create and amplify other differences within a culture, such as in the case of mainland China and Taiwan.

Unlike literature, which relies on written texts, specific to a language, cinema generally claims a certain universality beyond national boundaries, due to its emphasis on visuality. If literature plays an important role in the formation of a nation as "imagined community" – Benedict Anderson associates this with the origin of "print capitalism"[5] – cinema may function as a means of internationalization, as in the case of experimental films in China and in Taiwan in the 1980s and 1990s. One can say that national cinema is a contradiction in terms, because it often emerges in the process of internationalization, and its implied audiences are partially, if not essentially, international. For example, although both the Fifth Generation and the New Cinema filmmakers on both sides of the Taiwan Strait have occasionally claimed that they would like to build a well-recognized national cinema, they often have to privilege global audiences to the detriment of local ones. The reason is not difficult to understand: Recognition by the international film milieu (juries at international film festivals, for example) is the most efficient means of obtaining the status of representative of the national culture for these films, as well as further financial support for their directors from multinational corporations. The Zhang Yimou model represents an extreme case of the globalization of national cinema.[6] On the other hand, thanks to a lesser degree of commitment to nationalism, and partly due to cinematic dependence on visual means, films may also function as useful vehicles to problematize the very notion of national (cultural) identity in the era of globalization, as in the case of *Buddha Bless America* (*Taiping tianguo*), a Taiwan film released in 1996.

If a nation is defined as an "imagined political community" that holds various individuals together after the death of God, the death of the king (one may add, the death of Mao), and the death of man,[7] the Chinese on the mainland and in Taiwan are bound together by an imagined cultural community after half a century of political segregation. On both sides of the Taiwan Strait, the collective imaginary has changed so much through their respective processes of modernization to the point that their common ground has become considerably reduced, despite the common language.

Taiwan (Formosa) was first colonized by Holland at the beginning of the seventeenth century. In 1662, Zheng Chenggong, a Chinese loyalist of the bygone Ming dynasty during the Qing dynasty, took over their colonial power. The Japanese, who occupied Taiwan from 1895 to 1945, were arguably the last colonizers of this island. The majority of Taiwan's population are of ethnic Chinese origin, and the aboriginals, Taiwan's first inhabitants (the earliest ones, Yamei nationalities, supposedly started living on the island five to ten thousand years ago),[8] have been reduced to minority status by various colonizers, who killed them, starting with the Dutch government, helped by their missionaries.[9] During the seventeenth and eighteenth centuries, since the Qing government forbade Chinese immigrants to bring their families to Taiwan, in order to keep them from rebelling against their Manchu rulers, many intermarriages between Chinese men and aboriginal women occurred to the extent that the native population was greatly reduced.[10] Because the aboriginals nowadays mainly live in mountainous areas in Taiwan, they have obtained the title of Mountainous or High Mountain minorities (*shandi zu* or *gaoshan zu*) in the official language. Meanwhile, the Chinese settlers became the majority of the Taiwan population in the Qing dynasty. Since the Nationalist government's exodus from the mainland to Taiwan in 1949, it has heavily relied on American economic power and military protection – especially at the early stage of their economic development. As a result, Americans have wielded a type of colonial power despite the absence of colonial institutions. Furthermore, at the beginning of their power, partly to justify their own ruling status, the Nationalists from the mainland reinforced an ethnic division between the mainlanders (*waisheng ren*) and the Taiwanese (*bensheng ren*), although both belong to Chinese ethnicity.

Immanuel Wallerstein explains:

Wherever we find wage workers located in different kinds of household structures from more highly paid workers located in more "proletarianized" household structure, we tend to find at the same time that these varieties of household structures are located inside "communities" called "ethnic groups." That is, along with an occupational hierarchy comes the "ethnicization" of the work force within a given state's boundaries.[11]

During the early stage of the Nationalist government in Taiwan, few Taiwanese were considered trustworthy for leadership positions, because they had been "enslaved" by the Japanese.[12] Furthermore, during the fifty years of their occupation, the Japanese colonizers imposed their language on the population in Taiwan. It was only after the end of the Second World War that the Nationalist government changed the official language to Chinese. As a result, the postwar generation in Taiwan, who had received their education in Japanese during this half-century, suddenly found their education virtually useless. For these reasons, the division between the Taiwanese and the mainlander initially turned the "numerical majorities," namely, Taiwanese, into "social minorities,"[13] due to their lack of political and economic power. This situation started changing during the 1970s partly due to Jiang Jingguo's succession to his father's power and partly due to rapid economic development. Jiang was relatively more open to the Taiwanese. In 1987, he ended four decades of martial law, which had been imposed by the Nationalist government after the February 28 Incident. Meanwhile, economic changes, especially the real-estate boom in the 1980s, which greatly benefitted the Taiwanese due to their significant shares of landownership, have also improved their political situation.

Wu Nianzhen (Wu Nien-chen), formerly a Native Soil novelist and one of the most prolific New Cinema screenwriters, directed *Buddha Bless America* (*Taiping tianguo*), his second film, in 1996. *Buddha Bless America* is about a Taiwanese village, temporarily converted to a military base for American soldiers by the Nationalist government in the midst of the Vietnam War. All the villagers temporarily live in the twelve classrooms of the elementary school, to free up rooms for American soldiers who perform war games in their village. Initially, the villagers agree to accept this arrangement thanks to the government's offer of compensation for their economic loss and to persuasion by one of their own. This respected villager, called Brains (Xin) is the only educated adult in the village, and he has a seemingly unlimited admiration for American technology; secretly he hopes that American military doctors will be able to perform microsurgery on his brother's fingers, cut in the course of a work-related accident in a Japanese-owned factory. The film offers satirical portrayals of various people: Brains, the native intellectual, in his blind admiration of all that is related to the United States; American soldiers in their simplemindedness and insensitivity to the local culture; Nationalist officers, in their ingratiation with Americans and their royal contempt for local Taiwanese; and the Taiwanese villagers themselves, in their selfishness and ignorance. The plot is centered on multilayered conflicts surrounding the American temporary military base: conflicts between the Nationalists (mostly mainlanders) and the Taiwanese, between American soldiers and Taiwanese villagers, as well as among the villagers themselves.

A TRAGICOMEDY

In the prologue, a long take of a foggy and empty countryside appears on the screen. At the bottom of the screen is written, "South Taiwan in late 1960s." At the same time, a woman's mourning voice gradually fills the dimly lit horizon. After three successive long takes – the horizon, a field path, and a cabbage field – the camera traces the source of the wailing voice, an old lady, whom everyone in the village calls Granny (as we find out later in the film). Wearing a flowery scarf, kneeling before her husband's tomb, Granny talks to her dead husband as if he were alive and she were nagging at him on ordinary days. While complaining to him about her loss of voice, she states matter-of-factly that she has mourned enough for today: The wailing is simply a routine exercise for her. Accompanied by her two inseparable goats, Granny stands up and returns to the village. The camera, however, follows the same sinuous road as presented in the initial long takes – except in reverse order. In contrast with the tragic mourning sound, we hear a cheerful tune hummed by a female voice (Granny's?) as she and the two goats reenter the frame. The camera follows her back, until the image fades into the title screen. While humorous music soon replaces the tune, the

Chinese title for it, *Taiping tianguo* ("Peaceful Heavenly Kingdom," a title that rebellious peasants, vaguely influenced by Christian doctrine in mid-nineteenth-century China, attributed to their own short-lived regime), appears playfully on the screen. By then, all the tragic impressions created by the opening long take of dark and foggy horizon as well as the wailing sounds have been proven misleading. The comic effect is further reinforced by the revelation of the reason for Granny's mourning: a dream. In her dream of the previous night her husband stroked her breast – a gesture he had not been able to make for at least a dozen years, because of his premature death – as Granny later explains to her nephew, Brains. This prologue and title screen establish a pattern repeated throughout the film. As a rule, each potentially tragic situation in the end becomes absurdly humorous. Like the initial road followed by Granny, the itinerary of the departure and the return is the same except in reverse, but the tone that initially appeared tragic has always ended up becoming comic.

The miscommunication caused by a mixture of linguistic, cultural, and economic differences colors the drama created by the conflicts between the Taiwanese villagers and the American military, and filters it through a lens of comic absurdity, despite potentially or realistically tragic consequences. To this extent, the prologue forcefully sets the tone for the rest of the film. The same factors that turn a tragic situation into an absurd comedy are also the cause of the tragedy beneath comic appearances. Due to his misperception of the Americans, Brains loses respect from the villagers – a respect he had earned through hard work by successfully promoting scientific agriculture methods; his brother loses his fingers, since American doctors are not as miraculous as Brains has believed; and the villagers lose a major part of their harvest and part of their ancestors' tombs, smashed by the American tanks – despite their initial belief that they were getting a lucrative deal from governmental compensation. At the same time, American soldiers lose something as well: food cans, uniforms, beer, and two corpses in metal coffins – all stolen by villagers from their base. Since the villagers cannot work in their fields, stealing from the American military base becomes the only "productive" activity for them during this period. As a result, most villagers steal anything from the U.S. base. Sometimes they even do not have a clue about the functions of their stolen goods – from contraceptives to metal coffins. However, Taiwanese villagers and American soldiers do not suffer the same scale of loss, largely due to the imbalanced economic and political power in Taiwan. Despite its decolonization from Japan after the Second World War, the Taiwan Nationalist government still largely depends on American economic and military power, partly to protect itself from the communist power on the mainland, and partly to achieve a rapid industrialization. As a result, American soldiers enjoy the power of colonizers over Taiwanese villagers, even without an explicitly colonial institution.

As the only educated villager, Brains represents Taiwan intellectuals – Wu Nianzhen, the director, claimed in a phone conversation that his film is mostly "self-mockery."[14] Although he cannot distinguish a casket from an A-bomb, Brains still identifies with America through his ability to appreciate science and technology. Throughout the film, Brains enthusiastically promotes his belief in American superiority based on a misperception in which he equates technological and economic power with cultural and intellectual excellence. The sketchier his scientific knowledge is, the more easily he idealizes American technological power. The Nationalist government institutionalizes this misperception by inducing all villagers to leave their homes and fields for the sake of American soldiers' war games. Through its promise of compensation for their economic losses, the government succeeds in creating a free field for American operations out of a highly populated area. The U.S. government would not have been able to act in the same way for its army on its own land. The bar owner commercializes this misperception: He not only makes workers construct, overnight, a nightclub for American soldiers to "have fun" in, but also brings some "sexy" prostitutes to anticipate their arrival. In the final analysis, what is truly tragic in the film is not necessarily the conflict between the Taiwanese villagers and American soldiers, but rather that the Americans are perceived as the center in a foreign land at the governmental, educational, and cultural levels due to their military, technological, and economic power. This power allows them to act (often seemingly innocently) more unethically than they would be permitted to in their homeland. Since Americans' perceived superiority makes any serious confrontation between them and Taiwanese villagers impossible, these conflicts often appear comic in the film – as exemplified by a confrontational scene between villagers armed with stones and sticks, and American soldiers with machine guns and tanks.

"HELLO" AND "HEY YOU"

At the beginning of the film, villagers learn the alleged "state secret" in a community meeting: the arrival of the American militaries in the near future. As the elementary school will soon be closed to serve as temporary dormitory for the whole village, the schoolmaster takes advantage of her last class to teach children how to say "Hello" to American soldiers. Because "Americans are our best friends who have been helping us tremendously," she asks students to pronounce "Hello" with a cheerful smile and friendly wave whenever they encounter them. The aged astrologer, who happens to overhear the lesson outside the classroom, also learns this expression by heart, thanks to the teacher's diligence. In the course of the film, several villagers indeed use this expression. For example, Brain's only son, Asong, accompanied by his uncle, dutifully pronounces "Hello" to American soldiers in front of the nightclub, while waving to them with an artificial smile. Through his demonstrated friendliness, Asong hopes that an American soldier will help him find a doctor who will be able to reattach his uncle's severed fingers. However, the response from these soldiers to his "Hello" is, "We don't have any change." Ironically, when the teacher taught this lesson to her students, she wanted the children to show "the manners of a great civilized country" (namely, China); but his use of the greeting only makes the boy seem to be a beggar, since this is the image the Chinese have in the eyes of American soldiers. On another occasion, the village astrologer is confronted by American soldiers, who are ransacking the villagers' temporary dormitory in order to find stolen goods. The old man uses "Hello," which he accidentally learned outside the classroom, while taking off a pair of American military trousers in order to avoid punishment for his share of stolen goods. The soldiers pay no attention either to his words or to his suspicious conduct.

In both cases, this expression pronounced by Taiwanese villagers has no salutational effect on Americans. Moreover, the soldiers themselves never use this expression toward villagers. Instead, they use another expression, which is obviously less polite – even to villagers who do not understand a single word of English. Whenever American soldiers confront villagers, either in daily life or in conflict, they often yell at them, "Hey you!" As a result, village children learn this expression in a real-life situation, which seems to them much more effective than "hello" taught in their classroom. If "Hello" anticipates the Americans' arrival to this village, "Hey you" draws an interesting conclusion. After the village chief forcefully takes away the colorful disks (phonograph records) that Asong picked up in the empty nightclub right after the departure of American soldiers, the boy shouts "Hey you!" at the old man and his wife from a distance – as if it were the most powerful curse in the world. At the end of the film, a cheesy song comes from one of Asong's lost colorful disks. This song, originally used for the American nightclub, is broadcast through the loudspeaker to the entire village. In the final shot, this music accompanies villagers to their last community meeting in order to receive their compensation from the Nationalist government.

In this context, both interjections, "Hello" and "Hey you," are misinterpreted or misused by Taiwanese villagers: "Hello" in its overfriendliness and "Hey you" in its hostility. They are not the only words misinterpreted and misused, but not all misinterpretations are as unintentional and innocent as those of these two expressions. Three different languages are used in the film: Taiwanese, Mandarin, and English. The interpreters in three different languages, instead of bridging communication gaps as they are supposed to, often try to misinterpret speeches in both directions. The first deliberate misinterpretation occurs when Brains, the protagonist, delivers a speech at the community meeting in order to convince his fellow villagers to accept the government plan. At the request of the Mandarin-speaking military officers, the Taiwanese-speaking school principal translates his speech to the officers. In his speech, Brains expresses his fundamental hostility and mistrust toward the Nationalist government, and suggests to the villagers that they take advantage of this opportunity to make a lucrative deal and squeeze money from the usually stingy government. In the course of translation, however, Brains's criticism of the government becomes its unrestricted endorsement. This purposeful misinterpretation thus underlines the villagers' mistrust of the central government. In the following scene, Brains scolds his son Asong for not being able to follow his advice. According to the father, if teachers, government officials, or military personal – in short, any of the spokesmen and women for the official ideology – ask the son about anything, he should either answer, "I don't know" or he should tell a lie. Throughout the film, the difference between the official Mandarin and the popular Taiwanese overlaps with another cultural and linguistic line of demarcation: that between the Chinese and the Americans.

"ALL SMART PEOPLE NOWADAYS WANT TO BECOME AMERICAN"

The opening long shot of a courtyard cuts into a medium shot of Brains. In the dim light of the early morning and framed by a door, Brains is reading a magazine on his bed. His wife enters the frame, loudly complaining about men's laziness, since they still have not started working yet. After waking up his brother, Brains tells him that Americans are creators of space-age miracles, as he has just read of the replantation of a rabbit ear through microsurgery in the United States. Proud for being the only one in the village able to obtain news about American technological developments, Brains consciously or unconsciously identifies with Americans as his ego-ideal. As he explains to his brother, "All smart people nowadays want to become American." Because Brains obviously considers himself smart, it goes without saying that in this context he also speaks for himself. Furthermore, villagers implicitly agree with his self-perception by calling him "the one who understands ABC," although he seemingly never demonstrates this ability throughout the film. Partly due to this vague sense of identification with an alien culture, Brains uses his credibility among the villagers to convince them to accept the governmental plan of establishing a temporary American military base in the village, despite his fundamental distrust of the Nationalist government.

As the only native villager who can read and write well enough to teach elementary school (although he was dismissed from his teaching position due to his "subversive language"), Brains knows how to improve agricultural production by means of modern scientific methods, as well as how to interpret dreams according to an ancient Chinese fortune-telling book. The first set of skill earns him respect from all the villagers; the second keeps him rooted in the native soil. Furthermore, throughout the film, his admiration for modern Western (especially American) technology is intertwined with his belief in traditional Chinese astrology to the extent that they often become interchangeable. Like gods governing human fates, Americans are perceived as supernatural by Brains in that they are supposedly able to perform miracles in the name of science and technology. Furthermore, similar to his relation to traditional Chinese astrology, his contacts with Americans still remain at an abstract level, despite the physical presence of U.S. soldiers in his village. As an abstract cultural icon, America can easily be idealized, especially because this idealization is encouraged by the official discourse, educational system, and media propaganda in Taiwan. In the same vein, he thinks that any common American doctor will be able to perform micro-surgery on his brother's mutilated hand. Even after his wife mistakes these severed fingers for fresh ginger roots and put them in a jar full of preservatives and pickled ginger, Brains still believes that they remain replantable as long as American doctors agree to touch them with their own magic fingers.

At the same time, the film offers an ironic portrayal of American soldiers, despite their godlike appearance in Brains's eyes. For example, the first sign that anticipates the presence of American soldiers is the construction of a temporary nightclub. In order to make this club more appealing, according to the owner's order a contractor tries to paint the English words "Music, Dance, Liquor, and Hot Girls" on the facade of the building. However, as the painter cannot read English, he copies these letters from the back of the paper in reverse order. Looking at these unintelligible traces, the owner angrily comments: "What is this? What is this? Even an American scholar won't be able to understand this." The contractor believes that these words should be written from right to left – as in traditional Chinese; that's why he copied them backward. After his explanation, he mumbles to himself, "Why does a whorehouse need any sign?" In a sense, the reversed letters summarize Brains's understanding of American culture, since he also looks at this culture from an idiosyncratically distorted perspective, although his perspective is much more flattering. Furthermore, in this hilarious incident, one cannot help detecting a touch of irony toward films following the Zhang Yimou model, which were flourishing in the international market at this moment. All four of these elements – music, dance, liquid, and hot girls – usually weigh heavily in this type of film. If even an American scholar cannot recognize the distorted version of this sign, however, it is understandable that Brains and his brother are never able to communicate to Americans what they truly expect from them – not only because of their misperception of the Americans but also because of the Americans' misperception of the Chinese or the Taiwanese villagers.

After having learned about his brother's encounter with the soldiers, Brains believes that he failed to attract attention from their army doctors because he lacks knowledge about America. Armed with his proudly acquired knowledge and smartly dressed, Brains confidently looks for an American doctor in order to talk to him in person. Unfortunately, his own communication with the American military doctor is no more fruitful than his brother's previous encounter. When the American doctor gives him ten dollars after having witnessed his brother's severed fingers in the glass jar, Brains angrily and repeatedly protests in Mandarin, "We are not beggars." Questioned by the American military doctor, the interpreter misinterprets Brains' protestation and explains, "They think that ten dollars is too little, considering how rich Americans are, especially because you are a doctor." In other words, the misinterpretation reinforces the doctor's perception of the two brothers as greedy beggars. At this moment, three different languages as well as three different cultures are involved: English, spoken by Americans, representing technological and cultural superiority; Mandarin as the more "cultured" Chinese language despite its subordination to the masters' English; and Taiwanese, which is considered doubly inferior, as a third-world language, and further deemed uncultivated in its official cultural hierarchy. Regardless of how much he admires America, Brains's words are unable to reach the military doctor. The reason is simple: The distance between them is too great. The doctor is the master of the interpreter, and the interpreter considers himself superior to a Taiwanese villager – partly because of his higher position in the internal cultural hierarchy and partly because of his mastery of English. As Frantz Fanon points out: "A man who has a language consequently possesses the world expressed and implied by that language. What we are getting at becomes plain: Mastery of language affords remarkable power."[15] Following the same logic of the colonized, the interpreter who masters the master's language at least partially participates in the superior world inhabited by smart Americans. At the same time, since Brains's predominant language is Taiwanese, he is confined to his village in the eyes of the Mandarin-speaking interpreter or the English-speaking military doctor, regardless of his fantasy of identification with the latter's modernity.

Logically speaking, Brains's unfortunate encounter with his ego-ideal, a true American doctor who is supposedly a master of scientific knowledge, should somewhat shake his unlimited faith in the United States. In fact, although Brains is deeply disappointed, his faith in American power still remains intact. Žižek points out: "An ideology really succeeds when even the facts which at first sight contradict it start to function as arguments in its favor."[16] Despite his inability to make the doctor listen to him, Brains does not doubt for a single moment the miraculous power of American technology. Instead, he now considers his brother's permanent handicap to be caused by a fracture on his father's tombstone. In other words, his brother's misfortune reinforces Brains's faith in traditional astrology as a substitute for American technology. In the final analysis, his faith in American technology is no different from that in Chinese astrology, since both are worshiped as supernatural or/and superhuman forces and are often considered interchangeable. Furthermore, events in the film seemingly reinforce this interchangeability: In an early scene, for example, right after the astrologer predicts the oncoming heavenly wind to Brains's ancestor's tomb, an American helicopter flies low, almost touching his father's tomb, blowing away his paper money offered to his soul.

Nevertheless, unlike all the other villagers, Brains initially refuses to share in stolen goods from the American military base, throwing away a box of cans, which he calls "American shit." Ironically, between the American soldiers at the top of the colonialist chain and the Taiwanese villagers at the bottom, the stolen goods become their only means of contact. By stealing from American soldiers, villagers unconsciously fulfill the perception of them as beggars, because begging and stealing are both symptomatic of economic discrepancy. Since Brains tries to identify with Americans through his own mastery of scientific knowledge, it is difficult for him to accept stealing as his only means of communication with his ego-ideal. At the same time, he cannot persist in his refusal, despite his good will toward Americans, since he too has to steal in order to prove himself to the villagers, including his wife, as one of their own. As he wants to demonstrate his own distinction from the rest of villagers, the object that deserves his effort must have a distinguished quality, "an A-bomb" for example, as Brains repeatedly tells his disrespectful wife. Following his promise and helped by his brother, Brains proudly brings back two large metal boxes, which in his eyes are big enough to contain atomic bombs. To his disappointment, when villagers open the boxes, they find two corpses, one black and one white American soldier, covered with dry ice. Ironically, what Brains obtains from Americans – even through thievery – is not an A-bomb, symbol of their unlimited (technological) power, but death itself. Furthermore, by stealing these metal boxes, Brains inadvertently fulfils their perception of him as an economically and morally inferior being – either a beggar or a thief.

The villagers' communication with Americans are also tinged by traditional Chinese astrology. Two bowls of rice, with two pairs of chopsticks on top, are offered to the soldiers' souls in front of the metal coffins – as if they were Chinese ancestors. Villagers refuse to let Brains bury the two corpses near the school because they "cannot understand Chinese exorcists in case their souls are wandering around." After Brains and his brothers have brought the coffins back to the road, near the military base, they pray for the soldiers' souls in a traditional Chinese way. Meanwhile, the brother also imitates American TV detective series by erasing fingerprints from the metal coffins.

Instead of receiving a powerful weapon from his encounter with Americans, Brains obtained death – not only two dead bodies stolen from the military base, but the death of his brother's severed fingers, death of their hope, and death of his hard-earned respect from the other villagers. At the beginning, when Brains stands before them, everyone is silent in order to listen to him, as if he were indeed the "brains of the village." By the film's end, he has become a laughing-stock – his brother has to fight a group of people in an (unsuccessful) attempt to protect his reputation. Brains remains so powerless that he does not even rise from his bed to stop the villagers despite his wife's warning that they may be killing his brother. Ironically, the "death" that he steals from the military base only further proves to him the superiority of the American superpower, since even "their coffins are made in metal," as he explains to his wife. For this reason, he insists on sending his son to the United States in the future. In other words, if he himself cannot communicate with Americans in his lifetime, his descendant should eventually be able to identify with them in the place of the father.

STICKS AND TANKS

Contrary to Brains, who is so eager to communicate with Americans, the villagers are indifferent toward them, unless their interests are at stake. A brief anecdote prior to the arrival of American soldiers summarizes this relationship. When a truck preparing for their arrival twice prevents a tractor driver from going to the side to urinate, the driver curses them for not "attacking the mainland." In the eyes of these villagers, the only useful function for soldiers in Taiwan, be they American or Chinese, is to fight against the mainland communist government. At the beginning of the film, after having overheard that government officials told the school principal to keep a certain "state secret" from his students, several schoolchildren believe that the government will indeed attack mainland China; but to their surprise, they unravel the "state secret" by themselves, because they run into a construction site right after this news. There, construction workers are building a nightclub – or "whorehouse," to use a child's expression – for American soldiers. Ironically, the slogan of attacking the mainland in this film associates soldiers with an action that trivializes their function, whether it be hindering a villager from releasing his bladder or indulging in their own sexual excess. The only linguistic communication between the villagers and the soldiers consists of two English expressions: the "Hello" taught by the schoolmaster along with artificial expressions and gestures, and "Hey you," which American soldiers use to address villagers disdainfully. Both are interjections, one polite and the other impolite; at the same time, isolated, they are meaningless. Likewise, the villagers' perception of the Americans is empty, free from any significance. Furthermore, it is distorted – just like the backward letters initially painted on the nightclub by a contractor who does not read English. Things from the military base sometimes reach villagers: cans, contraceptives, disks, and a magazine in which "American women do not wear panties." These scattered objects form a fragmented picture of "the American," one that differs greatly from the flattering descriptions of the official discourse or Brains's enthusiastic praises, although those are equally distorted.

If for Brains America stands for technology, knowledge, and progress – in short, modernity – for the villagers, who are mostly illiterate, American soldiers are seen at a much more literal level. In other words, the soldiers stand for what they are seen as in the village. Besides other useful or useless goodies that villagers steal from the base, tanks are the most visible objects associated with the American presence in this film. Furthermore, these are also directly responsible for the villagers' economic loss, since they destroy crops and crush tombs scattered in the field in the process of war games. Instead of symbolizing unlimited American power – as Brains might have understood it – to villagers these armored vehicles are like incomprehensible but harmful mechanical beasts.

In order to prevent the tanks from disturbing their lives, the villagers try to beat them with sticks. After a confrontation, most villagers give up direct conflict and resort to indirect means – thievery – since they realize that their sticks are no match for the tanks. However, the villager who first started using a stick to communicate in this way never ceases to do so until after the American soldiers depart. This person, Granny, is in a sense portrayed as the true heroine of the film, albeit with a comic twist.[17] Granny is the only one who is beyond all linguistic and cultural confusions – by simply refusing to speak any language that she does not understand. Her only means of communication with the Americans and their followers is her stick: It speaks for her against whoever contributes to the American settlement in the village, which disturbs the normal course of her life. With the stick, she beats both a Taiwanese soldier and her own nephew Brains, for their support for the American military base in the village. When she realizes that tanks crushed some tombs in some other people's field, and that her husband's tomb may also suffer the same fate, Granny immediately decides to use her stick to protect her dead husband from the ravages of these tanks. She stays in front of her husband's tomb day and night, sleeping in a small tent and eating food from a lunchbox brought by her grandnephew Asong. Whenever she hears the tanks, she stands up and runs left and right to chase them out of her field with her stick. Since the American soldiers do not know how to deal with this stubborn old lady, they in the end must spare her husband's tomb, as well as her family's cabbage patch, in order to avoid crushing her. In this sense, Granny with her stick uses exactly the same language as American soldiers with their tanks, a wordless language that is incomprehensibly threatening and annoying. Inadvertently, Granny returns the tanks' language by assuming its inherent logic.

As noted earlier, the film's Chinese title, *Taiping tianguo,* literally translates as "Peaceful Heavenly Kingdom," the name of the empire of rebellious peasants against the Qing dynasty in mid-nineteenth-century China, partially inspired by their unorthodox Christian beliefs. Hong Xiuquan, the leader of this kingdom, was also the hero of Sun Zhongshan, father of the Republic of China, whose Three People's Principles (*sanmin zhuyi*) has served as an important part of the state ideology for the Nationalist government. In fact, Hong's slogan "Rebelling against the Qing [Manchu] to Restore the Ming [Han Chinese]" (*fan Qing fu Ming*) had partly inspired Sun's idea of nationalist revolution in his youth. Peasant rebellion in the film is barely noticeable, however, except at the rather comic level represented by Granny. Granny, a childless and uneducated widow, lives in the household of her nephew, Brains. In terms of gender, education, and class, she occupies the position of subaltern par excellence.[18] As a subaltern, her body is turned into a comic spectacle, which at the same time speaks for chastity (a great female virtue in the traditional patriarchy) as well as the otherwise silenced national pride (a modern patriarchal value). Uneducated and confined in her idiosyncratic world, Granny is "uncontaminated" by the discourse of modernity. In other words, she represents a past, a zero degree of modernity, which seems to suggest an alternative to the implicit logic of the "universal" cultural hierarchy implied in the discourse. Nevertheless, the return to this past is no longer either possible or desirable, however much the film tries to show her in a relatively positive light. On the one hand, anyone still in Granny's position at the beginning of the twenty-first century is certainly much more "contaminated" by modern technology and globalization, taking into consideration the current life-style in

Taiwan. On the other hand, Granny's alleged "purity" is in fact a reversed mirror image of the dichotomy of the modern West and the traditional East – part of the orientalist component in the discourse of modernity – as in the case of opposition between Western technology and Chinese astrology. Furthermore, this purity can be reached only through the body language of a subaltern, which is both idealized and yet ridiculed in the film. However, the film seems to problematize the cultural hierarchy more effectively from a different angle: through its ironic and critical portrayal of the native intellectual, Brains.

Who is Brains? As the only educated native in the village, Brains represents a "self-mockery" (to use Wu's own expression) of the director, or of local intelligentsia, caught between his traditions and his desire to identify with modernity and progress. In the "universal" discourse of modernity, these two forces have constantly been associated with the West, largely because of Western science and technology. In this sense, Brains's statement, "All smart people nowadays want to become American," is no longer as laughable as it first appeared because it has been embedded in the implicit logic of the "universal" discourse of modernity. Technological advances are expressions of modernity, which supposedly measure the level of cultural excellence. Following this fetishistic logic,[19] citizens of the most technologically powerful country, the United States, are supposedly "the smartest" people in the world.

By contrasting Brains's idealized images of Americans with the presence of American soldiers in his village, the film undermines a fundamental logic in the discourse of modernity. This capitalistic logic, which equates technological development with cultural excellence, sustains the orientalist component in the discourse. Various versions of this discourse are embedded in school systems in different countries. Like Brains, none of us can be immune to the influence of this logic. At the same time, the film also demystifies the function of third-world intellectuals in their relations to this discourse. They are not necessarily innocent victims or even bystanders. In their eagerness to modernize their own countries, native intellectuals, like Brains, have often inadvertently played important roles in spreading the orientalist component of the discourse of modernity in their own countries – relying upon their credibility among their own peoples. Lu Xun, the well-known May Fourth radical intellectual, for example, suggested that Chinese youth not read any Chinese books.[20] On the other side of the ideological spectrum, Hu Shi, a May Fourth humanist scholar, told his "young [Chinese] friends": "We must admit that we are inferior in everything, not only in terms of material possession and technological development, but also in terms of political institution, morality, knowledge, literature, music, arts, and physical health."[21] In other words, both intellectuals, despite their ideological and political differences, implicitly accept the imperialistic cultural logic: The West is the source of universal standards and measurements for different aspects in a society, from human nature to cultural product. Like Brains among his fellow villagers, these intellectuals, thanks to their important positions in their own culture, have been among the most influential thinkers for the Chinese from generation to generation. As a matter of fact, as in Brains's case, in the process of promoting modernization and reform, they have also inadvertently contributed to sustaining and universalizing the orientalist component of the discourse of modernity. This logic is largely responsible for sustaining the cultural hierarchy between the East and the West, initially a by-product of Western imperialist expansion. That hierarchy, thanks in part to the endorsement of well-meaning third-world intellectuals like Brains, still plays an important role in the ideological superstructure and collective political unconsciousness in third-world countries.

What Wu's film succeeds in doing is to point out the absurd logic sustaining this cultural hierarchy. After all, one does not need to become American to remain smart even in "our space age," or to idealize Granny to resist their imperialist power: American soldiers and Taiwanese villagers are neither superior nor inferior to each other, despite different stages of technological development in their respective societies at this particular historical moment.

EPILOGUE

More than a century and a half has passed since the First Opium War. During this time, China and Taiwan have rapidly modernized economically, culturally, and ideologically, while following separate paths. This is especially true since the communist victory in 1949. Modernization means changes at different levels. Economic, political, and social changes, which destabilized traditional cultures, have led to formations of new axiological systems. On the surface, these systems bear little resemblance to their respective pasts, although they may be haunted on deeper levels by what has happened historically. Since the formation of a cultural identity largely depends on how people view and relate to their cultural heritages, Chinese cultural identity, after several decades of political segregation between the mainland and Taiwan, has often taken different forms on the two sides of the Taiwan Strait.

The expression "discourse of modernity" here includes various versions of Western enlightenment concepts. These concepts, especially social Darwinist theory, which were imported to China at the turn of the twentieth century, influenced modern Chinese thinkers across a vast ideological spectrum. During the first half of the century, the importation of these ideas triggered various revolutions and reforms (for example, the Nationalist Revolution in 1911 and the New Culture movement that soon followed). These revolutions and reforms brought a sea change to China and its culture(s). The Nationalist and Communist parties, as the two main political forces in China since the beginning of the twentieth century, have governed their respective territories with nearly opposite ideological agendas. Along with other external and internal forces, these parties have, in their separate ways (both in their ideological trends and their reactions to events), contributed to changing Chinese culture considerably, to the extent that modern Chinese cultures have definitely become plural.

Here, there is one point I would like to emphasize: Although I have juxtaposed films made in Taiwan and mainland China in this book, I have no intention of equating their vastly different cultural, economic, political, and ideological experiences. On the contrary, through close readings of these films, I have tried to show how two cultures, despite their roughly common language and origin, have taken two entirely different paths to modernity, while redefining new cultural identities in almost unrelated ways. Consequently, Chinese cultural identity acquires different meanings partly in accordance with its geopolitical locations. At the same time, despite different versions of modernization processes, the cultural hierarchy and Eurocentrism inherent in the discourse of modernity still shape ways of thinking on both sides of the Taiwan Strait.

The works I have chosen to examine in this book can be considered products of the late stages of modernization, thanks to cinema's intimate relationships with technology in general and these works' emphasis on formal experiments in particular. While studying these films, I have greatly enjoyed their daring formal innovations as well as their critical edge regarding dominant ideologies. At the same time, I have also realized to what extent these works remain limited by one element that they inherited from the discourse of modernity: the cultural hierarchy of East and West. Social Darwinism, which tends to equate technological development with cultural excellence, has shaped the thinking of previous generations of modern Chinese intellectuals. At the beginning of the twenty-first century, its influence is still visible in both Taiwan and mainland China. This influence may take different forms – cultural nihilism or cultural pride. The latter form associates the East with a spiritual past and the West with the materialistic present. In other words, modernity, be it beneficial or destructive, belongs to the West, whereas the East has little to contribute to it except its forlorn past. In this context, Western culture still remains the source of the universal standards by which the modern world is judged. Wu Nianzhen's *Buddha Bless America,* analyzed in Chapter 7, however, represents an emerging postcolonial consciousness among nonwestern intellectuals, who have begun to question the dominance of this fetishist logic.

Cultural identity appears to be increasingly shifting in the era of globalization, since it has constantly been redefined by recent changes. Partly because of the difference in the attitudes toward their cultural traditions, Chinese identity on the two sides of the Taiwan Strait is expressed in different forms. The first two parts of this book study works of two mainland and two Taiwan directors, whose films (especially the earlier ones) are characterized by formal innovations.

As rebellious offspring of the May Fourth movement and the Communist Revolution, the Fifth Generation directors, such as Chen Kaige and Tian Zhuang-zhuang, demonstrated in their works an uneasiness vis-à-vis their past, whether defined as traditional or as communist, since modernity in this context often implies a fundamental rupture from traditional China. Furthermore, Mao Zedong's revolution was a radical attempt at modernizing China, particularly at an ideological level, through communist ideology. This ideological modernization can be summarized by Mao's famous concept of "continuous revolution" (*buduan geming*), which expresses a longing for constant change. The Cultural Revolution, Mao's last grandiose political gesture, epitomizes this idea. Mao initially intended to destroy anything related to the past through this revolution. The movement started with the "destruction of the four olds" (*po sijiu*) in order to build a brand-new world. The "four olds" include "old ideas, old culture, old customs, and old habits" (*jiu sixiang, jiu wenhua, jiu fengsu, jiu xiguan*). Mao's idea, however, was not new, since it had been shared, to differing degrees, by many May Fourth radical intellectuals at the beginning of the twentieth century.[1] Instead of creating a "communist paradise" characterized by "unlimited material wealth and spiritual civility," however, this cultural nihilist practice resulted in a decade of social and political chaos, which led to poverty, terror, and disillusionment with the communist ideology among the Chinese.

As former Red Guards as well as victims of this movement, Chen and Tian are children of the Cultural Revolution. Ironically, this generation of former Red Guards, who are now thoroughly disillusioned with the Communist Revolution, in fact pushed Mao's logic to its extreme. Mao encouraged young people to question any authority. At the same time, although he never explicitly stated this, his own authority remained unquestionable: Those who questioned it would lose their political and personal freedom during the Cultural Revolution, being labeled as enemies of the people. As representatives of the first generation of post–Cultural Revolution filmmakers, Chen and Tian in their early works precisely tried to question any authority, including Mao's own. In their iconoclastic world, they could no longer find any firm ground, either in the Confucian tradition or in the communist ideology. Consequently, they looked for marginal spaces and cultures as points of departure for articulating their subversive stances. In order to cut clean from their own traditions, be they communist or Confucian, both filmmakers early in their careers chose to depict either remote regions or minority cultures in order to criticize the mainstream cultural center. Through this spatial movement, they were able to occupy a more "modern" space than that of Mao's ideological modernization.

In the course of modern Chinese history, "traditional China," usually expressed as various forms of past according to collective memories, has become a vague notion. Reconstructed pasts in their turns contribute to reinventing different Chinese cultural identities. Chen and Tian's notion of Chinese tradition was largely defined by Mao's ideological modernization, despite, or more precisely because of, their own subversion of Maoist ideology. At the same time, through their spatial journey, they have also included Mao's modernization program as part of Chinese tradition, which they would like to change. As a result, the Maoist past, especially the Cultural Revolution, has in various ways become an equivalent to an important part of Chinese tradition in their films, through which the cultural identity is redefined.

Across the strait, Taiwan can be regarded as a belated model of successful modernization for a non-Western region. At the same time, a high price has been paid for this success. The government's reliance on Western (especially U.S.) investments and its single-minded focus on rapid economic development have often worked to the detriment of other areas, such as ecological preservation and cultural continuity. In this sense, Taiwan's situation is similar to that of other Asian countries, such as Malaysia, Singapore, the Philippines, and South Korea, whose economic successes have often been paralleled by radical changes in value systems and personal relationships. Cai Mingliang, a new-wave Taiwan director of a slightly younger generation than those studied in this book, was born and raised in Malaysia. He has noted: "Deprived of a long-term plan, the [Taiwan] government does not pay attention to ecological and cultural environments, which have been continuously undermined and destroyed. Can such a high-priced miracle be used as example [for other Asian nations]?"[2] These changes have created a sense of loss among local peoples, despite the relative improvement of living standards. Partly to overcome the sense of loss, Hou Xiaoxian in his films often searches for a new identity through the indigenous past, in the midst of the changing world. This past is personified by a father figure, which reveals the patriarchal nature of his search. Edward Yang, by contrast, portrays modernity as a homeless state. Rapid urbanization and commercialization in Taiwan brought radical changes in the traditional value system. Traditional family ties and personal relationships have gradually been replaced by an abstract symbol: money.

To a large extent, Taiwanese society portrayed in films made by Taiwan New Cinema directors, especially Edward Yang, underscores a crucial problem in the Asian model of rapid economic modernization. This process of modernization often proceeded on a faulty basis: The West lives in the present with its technological advance and humanitarian moral superiority, and the East lives in the past with its memory of a spiritual tradition. Consequently, a non-Western subject must implicitly or explicitly break away from his or her past in order to become part of the modern world by adopting the Western scientific and rational value system. As a by-product of this reductive logic, the West also represents material wealth. In other words, the worship of money as a trademark of consumer society also roughly symbolizes the "modern" and "westernized" value system in various developing countries, as it does in Taiwan. Imported along with technology, through its simplification and abstraction, an advanced monetary system transformed a traditional agricultural society into a consumer society. In this process, it also directly or indirectly repressed indigenous values, such as traditional social and family ties often based on kinship, by making them look "irrational" and "impractical." As Yang's films demonstrate, the radical break from the past of local people has left an empty space in their lives, one that cannot be refilled by material wealth. Although the Nationalist government has praised traditional Chinese culture from the very beginning of their settlement in Taiwan, this culture, thus sanctified, has the luster of an object preserved in an orientalist museum. Due to the deliberate omission of the May Fourth movement, the official idealization of traditional Chinese culture indirectly reinforces the dichotomy between the modern West and traditional China, as if the Chinese past, which serves mostly as aesthetic object despite its moral superiority, had little to do with the modern world. Following the same logic, the "modern" space is predominantly Western, the pleasant flavor of traditional Chinese culture notwithstanding.

At the turn of the millennium, Taiwan and mainland China have approached each other culturally. Paradoxically, this rapprochement has been caused more by globalization than by the common cultural origin. Despite its political differences from Taiwan, mainland China has joined other Asian countries by following a road similar to the one that led to Taiwan's economic success. In the same vein, they have tried to attract oversea investments, including a considerable amount from Taiwan entrepreneurs. These entrepreneurs usually consider China as a vast market that does not require foreign-language learning. Along with its investments, Taiwan culture has also become influential on the mainland. Moreover, this influence is not a one-way street. Cultural exchanges between the two regions have become increasingly significant despite constant political clashes at the governmental level. Meanwhile, since the 1990s, mainland and Taiwan filmmakers, who have recently increased their cultural exchanges, have started dealing with a problem that confronts them both: how to face changes brought on by the globalization process, as Part III of this book has demonstrated.

While analyzing films in the present volume, I have tried to pinpoint the influences of the cultural hierarchy and Eurocentrism embedded in the discourse of modernity in the works of these new-wave filmmakers. Nevertheless, I do not intend to criticize them in a judgmental way, but rather to show to what extent this cultural bias still governs their ways of thinking in the era of globalization. The same bias remains influential among third-world intellectuals, including those who have engaged in rethinking their own cultures in relation to globalization critically and self-reflexively. At different levels, I can identify my position with these filmmakers. For decades, postcolonial- and cultural-studies scholars have criticized Eurocentrism. However, as intellectuals coming from third-world cultures and committed to postcolonial and cultural studies ourselves, if we do not identify Eurocentrist influences in our thinking, we often still criticize Eurocentrism from a standpoint situated within the same ideological space. As a result, the West is still the ultimate measurement for the modern world.

As Edward Said notes in his pathfinding work *Orientalism,* the West invented the East as a convenient Other to redefine itself in the midst of imperial expansion. The residue of this invention still remains as influential as ever in the era of globalization. To different degrees, its residual influence still governs our self-perception according to which we have been consciously and unconsciously reinventing ourselves based on the dichotomy between the progressive (materialist) modern West and the backward (spiritual) traditional East. While studying some of the most formally interesting mainland and Taiwan films at the end of the twentieth century, this book also has intended to point out the hidden "white mask" – to borrow Frantz Fanon's expression[3] – which these films as well as ourselves have internalized as part of the discourse of modernity. We need to recognize the existence of this mask in order to remove it. Only then will it be possible to break out of this circle of self-Othering and self-reinventing according to the orientalist images of the East provided by the discourse of modernity. Only then will it be possible to conduct cultural exchanges on a more balanced basis, instead of using the West as the ultimate reference point for modernity.

NOTES

INTRODUCTION

1. For example, Zhou Dunyi, a Confucian scholar of the Song Dynasty, said, "How can writing not carry Tao? It is just as if one decorated a vehicle, but never used it – vain decoration." "Wenci," *Tongshu* (letters).
2. Lu Xun, for example, notes, "Nowadays, the most ingenious theory in literature is art for art's sake. This school, however, was subversive during the May Fourth movement, which at that time attacked 'literature must carry Tao.'" "Helpful Literature and Idle Literature" ("Bangmang wenxue yu banxian wenxue"), *Ji wai ji shiyi, Lu Xun quanji*, vol. 7 (Beijing: Renmin wenxue chubanshe, 1981), pp. 382–4.
3. I use the expression "discourse of modernity" in a broad sense, to refer to various versions of Western ideologies related to Enlightenment, which were imported to China at its early stage of modernization, especially after Yan Fu's translation of Thomas Huxley's *Evolution and Ethics* in 1898. Naturally, these versions have been changing in the course of history.
4. Enrique Dussel, "Beyond Eurocentrism: The World-System and the Limits of Modernity," trans. Eduardo Mendieta, in Fredric Jameson and Masao Miyoshi, eds., *The Cultures of Globalization* (Durham, N.C.: Duke University Press, 1998), pp. 3–31, at 15. In his article, Dussel refers to the American continent as Amerindia to emphasize that this land originally belonged to Native Americans. I adopt his expression because I believe that this forcefully indicates a close tie between modernization and colonization, since America exemplifies modernity in many aspects.
5. Walter D. Mignola, "Globalization, Civilization Processes, and the Relocation of Language and Culture," in ibid., pp. 32–53.
6. Russell Ferguson, "Introduction: Invisible Center," in Russell Ferguson et al., eds., *Out There: Marginalization and Contemporary Culture* (New York: New Museum of Contemporary Art/Cambridge, Mass: MIT Press, 1990), pp. 9–14.
7. John K. Fairbank, Edwin O. Reischauer, and Albert M. Craig, *East Asia: Tradition and Transformation* (Boston: Houghton Mifflin, 1973), p. 460.
8. Ibid., p. 461.
9. Hu Sheng, *From the Opium War to the May Fourth Movement* (*Cong yapian zhanzheng dao wusi yundong*), vol. 1 (Beijing: Renmin wenxue chubanshe, 1981), pp. 25–6. Also see Zhongguo jindaishi bianxie zu (Editorial Board of Modern Chinese History), "The Opium War" ("Yapian zhanzheng"), *Modern Chinese History* (*Zhongguo jindaishi*) (Beijing: Zhonghua shuju, 1979), pp. 1–50.

10. Fairbank et al., "China's Response to the West," *East Asia,* pp. 558–96.
11. James M. Polachek, *The Inner Opium War* (Cambridge, Mass.: Council on East Asian Studies/Harvard University Press, 1992), p. 150.
12. See Toni Morrison's brilliant analysis on this subject in her introduction to *Race-ing Justice, En-gendering Power: Essays on Anita Hill, Clarence Thomas, and the Construction of Social Reality* (New York: Pantheon Books, 1992), pp. vii–xxx.
13. The Three People's Principles of Sun Zhongshan (Sun Yat-sen) and the Nationalist Party are outlined later in this section.
14. Among Western historians, mostly of the younger generation, to have supposedly adopted the "Chinese-centered approach" are, for example, Frederic Wakeman Jr. in his *Strangers at the Gate: Social Disorder in South China, 1839–1861* (Berkeley: University of California Press, 1966), and later Paul Cohen in his *Discovering History in China: American Historical Writing on the Recent Chinese Past* (New York: Columbia University Press, 1984).
15. Prasenjit Duara, *Rescuing History from the Nation: Questioning the Narratives of Modern China* (Chicago: University of Chicago Press, 1995), p. 26.
16. Ibid., p. 49.
17. Polachek, *Inner Opium War,* p. 9.
18. See, for example, Yan Zhongping, ed., *History of Modern Chinese Economy: 1840–1894 (Zhongguo jindai jingjishi: 1840–1894),* vol. 1 (Beijing: Renmin wenxue chubanshe, 1989), p. 1.
19. Karl Marx, *Marx on China: 1853–1860* (London: Lawrence and Wishart, 1951), p. 4.
20. Duara, *Rescuing History,* p. 141.
21. *On the Hunting Ground (Liechang zasa,* 1984) and *Horse Thief (Daoma zei,* 1985), about which see Chapter 2 of the present volume.
22. Marx, *Marx on China,* p. 4. Tianxian bianji (Editorial Board under Heaven [Yin Yunfan et al.]) also quotes Marx in its official two-volume history on Taiwan, *Discovering Taiwan (Faxian Taiwan)* (Taipei: Tianxia zazhi, 1992), vol. 1, p. 148.
23. See Benjamin Schwartz, *In Search of Wealth and Power: Yen Fu and the West* (Cambridge, Mass.: Belknap Press, 1964).
24. Later, Hu Shi softened his initial position somewhat in his essay "Full Universalization and Complete Westernization" ("Chongfen shijie hua yu quanmian xihua"), *Hu Shi wencun,* vol. 4 (Taipei: Yuandong chubanshe, 1953), pp. 541–4.
25. Lu Xun, "Preface to 'Cheering from the Sidelines'" in *Diary of a Madman and Other Stories,* trans. William A. Lyell (Honolulu: University of Hawaii Press, 1990), pp. 21–8, at 27–8.
26. *Hu Shi wencun,* vol. 4, pp. 431–2.
27. James Reeve Pusey, *China and Charles Darwin* (Cambridge, Mass.: Harvard East Asian Monographs, 1983), p. 201.
28. For example, after 1927 women were even killed for carrying physical marks that might associate them with the New Cultural movement, such as unbound feet or bobbed hair. Wendy Larson, *Women and Writing in Modern China* (Stanford: Stanford University Press, 1998), p. 166.
29. Larson provides an extensive description of women's fate in modern China in "Women's Writing and Social Engagement," in ibid., pp. 166–97.
30. Thomas Huxley (Huoxuli), *Evolution and Ethics (Tianyan lun),* trans. Yan Fu (Beijing: Shangwu shudian Beijing faxingshe, 1981) (1st ed., 1898).
31. Li Zehou, *On Modern Chinese History of Thought (Zhongguo jindai sixiangshi)* (Beijing: Renmin wenxue chubanshe, 1979), p. 364.

32. Lin Yü-sheng, *The Crisis of Chinese Consciousness: Radical Antitraditionalism in the May Fourth Era* (Madison: University of Wisconsin Press, 1979), pp. 56–7. Although Lin criticized the "iconoclastic totalism" of May Fourth intellectuals, with a typical "May Fourth" gesture, Lin blamed their ideological standard on traditional Chinese culture and its concept of "universal kinship." Ibid., p. 17.

33. Stuart Hall explains how this fetishistic logic works: "The Falseness therefore arises, not from the fact that the market is an illusion, a trick, a sleight-of-hand, but only in the sense that it is an *inadequate* explanation of a process. It has also substituted one part of the process for the whole – a procedure which, in linguistics, is known as 'metonymy' and in anthropology, psychoanalysis and (with special meaning) in Marx's work, as *fetishism*." Stuart Hall, "The Problem of Ideology: Marxism without Guarantees," in David Morley and Kuan-hsing Chen, eds., *Stuart Hall: Critical Dialogues in Cultural Studies* (London: Routledge, 1996), pp. 25–46, at 37.

34. I have deliberately chosen the masculine pronoun to designate modern Chinese intellectuals for two reasons: First, at the beginning of the twentieth century, women's voices to a great degree were marginalized in the modernization process, despite the crucial allegorical roles that they played in this process. For example, Qiu Jin, the well-known revolutionary at the end of the Qing Dynasty, wrote extensively on feminist issues; yet regardless of her fame, her radical feminist writings were mostly repressed in the official cultures on both sides of the Taiwan Strait. See Amy Dooling and Kristina Torgeson, eds., *Writing Women in Modern China: An Anthology of Women's Literature from the Early Twentieth Century* (New York: Columbia University Press, 1998). Also, during the May Fourth movement, women intellectuals often deliberately chose marginal positions to articulate their own agendas. In the heart of nationalist fervor in the 1930s, Xiao Hong privileged gender issues over those of national salvation in her writings. See Lydia H. Liu, "The Female Body and Nationalist Discourse: Manchuria in Xiao Hong's *Field of Life and Death*," in Angela Zito and Tani E. Barlow, eds., *Body, Subject and Power in China* (Chicago: University of Chicago Press, 1994), pp. 157–77. To a lesser extent, Ding Ling also expressed her feminist agenda at the earlier stage of her writings despite the pressure of the party. See Yi-tsi Mei Feuerwerker, *Ding Ling's Fiction: Ideology and Narrative in Modern Chinese Literature* (Cambridge, Mass.: Harvard University Press, 1982). Since the voice of a woman intellectual was generally either marginalized or dissident due to the essentially patriarchal nature of the modernization process, I have chosen the masculine pronoun to indicate a "modern intellectual." However, the current situation differs a great deal from the beginning of the previous century, although we still cannot say that gender hierarchy has changed fundamentally. Furthermore, due to the dominance of the party's minority discourse, contemporary women intellectuals on the mainland are less inclined to take feminist stances openly (as I explain in Chapter 6). Because of the massive globalization as well as the migration and mobility of Chinese intellectuals, I use the expression "third-world intellectuals" to designate the contemporary Chinese educated class on both sides of the Taiwan Strait.

35. See Jacques Derrida, *Of Grammatology*, trans. Gayatri Chakravorty Spivak (Baltimore: Johns Hopkins University Press, 1976).

36. Jacques Derrida, "Plato's Pharmacy," *Dissemination*, trans. Barbara Johnson (Chicago: University of Chicago Press, 1983), pp. 61–84.

37. Dussel, "Beyond Eurocentrism," p. 19.

38. See, for example, Li Suyuan and Hu Jubin, *History of Chinese Silent Films* (*Zhongguo wusheng dianying shi*) (Beijing: Zhongguo dianying chubanshe, 1996), p. 73.

39. See Ni Zhen's *Memoirs from the Beijing Film Academy: The Early Days of China's Fifth Generation*, trans. Chris Berry (Durham, N.C.: Duke University Press, forthcoming).

40. See Arif Dirlik, *Origins of Chinese Communism* (Oxford: Oxford University Press, 1989).

41. Unfortunately, there are very few available sources in English about Taiwan New Cinema directors. However, one can read books about them in Chinese written by well-known participants in this movement. Xiao Ye (Hsiao Yeh), *The Beginning of a Movement* (*Yige yundong de kaishi*) (Taipei: Shibao wenhua chubanshe, 1986), and Jiao Xiongping, *Taiwan New Cinema* (*Taiwan xin dianying*) (Taipei: Shibao wenhua chubanshe, 1988), are two important works that describe this movement from the outset.

42. See Lin Qixu, *A Synthetic Study of the February 28 Incident in Taiwan* (*Taiwan ererba shijian zonghe yanjiu*) (Long Island, N.Y.: Taiwan Tribune, 1984); and Su Xin, *Angry Taiwan* (*Fennu de Taiwan*) (Taipei: Shibao wenhua chubanshe, 1993).

43. Peng Ruijin, *Forty Year New Literature Movement in Taiwan* (*Taiwan xin wenxue yundong sishi nian*) (Taipei: Zili wanbao, 1991).

44. Sun Zhongshan [Sun Yat-sen], "Second Lecture on Democracy" ("Minquan zhuyi dier jiang"), in *Complete Works of the Father of the Nation* (*Guofu quanshu*) (Taipei: Zhongguo xinwen chuban gongsi, 1960), pp. 221–6.

45. Abdul R. JanMohamed and David Lloyd, "Introduction: Toward a Theory of Minority Discourse: What Is to Be Done?" in JanMohamed and Lloyd, eds., *The Nature and Context of Minority Discourse* (Oxford: Oxford University Press, 1990), pp. 1–16, at 7.

46. Esther Yau, "*Yellow Earth:* Western Analysis and a Non-Western Text," *Film Quarterly* 41(2) (1987–8): 22–33.

47. See, for example, *Wide Angle* 11(2) (1989) and *Camera Obscura* 6 (1989).

48. For example, Chris Berry, ed., *Perspectives on Chinese Cinema* (London: BFI, 1991); and George S. Semsel, ed., *Chinese Film: The State of the Art in the People's Republic* (New York: Praeger, 1987).

49. Rey Chow, *Primitive Passions: Visuality, Sexuality, Ethnography, and Contemporary Chinese Cinema* (New York: Columbia University Press, 1995). Zhang Xudong also devotes to the Fifth Generation half of his recent book *Chinese Modernism in the Era of Reform* (Durham, N.C.: Duke University Press, 1997).

50. Hannah Arendt, *On Violence* (San Diego: Harvest, 1970), pp. 55–6.

51. Fredric Jameson, "Nostalgia for the Present," *South Atlantic Quarterly* 88(2) (1989): 517–37.

52. See, e.g., Alan Stanbrook, "The Worlds of Hou Hsiao-hsien," *Sight and Sound* 59(2) (Spring 1990): 120–4; Tony Rayns, "Lonesome Tonight," *Sight and Sound* n.s. 3(13) (March 1993):14–17; Antoine de Baecque, "Le Temps suspendu," *Cahiers du cinéma* no. 438 (December 1990): 24–8; Thierry Jousse, "Plus de Lumière," *Cahiers du cinéma* no. 454 (April 1992): 25–9; and Jean-François Rauger, "Naissance d'une nation," *Cahiers du cinéma* no. 469 (July 1994): 18–19.

53. For example, *Cinemaya* and *East West Film Journal*.

54. Nick Browne et al., eds., *New Chinese Cinemas: Forms, Identities, Politics* (Cambridge: Cambridge University Press, 1994); Lu Hsiao-peng, ed., *Transnational Chinese Cinemas: Identity, Nationhood, Gender* (Honolulu: University of Hawaii Press, 1997); and Kwok-kan Tam and Wimal Dissanayake, ed., *New Chinese Cinema: Images of Asia* (Oxford: Oxford University Press, 1998).

55. See, for example, Bai Chongxi's statement after the February 28 Incident of 1947, in Lin Qixu, *Synthetic Study,* p. 180.
56. Nikos Papastergiandis, *Dialogues in the Diasporas: Essays and Conversations on Cultural Identity* (London: River Oram Press, 1998), p. 8.
57. Arjun Appadurai, *Modernity at Large: Cultural Dimensions of Globalization* (Minneapolis: University of Minnesota Press, 1996), p. 44.
58. Ferguson, "Introduction: Invisible Center," p. 9.
59. See, for example, Huang Chunming's *I Love Mary* (*Wo ai mali*) (Taipei: Yuanjing chubanshe, 1975), and Wang Zhenho's *Rose, Rose I Love You* (*Meigui meigui wo ai ni*) (Taipei: Yuanjing chubanshe, 1984).

PART I. ON THE CULTURAL AND IDEOLOGICAL MARGINS

1. CONTINUITY AND SUBVERSION

1. Chen Wanying, "Interview with Chen Kaige, Director of *King of the Children, Yellow Earth*" ("Fangwen Chen Kaige, *Haizi wang, Huang tudi* daoyan"), *Playboy* (Chinese ed.) 22 (May 1988): 41–5, at 45.
2. Chen likely had in mind the Taiwanese pamphlet writers Bo Yan and Song Longji.
3. *A Time to Live and a Time to Die* (*Tongnian wanshi*) is based on the director's own memory of this period; *A Summer at Grandpa's* (*Dongdong de jiaqi*), on that of one of his screenwriters, Zhu Tianwen, although the film was shot from the perspective of a boy, not that of a girl; and *Dust in the Wind* (*Lianlian fengchen*), on the recollection of his other scriptwriter, Wu Nianzhen.
4. Chen delivered this public lecture addressing students in my class in Chinese cinema at the University of Minnesota in July 1989.
5. The famous director of an older generation, Lin Zifeng, criticizes the "pictureness" of *Yellow Earth*: "The cinematographic search is dissociated from the content. Cinema is a dynamic art form, different from stage performance, plastic arts, or photography." *Huashuo "Huang tudi"* [*On "Yellow Earth"*] (Beijing: Zhongguo dianying chubanshe, 1986), p. 18. Hu Bingliu argues: "The film has a large number of still shots, which are nevertheless not dull. It's even more unconvincing to compare them with photography. Its moving dynamism resides in its conceptualization of deep and complicated thought behind the fixity of the camera eye. The conceptualization inspires the audience to think about limitless subjects. This is an original movement, a movement of consciousness." Ibid., p. 32.
6. See Chen Wanying, "Interview with Chen Kaige," p. 44.
7. Concerning the relationship between representation and recording in *Yellow Earth,* see Rey Chow, *Primitive Passions: Visuality, Sexuality, Ethnography, and Contemporary Chinese Cinema* (New York: Columbia University Press, 1995).
8. Chen Kaige, "With a Childlike Sincerity" ("Huaizhe yipian zhencheng de chizi zhi xin"), *Huashuo "Huang tudi,"* pp. 264–84, at 278–9.
9. Ibid., p. 280.
10. Ibid., p. 278.
11. Nagisa Oshima singles out this association in his interview with Chen Kaige. "The Dialogue between Chen Kaige and Oshima" ("Chen Kaige yu Dadao zhu de duihua"), in Jiao Xiongping, ed., *Life on a String* (*Bianzou bianchang*) (Taipei: Wanxiang, 1991), pp. 150–72.

12. See Kaja Silverman, *The Acoustic Mirror: The Female Voice in Psychoanalyis and Cinema* (Bloomington: Indiana University Press, 1988), and Michel Chion, *Audio-vision: Sound on Screen,* trans. Claudia Gorbman (New York: Columbia University Press, 1994).

13. Silverman, *Mirror,* p. 64.

14. Ibid., p. 54.

15. Ibid., p. 63.

16. See Stephen Heath, "On Suture," *Questions of Cinema* (Bloomington: Indiana University Press, 1981), pp. 76–112.

17. Rey Chow, "Silent Is the Ancient Plain: Music, Film-Making, and the Concept of Social Change in the New Chinese Cinema," *Discourse* 12(2) (1990): 82–109; reprinted in *Primitive Passions: Visuality, Sexuality, Ethnography, and Contemporary Chinese Cinema* (New York: Columbia University Press, 1995), pp. 79–107, at 97.

18. Ibid.

19. Fredric Jameson, *The Geopolitical Aesthetic: Cinema and Space in the World System* (Bloomington: Indiana University Press, 1992), p. 117.

20. Jameson, *The Seeds of Time* (New York: Columbia University Press, 1994), p. 74.

21. Ibid., pp. 117–19.

22. Millicent Marcus, *Italian Film in the Light of Neorealism* (Princeton: Princeton University Press, 1986), p. 74.

23. "We shot this scene with great passion. When we finished the last shot – waist-drum dancers emerged from the back of the hill – all the comrades in the team applauded enthusiastically – they were so excited as if they were mad. Unfortunately, we didn't have another camera to shoot at this image of the working team." Chen Kaige, "With a Child-like Sincerity," p. 267.

24. Ibid., p. 268.

25. Jameson, *Seeds of Time,* pp. 74–5.

26. Esther Yau, "*Yellow Earth:* Western Analysis and a Non-Western Text," *Film Quarterly* 41(2) (1987–8): 22–33, at 31.

27. Jameson, *Seeds of Time,* p. 90.

28. Kaja Silverman, *Male Subjectivity at the Margins* (New York: Routledge, 1992), p. 34.

29. Slavoj Žižek, *The Metastases of Enjoyment: Six Essays on Woman and Causality* (London: Verso, 1994), pp. 21–2.

30. Silverman, *Male Subjectivity,* p. 50.

31. Chen Kaige, *Tree of Dragon Blood* (*Longxue shu*) (Hong Kong: Tiandi, 1992), p. 133.

32. Žižek, *Metastases of Enjoyment,* p. 17.

33. Ibid., p. 20.

34. Peng Xing'er, "Who Is Able to Observe the World Without Emotion? Using the Ideology of Educated Youth to Explain Chen Kaige's *King of the Children*" ("Shui neng lengyan kan shijie? Yong zhiqing yishi xingtai dujie Chen Kaige de yingpian *Haizi wang*"), *Dangdai dianying* 29 (February 1989): 105–15, at 107.

35. During the Cultural Revolution, all the high schools and colleges were closed because most students, who joined the Red Guards, were to attack capitalistic fortifications, including the educational system itself. Once their tasks were accomplished, most of these youngsters were sent to the countryside in order to be "reeducated" by peasants – as Mao suggested. These youth who moved from big cities to the (usually remote) countryside are called "educated youth."

36. Peng Xing'er, "Who Is Able to Observe . . . ?" p. 107.

37. Chen Kaige, "Life Reflection: Self-Examination" ("Sikao rensheng: shenshi ziwo"), *Dianying yishu cankao ziliao* 183 (1987): 10–30.
38. Su Dongpo (Su Shi), "First Prose Poem on the Red Cliff" ("Qian Chibi fu"), in *Selected Poems of Su Tung-p'o,* trans. Burton Watson (Port Townsend, Wash.: Copper Canyon Press, 1994), pp. 94–6. In his interview, Chen also emphasizes the influence of this prose poem. Ibid., p. 31.
39. Ibid., p. 30.
40. Ibid., p. 19.
41. Chen Wanying, "Interview with Chen Kaige," p. 43.
42. Gilles Deleuze, *Critique et clinique* (Paris: Minuit, 1993), pp. 137–8.
43. Terry Eagleton, "Nationalism: Irony and Commitment," Pamphlet 13 (Derry: Field Day Theatre Company, 1988); reprinted in Terry Eagleton, Fredric Jameson, and Edward W. Said (with an Introduction by Seamus Deane), *Nationalism, Colonialism, and Literature* (Minneapolis: University of Minnesota Press, 1990), pp. 23–42, at 29.
44. Chen Kaige, "Life Reflection," p. 28.
45. Rey Chow, *Primitive Passions,* p. 131.
46. Chen Kaige, *Tree of Dragon Blood.*
47. Chen Kaige, "Life Reflection," p. 28.
48. Rey Chow, *Primitive Passions,* p. 137.
49. Li Tong, "Questions and Answers on *King of the Children* at Canne" ("*Haizi wang* gena dawen"), *Dangdai dianying* 28 (June 1988): 57–9, at 58–9.
50. Lu Xun, "Diary of a Madman," in *Diary of a Madman and Other Stories,* trans. William A. Lyell (Honolulu: University of Hawaii Press, 1990), pp. 29–41, at 41.
51. Chen Kaige, "Life Reflection," p. 28.
52. See an interesting explanation regarding this subject in Chow's *Primitive Passions,* pp. 127–8.
53. See Žižek, *Sublime Object of Ideology,* pp. 206–7. Concerning the interpretation of this passage, see also Rey Chow, *Primitive Passion,* p. 130.

2. ALLEGORICAL AND REALISTIC PORTRAYALS OF THE CULTURAL REVOLUTION

1. Melvyn Goldstein and I had our phone conversation on December 10, 1998.
2. In an informal interview with me in August 1993 in Beijing, Tian repeatedly expressed this idea.
3. Gina Marchetti, "Two from China's Fifth Generation: Interviews with Chen Kaige and Tian Zhuangzhuang," *Continuum* 2(1) (1988–9): 128–34, at 134.
4. See Tian's interview with Zhang Wei, "Talking about Zhuangzhuang with Zhuangzhuang" ("Yu Zhuangzhuang tan Zhuangzhuang"), *Dangdai dianying* 29 (January 1989): 37–44, at 38.
5. Marchetti, "Two from China's Fifth Generation," p. 134.
6. Name of the Father (*nom-du-père*). This concept derives, in a sense, from the mythical, symbolic father of Freud's *Totem and Taboo.* In terms of Lacan's three orders, it refers neither to the real father, nor to the imaginary father (the paternal imago), but to the symbolic father. Freud, says Lacan, was led irresistibly "to link the appearance of the signifier of the Father, as the author of the Law, to death, even to the murder of the Father, thus showing that although this murder is the fruitful moment of the debt through which the subject binds himself for life to the Law, the symbolic Father, in so far as he signifies this Law, is certainly the dead Father." Alan Sheridan, translator's notes to Jacques Lacan, *Écrits: A Selection* (New York: W. W. Norton, 1977), p. 11.

7. For example, so-called Wound Literature, which prevailed during the late 1970s, focuses on traumatic experiences of individuals during the Cultural Revolution. Most Wound Literature heroes are depicted as innocent victims tyrannized by bad officials or Red Guards in an overly melodramatic way.

8. Chen Kaige, *Tree of Dragon Blood* (*Longxue shu*) (Hong Kong: Tiandi, 1992), p. 85.

9. See Xiao Ye, "Debate on *Horse Thief*" ("*Daoma zei* bianlun"), *Dianying yishu* 186 (July 1986): 3–24.

10. Yang Ping, "A Director Who Is Trying to Change the Audience: A Chat with Young Director Tian Zhuangzhuang," *Continuum* 2(1) (1988–9): 109, 111, 113; reprinted in Chris Berry, ed., *Perspectives on Chinese Cinema* (Worcester: Trinity Press /London: BFI, 1991), 127–30, at 128.

11. Tian told me this anecdote during our conversation in August 1993.

12. Liu Shusheng, "The Religious Mood in *Horse Thief* " ("*Daoma zei* de zongjiao qingxu"), *Yingshi wenhua* 6 (March 1993): 88–108, p. 105.

13. Ibid., p. 93.

14. Xiao Ye, "Debate," p. 15.

15. Slavoj Žižek, *The Sublime Object of Ideology* (London: Verso, 1989), p. 97.

16. Ibid.

17. Ibid., p. 37.

18. Chen made this statement in a conversation with me during a visit to Minneapolis in August 1989.

19. See Laura Mulvey, "Visual Pleasure and Narrative Cinema," *Screen* 16(3) (1975): 8–18; reprinted in *Visual and Other Pleasures* (Bloomington: Indiana University Press, 1989), pp. 14–26.

20. Xiao Ye, "Debate," p. 15.

21. Liu Shusheng, "Religious Mood," p. 107.

22. Rey Chow, *Writing Diaspora: Tactics of Intervention in Contemporary Cultural Studies* (Bloomington: Indiana University, 1993), p. 61.

23. E. T. A. Hoffmann, "The Sand Man," from *Eight Tales of Hoffmann*, trans. J. M. Cohen (London: Pan Books, 1952); originally in *Nachtstücke*, 2 vols., 1816–17.

24. Chow, *Writing Diaspora*, p. 62.

25. In August 1993, I interviewed Tian Zhuangzhuang in Beijing.

26. Marchetti, "Two from China's Fifth Generation," p. 134.

27. During this period, Tian made four films: *The Street Players* (*Gushu yiren*, 1987), *Rock Kids* (*Yaogun qingnian*, 1988), *The Imperial Eunuch* (*Da taijian Li Lianying*, 1990), and *Unforgettable Life* (*Teshu shoushushi*, 1992).

28. According to my interview with him in Beijing.

29. "Ce que je recherche, dans notre tradition, ce sont les évocations des rapports entre l'individu et un pouvoir. Comment un pouvoir naît, se développe. Comment, inévitablement, il est amené à porter atteinte à l'expression, comme un jardinier taille un arbre." "Le Fils du dragon: Un Cinéaste de la cinquième génération: Tian Zhuangzhuang," *Cahiers du cinéma* no. 392 (1987): 63–4, at 63.

30. Tian mentioned this in his interview with me in August 1993. Also see Robert Sklar, "People and Politics, Simple and Direct: An Interview with Tian Zhuangzhuang," *Cinéaste* 20 (April 1994): 36–8.

31. See Chapter 5 of the present volume.

32. "Tian Zhuangzhuang, Fifth Generation Director," in George S. Semsel, ed., *Chinese Film: The State of the Art in the People's Republic* (New York: Praeger, 1987), pp. 128–34, at 132.

33. As I noted earlier in the text, the Tibetan actor who played Norbu felt reluctant to act as the evil river ghost in one of the religious rituals due to his fear of the possible perception among his fellow Tibetans prompted by this performance. Tian told me this anecdote in order to show how truthfully these rituals in the film were portrayed. However, the usually timid director did not seem to hesitate to impose his views in this respect.

34. See Étienne Balibar, "Racism and Nationalism," in Étienne Balibar and Immanuel Wallerstein, *Race, Nation, Class: Ambiguous Identities,* trans. Chris Turner (London: Verso, 1991), pp. 37–67, at 50.

35. An expression to indicate films on remote regions, mainly the countryside in the northern and western parts of China. Since transportation conditions and natural and cultural environments are often unusually difficult, only a relatively small peasant population, either Han majority or non-Han minority, live there.

36. See Zhang Yinjun, "From 'Minority Film' to 'Minority Discourse': Questions of Nationhood and Ethnicity in Chinese Film Studies," *Cinema Journal* 36(3) (Spring 1997): 73–90.

37. See Esther Yau, "Is China the End of Hermeneutics? Or, Political and Cultural Usage of Non-Han Women in Mainland Chinese Films," *Discourse* 11(2) (1989): 115–36; reprinted in Diane Carson, Linda Dittmar, and Janice R. Welsch, eds., *Multiple Voices in Feminist Film Criticism* (Minneapolis: University of Minnesota Press, 1994), pp. 280–92.

38. Balibar, "Racism and Nationalism," p. 50.

39. See Prasenjit Duara, *Rescuing History From the Nation: Questioning the Narratives of Modern China* (Chicago: University of Chicago Press, 1995), p. 139–44.

40. Zhang Chengzhi, a Chinese writer who returned to his Muslim roots later in life, wrote the novel *History of the Soul* (*Xinling shi*) (Guangzhou: Huacheng chubanshe, 1991), in which he described the ethnic conflicts between the Han government and Muslim rebels in the Qing dynasty and the Republic period.

PART II. IN SEARCH OF TRADITION IN THE MIDST OF MODERNIZATION

3. FROM A VOICELESS FATHER TO A FATHER'S VOICE

1. Jiao Xiongping, "The Tie to the Mainland in Taiwanese Cinema" ("Taiwan dianying de dalu qingjie"), *Jintian* 17 (February 1992): 84–93, at 92.

2. See, for example, Bai Chongxi's statement after the February 28 Incident of 1947, in Lin Qixu, *A Synthetic Study of the February 28 Incident in Taiwan* (*Taiwan ererba shijian zonghe yanjiu*) (Long Island, N.Y.: Taiwan Tribune, 1984), p. 180.

3. Shi Ming's *The Four-Hundred-Year History of the Taiwanese* (*Taiwan ren sibai nian shi*) was first published in 1962 in Japanese, and the revised Chinese version was first published in 1980 (San Jose, Calif.: Paradise Culture Associates, 1980). Zhang Yanxian, "New Spirit in the Research on Taiwan History" ("Taiwan shi yanjiu de xin jingshen"), in *Taiwan shiliao yanjiu* 1 (February 1993): 76–86, at 83.

4. Peng Ruijin, "Return to Realism and the Native Soil Movement (1970–1979)" ("Fan xiezhen yu bentu hua yundong [1970–1979]"), in *Forty Year New Literature Movement in Taiwan* (*Taiwan xin wenxue yundong sishi nian*) (Taipei: Zili wanbao, 1991), pp. 149–94.

5. Xie Renchang, "Hou Xiaoxian on *Puppetmaster:* A Report in the Process of My Life"

("Hou Xiaoxian tan *Ximeng rensheng:* wo shengming guocheng de yige baogao"), *Dianying xinshang* 64 (July–August 1993): 46–62, at 55.

6. Ibid.

7. Lan Bozhou, *Sinking Bodies, Exile, February 28 Incident (Chenshi liuwang, ererba)* (Taipei: Shibao wenhua chubanshe, 1992).

8. Gilles Deleuze, *Critique et clinique* (Paris: Minuit, 1993), p. 11.

9. Lu Kuang, "A Film Not Fitting Its Title?: Space and Narration in *City of Sadness*" ("Liti de dianying: *Beiqing chengshi* de kongjian yu xushi"), in Mi Zou and Liang Xinhua, eds., *The Death of the New Cinema: From "All for Tomorrow" to "City of Sadness"* (*Xin dianying zhi si: cong "Yiqie wei mingtian" dao "Beiqing chengshi"*) (Taipei: Tang-shan chubanshe, 1991), 141–7.

10. Jiao Xiongping, "*City of Sadness:* A Tentative Epic of Taiwan History" ("*Beiqing chengshi:* shifu Taiwan shishi"), in *Authors and Types in Taiwan and Hong Kong Cinemas (Tai gang dianying zhong de zuozhe yu leixing)* (Taipei: Yuanliu, 1991), pp. 48–59, at 56.

11. Zhu Tianwen, "Thirteen Questions on *City of Sadness*" ("*Beiqing chengshi* shisan wen"), *Jintian* 17 (February 1992): 94–110, at 109.

12. Concerning the function of actions in the narrative, see, for example, Brigitte Peuker's discussion on Griffith's films ("Miscegenation and the Sister Arts: Griffith's *Broken Blossoms*") in her *Incorporating Images: Film and the Rival Arts* (Princeton: Princeton University Press, 1995), 57–66, at 61.

13. Huang Jianye, "*City of Sadness:* Hushed Requiem on the Porch of History"("*Beiqing chengshi:* lishi menlang zhong yinya de anhun qu"), in *Pursuit of Humanistic Films (Renwen dianying de zhuiqiu)* (Taipei: Yuanliu, 1990), 81–4, at 83; Yang Mingmin, "*City of Sadness* under the Photos/Visual Images" ("Zhaopian/yingxiang xia de *Beiqing chengshi*"), in Mi and Liang, eds., *Death of the New Cinema*, 148–52, at p. 152.

14. Xie Renchang, "Hou Xiaoxian on *Puppetmaster,*" p. 48.

15. Ibid., p. 60.

16. During my informal interview with Hou Xiaoxian, he twice mentioned how much he admires Li Tianlu's pure Taiwanese. According to Hou, even Wu Nianzhen, who spoke Taiwanese almost perfectly, could not compare with Li's Minnan dialect.

17. Li Tianlu, *Life as Performance: Li Tianlu's Memoir (Ximeng rensheng: Li Tianlu hu-yilu)*, ed. Zeng Yuwu (Taipei: Yuanliu, 1991), p. 128.

18. Xie Renchang, "Hou Xiaoxian on *Puppetmaster,*" p. 46.

19. Ibid.

20. In my interviews with Taiwanese filmmakers and film critics, such as Wu Nianzhen and Li Yu, they all mentioned this father–son bond. In fact, Wu once described Li as a father figure for their whole group. Hou himself also said on different occasions that Li was like a father to him.

21 Benedict Anderson, *Imagined Communities* (London: Verso, 1983), p. 36.

4. MELODRAMA OF THE CITY

1. Georg Simmel, *The Philosophy of Money (Philosophie des Geldes)*, trans. Tom Bottomore and David Frisby (London: Routledge, 1991) (first German edition, 1900).

2. I have chosen to use the masculine pronoun in this context because of Simmel's original patriarchal implication.

3. Ibid., p. 236.

4. Ibid., p. 296.
5. Ibid., p. 335.
6. Huang Jianye, *Studies of Edward Yang's Films* (*Yang Dechang dianying yanjiu*) (Taipei: Yuanliu, 1995), p. 44.
7. Stuart Hall in David Morley and Kuan-hsing Chen, eds., *Stuart Hall: Critical Dialogues in Cultural Studies* (London: Routledge, 1996), p. 436.
8. Li Bo, "Ch'ang-kan Village Song" ("Changgan xing"), trans. David Hinton, *Selected Poems of Li Po* (New York: New Directions, 1996), pp. 12–13.
9. For example, another of Yang's films, *Gulingjie shaonian sharen shijian*, literally translated as "Murder Case by a Youngster on Guling Street," has the English title *A Brighter Summer Day*, and his *Duli shidai*, literally "Independence Era," is retitled *Confucius's Confusion*. Likewise, Hou Xiaoxian's *Tongnian wangshi*, literally "Reminiscence of My Childhood," is called *A Time to Live and a Time to Die* in English. His *Ximeng rensheng*, literally "Life as Performance and Dream," has the English title *The Puppet-master*.
10. As Huang Jianye mentions: "This is a story about the city" ("*Qingmei zhuma:* Yang Dechang de Taipei gushi"), in *Pursuit of Humanistic Films* (*Renwen dianying de zhuiqiu*) (Taipei: Yuanliu, 1990), pp. 89–91, at 89.
11. See Wei Qing, "*Taipei Story:* Edward Yang's Cultural Reflection" ("*Qingmei zhuma:* Yang Dechang de wenhua fanxing"), *Dianying yishu* 2 (1992): 79–85, at 80.
12. Slavoj Žižek, *The Indivisible Remainder: An Essay on Schelling and Related Matters* (London: Verso, 1996), p. 4.
13. Simmel, *Philosophy of Money*, p. 301.
14. See Huang Jianye, "*Terrorizers:* Crisis of Complicity among City Dwellers" ("*Kongbu fenzi:* duhui gongfan de weiji"), *Studies of Edward Yang's Films*, pp. 127–49, at 136.
15. Ibid., p. 135.
16. Here, I use the term "melodramatic" by borrowing Thomas Elsaesser's definition: "Considered as an expressive code, melodrama might therefore be described as a particular form of dramatic mise en scene, characterized by a dynamic use of spatial and musical categories, as opposed to intellectual or literary ones." Thomas Elsaesser, "Tales of Sound and Fury: Observations on the Family Melodrama," *Monogram* 4 (1972): 2–15; reprinted in Christine Gledhill, ed., *Home Is Where the Heart Is: Studies in Melodrama and the Woman's Film* (London: BFI, 1987), pp. 43–69, at 51.
17. Fredric Jameson, *The Geopolitical Aesthetic: Cinema and Space in the World System* (Bloomington: Indiana University Press, 1992), p. 120.
18. In terms of "supplement," see Jacques Derrida, trans. Gayatri Chakravorty Spivak, *Of Grammatology* (Baltimore: Johns Hopkins University Press, 1976), p. 145.
19. Huang Jianye, "*Terrorizers,*" p. 136.
20. See Chapter 3 of the present volume.
21. Yang Dechang, "Interview with Yang Dechang" ("Yang Dechang fangwen ji"), in Huang Jianye, *Studies of Edward Yang's Films*, 187–244, at 226.
22. Fredric Jameson, "Postmodernism and Consumer Society," *Amerikastudien/American Studies* 29(1) (1984): 55–73; reprinted in in John Belton, ed., *Movies and Mass Culture* (New Brunswick: Rutgers University Press, 1996), pp. 185–202, at 190.
23. Yang Dechang expressed a hope in his promotional materials for *Confucius's Confusion* that his film would remind the audience of Woody Allen. Huang Jianye, *Studies*, p. 175.
24. "Affection between the father and son, righteousness between the ruler and his subjects, difference between the husband and wife, respect for elders, trust between friends."

"Teng Wengong," pt. I, Mengzi, *Mencius (Mengzi),* in Guoxue zhengli she, ed., *Zhuzi jicheng,* vol. 1 (Beijing: Zhonghua shuju, [1954] 1986), pp. 185–240, at 218.

25. Jameson, "Postmodernism and Consumer Society," p. 188.
26. I use the term "homoerotic" since these relationships are not explicitly sexual in nature.
27. Kaja Silverman, *The Threshold of the Visible World* (New York: Routledge, 1996), p. 64.
28. Mary Ann Doane, "Film and Masquerade: Theorizing the Female Spectator," in *Femme Fatale: Feminism, Film Theory, Psychology* (London: Routlege, 1991), pp. 17–32.
29. Peter Brooks, "Melodrama, Body, Revolution," in Jacky S. Bratton, Jim Cook, and Christine Gledhill, eds., *Melodrama: Stage Picture Screen* (London: BFI, 1994), pp. 11–24, at 19.
30. Arif Dirlik, *The Postcolonial Aura: Third World Criticism in the Age of Global Capitalism* (Boulder, Colo.: Westview, 1997), pp.113-14.

PART III. THE THIRD-WORLD INTELLECTUAL IN THE ERA OF GLOBALIZATION

5. THE ZHANG YIMOU MODEL

1. Laura Mulvey, "Visual Pleasure and Narrative Cinema," *Screen* 16(3) (1975): 8–18; reprinted in *Visual and Other Pleasures* (Bloomington: Indiana University Press, 1989), pp. 14–26, at 14.
2. For a discussion of the latter film, see Chapter 1 in this book.
3. See a comprehensive description of this term by Zhang Xudong, "Generational Politics: What Is the Fifth Generation?" *Chinese Modernism in the Era of Reform* (Durham, N.C.: Duke University Press, 1997), pp. 215–31.
4. See Chapters 2 and 1 in this book, respectively.
5. I would like to thank Zhang Yiwu for his insights on this subject.
6. Mulvey, "Visual Pleasure," p. 14.
7. Ibid., p. 19.
8. Ibid.
9. Ibid.
10. Su Tong, "A Man and His Wives" ("Qiqie chengqun"), in *Qiqie chengqun* (Taipei: Yuanliu, 1990), pp. 161–230, at 197.
11. Rey Chow, "Against the Lures of Diaspora: Minority Discourse, Chinese Women, and Intellectual Hegemony," in *Writing Diaspora: Tactics of Intervention in Contemporary Cultural Studies* (Bloomington: Indiana University Press, 1993), pp. 99–119, at 110–11.
12. See, for example, Kang-I Sun Chang, *The Evolution of Chinese Tz'u Poetry: From Late T'ang to Northern Sung* (Princeton: Princeton University Press, 1980).
13. On this subject, see Meng Yue and Dai Jinhua, *Emerging on the Surface of History (Fuchu lishi biaomian)* (Zhengzhou: Henan renmin chubanshe, 1989); Rey Chow, *Chinese Woman and Modernity* (Minneapolis: University of Minnesota Press, 1991); and Lu Tonglin [as Tonglin Lu], ed., *Gender and Sexuality in Twentieth-Century Chinese Literature and Society* (Albany: SUNY Press, 1993).
14. Slavoj Žižek, *The Sublime Object of Ideology* (London: Verso, 1989), pp. 186-7.
15. Mulvey, "Visual Pleasure," p. 17.
16. See Rey Chow, "The Unclassified Seduction: Discussion on Ambiguity in *Temptress Moon*" ("Bulun bulei de youhuo: mentan Chen Kaige dianying *Fengyue* de aimei xing"), in Jian Yingying, ed., *Identity, Difference, and Subjectivity: From Feminism to*

Post-colonial Cultural Imagination (Rentong, chayi, zhuti xing: cong nüxing zhuyi dao hou zhimin wenhua de xianxiang) (Taipei: Furen [Fu-jen] University, 1997), pp. 217–36.

17. Slavoj Žižek, *The Metastases of Enjoyment: Six Essays on Woman and Causality* (London: Verso, 1994), p. 2.

18. Ibid.

19. See *Encyclopedia of Chinese Cinema: Feature and Stage Films from 1977–1994 (Zhongguo yingpian dadian: gushi pian xiju pian 1977–1994)* (Beijing: Zhongguo dianying chubanshe, 1995).

20. See Zhang Yiwu, "The Anxiety of the Gaze" ("Ningshi de jiaolü"), in *From Modernity to Postmodernity (Cong xiandaixing dao hou xiandaixing)* (Nanning: Guangxi jiaoyu chubanshe, 1997), pp. 167–76.

21. Immanuel Wallerstein, "The Ideological Tensions of Capitalism: Universalism versus Racism and Sexism," in Étienne Balibar & Immanuel Wallerstein, *Race, Nation, Class: Ambiguous Identities*, trans. Chris Turner (London: Verso, 1991), pp. 29–36, at 31.

22. Frederick Buell, *National Culture and the New Global System* (Baltimore: Johns Hopkins University Press, 1994), p. 52. Junichiro Tanizaki, *Some Prefer Nettles (Tade kuu mushi*, 1928/9), trans. Edward G. Seidensticker (New York: Alfred A. Knopf, 1955; reprints New York: Perigee, 1981; New York: Vintage Books, 1995); idem, *Naomi (Chijin No Ai*, 1924), trans. Anthony H. Chambers (New York: Alfred A. Knopf, 1985; paperback, New York: Perigee/Putnam, 1986).

6. CULTURE AND VIOLENCE

1. An unwritten law that binds members of a community together and implicitly encourages them to transgress the written law as a mark of their common bond. Slavoj Žižek, *The Metastases of Enjoyment: Six Essays on Woman and Causality* (London: Verso, 1994), p. 37.

2. Gabriel García Márquez, *Chronicle of a Death Foretold (Cronica de una muerte anunciada)*, trans. Gregory Rabassa (New York: Alfred Knopf, 1983).

3. Ibid., pp. 12–13.

4. Rey Chow, "'Returning to Nature': Visuality in Films of the 1980s and Early 1990s," in *Primitive Passions: Visuality, Sexuality, Ethnography, and Contemporary Chinese Cinema* (New York: Columbia University Press, 1995), pp. 35–43.

5. Žižek, *Metastases of Enjoyment*, p. 54.

6. Ibid., p. 38.

7. Ibid., p. 55.

8. Ibid., p. 55.

9. Ibid., p. 38.

10. Ibid., p. 57.

11. Niu Haiyan, "It Is Difficult for Women to Make Films: Interview with Li Shaohong" ("Nüren pai dianying nan: Li Shaohong fangwen ji"), in Wang Lan, ed., *Interviews with VIPs (Fengyun renwu fangwen ji)* (Nanjing: Jiangsu wenyi chubanshe, 1993), pp. 306–17, at p. 308.

12. Ibid., 309–10.

13. Zhang Wei and Ying Xiong, "Getting Out from the Fixed Model: Talking with Li Shaohong about Her Filmmaking" ("Zouchu dingshi, yu Li Shaohong tan Li Shaohong de dianying chuangzao"), *Dangdai dianying* 35 (May 1995): 46–52.

14. This section was delivered as a talk at the Conference of the Studies of Cinema Societies in Florida in 1999. I would like to thank Patricia Erens for her helpful comments.

15. Niu Haiyan, "It Is Difficult for Women," pp. 316–17.
16. The interview took place in her home in Beijing on June 25, 1995.
17. See Rey Chow, "Against the Lures of Diaspora: Minority Discourse, Chinese Women, and Intellectual Hegemony," in *Writing Diaspora: Tactics of Intervention in Contemporary Cultural Studies* (Bloomington: Indiana University Press, 1993), pp. 99–119.
18. Luce Irigaray, *This Sex Which Is Not One*, trans. Catherine Porter (Ithaca: Cornell University Press, 1985); idem, *Speculum of the Other Women*, trans. Gillian Gill (Ithaca: Cornell University Press, 1985); and idem, *An Ethics of Sexual Difference*, trans. Carolyn Burke and Gillian Gill (Ithaca: Cornell University Press, 1993).
19. See my introduction to *Gender and Sexuality in Twentieth-Century Chinese Literature and Society* (Albany: SUNY, 1993).
20. See Lu Tonglin, *Misogyny, Cultural Nihilism, and Oppositional Politics: Contemporary Chinese Experimental Fiction* (Stanford: Stanford University Press, 1995).
21. Ibid., pp. 129–54.
22. Actually, this problem has its currency in contemporary China. An article published in the April 1996 issue of a popular journal, *Jiating* (*Family*), discusses whether girls who lost their virginity prior to their marriages need to repair their hymen through operations.
23. Jia Leilei, "The Language Strategy and Ritual Pattern in Narrative Form: Interpretation of the Film *Bloody Dawn*" ("Xushi zhong de yuyan celüe yu yishi yuanxing: yingpian *Xuese qingchen* chanshu lun"), *Yingshi wenhua* 5 (September 1992), at p. 249.

7. A POSTCOLONIAL REFLECTION

1. Gayatri Chakravorty Spivak, *A Critique of Postcolonial Reason: Toward a History of the Vanishing Present* (Cambridge, Mass.: Harvard University Press, 1999), p. 37.
2. Gregory Jusdanis, in his *Belated Modernity and Aesthetic Culture: Inventing National Literature* (Minneapolis: University of Minnesota Press, 1991), explores the "key role played by literature in the construction of national identities" in a peripheral culture such as that of Greece, whose traditional local culture is perceived as at odds, if not in conflict, with western European norms of modernity. As a result, literature functions almost as a glue that holds the "imaginary community" together as a nation, despite a certain inferiority complex that the local intelligentsia feels in regard to modernity based on Eurocentric norms.
3. See Edward Said, *Orientalism* (New York: Columbia University, 1979), p. 3.
4. See Spivak, *Critique of Postcolonial Reason*, p. 364.
5. Benedict Anderson, *Imagined Communities* (London: Verso, 1983), p. 36.
6. See Chapter 5 of the present volume.
7. Anderson, "Cultural Roots," in *Imagined Communities*, pp. 9–36.
8. Hu Zhiqian, ed., *Republic of China Toward the Twenty-First Century* (*Zhonghua minguo maixiang ershiyi shiji*) (Taipei: Xingzheng yuan xinwen ju, 1992), p. 84.
9. Leonard Blussé, "Retribution and Remorse: The Interaction between the Administration and the Protestant Mission in Early Colonial Formosa," in Gyan Prakash, ed., *After Colonialism: Imperial Histories and Postcolonial Displacement* (Princeton: Princeton University Press, 1995), pp. 153–82.
10. Tianxian bianji (Editorial Board under Heaven [Yin Yunfan et al.]), *Discovering Taiwan* (*Faxian Taiwan*), vol. 1 (Taipei: Tianxia zazhi, 1992), p. 68.
11. See Immanuel Wallerstein, "The Construction of Peoplehood: Racism, Nationalism,

Ethnicity," in Étienne Balibar & Immanuel Wallerstein, *Race, Nation, Class: Ambiguous Identities,* trans. Chris Turner (London: Verso, 1991), pp. 71–85, at 83.

12. See, for example, Bai Chongxi's statement after the February 28 Incident of 1947, in Lin Qixu, *A Synthetic Study of the February 28 Incident in Taiwan* (*Taiwan ererba shijian zonghe yanjiu*) (Long Island, N.Y.: Taiwan Tribune, 1984), p. 180.

13. Ibid., p. 83.

14. Wu Nianzhen had this conversation with me in April 1996.

15. Frantz Fanon, *Black Skin, White Masks,* trans. Charles Lam Markman (New York: Grove, 1967), p. 18.

16. Slavoj Žižek, *The Sublime Object of Ideology* (London: Verso, 1989).

17. See, for example, the director's own comment on this subject. Wu Nianzhen, *In Search of "Buddha Bless America"* (*Xunzhao "Taiping tianguo"*) (Taipei: Maitian, 1996).

18. See Gayatri [Chakravorty] Spivak, "Can the Subaltern Speak?" in Cary Nelson and Lawrence Grossberg, eds., *Marxism and the Interpretation of Culture* (Urbana and Chicago: University of Illinois Press, 1988), pp. 271–313.

19. Stuart Hall, "The Problem of Ideology: Marxism without Guarantees," in David Morley and Kuan-hsing Chen, eds., *Stuart Hall: Critical Dialogues in Cultural Studies* (London: Routledge, 1996), pp. 25–46, at 37.

20. Lu Xun, "List of Books the Youth Must Read" ("Qingnian bidu shu"), *Lu Xun quanji,* vol. 3 (Beijing: Renmin wenxue chubanshe), pp. 12–13, at 13.

21. Hu Shi, "Introducing My Own Thinking" ("Jieshao wo ziji de sixiang"), *Hu Shi wencun,* vol. 4 (Taipei: Yuandong chubanshe, 1953), pp. 616–21, at 618.

EPILOGUE

1. See, for example, Lu Xun's *Wild Grass* (*Ye cao*), trans. Yang Xianyi (Beijing: Foreign Language Press, 1974).

2. Cai Mingliang, "Cai Mingliang on *The Hole*" ("Cai Mingliang tan *Dong*"), in Jiao Xiongping and Cai Mingliang, eds., *The Hole* (*Dong*) (Taipei: Wanxiang, 1998), pp. 101–27, at 105.

3. Frantz Fanon, *Black Skin, White Masks,* trans. Charles Lam Markman (New York: Grove, 1967).

GLOSSARY

ai	爱
Aiqing wansui	爱情万岁
Baimao nü	白毛女
bali	芭梨
Bawang bieji	霸王别姬
Beigao Shangang ye	被告山杠爷
Beiqing chengshi	悲情城市
bensheng ren	本省人
bie xiajiao	别瞎叫
buduan geming	不断革命
Cai Mingliang	蔡明亮
canlan	灿烂
chaqu	插曲
Chen Kaige	陈凯歌
Da hong denglong gaogao gua	大红灯笼高高挂
da shuikeng	大水坑
da Taibei	大台北
Da taijian Li Lianying	大太监 李莲英
Da yuebing	大阅兵
danwei	单位
Daoma zei	盗马贼
Dazhong dianying	大众电影
dianxian gan	电线杆
dianying	电影
Dongdong de jiaqi	冬冬的假期
doushi haizi	都是孩子
Duli shidai	独立时代
Duosang	多桑
Dushen nüren	独身女人
facai zhuyi	发财主义
fan	蕃
fan Qing fu Ming	反清复明
Fan Yuan	范元
Fenggui laide ren	风櫃来的人
Fengyue	风月

gaoshan zu	高山族
gaoxiong xianzhengfu sushe	高雄县政府宿舍
gele yibeizi ming, hai ge?	革了一辈子命，还革？
genju di	根据地
gongchan dang	共产党
Gu Rong	古榕
guiju	规矩
Gulingjie shaonian sharen shijian	古岭街少年杀人事件
Gushu yiren	鼓书艺人
Haitan de yitian	海滩的一天
Haizi wang	孩子王
haoren bu dangbing, haotie bu dading	好人不当兵，好铁不打钉
He Ping	何平
heshan	河山
Hong gaoliang	红高粱
Hong xiang	红象
Hongchen	红尘
Hongfen	红粉
Hongse niangzi jun	红色娘子军
Hou Xiaoxian	侯孝贤
hu	胡
Hu Shi	胡适
Huang Jianxin	黄健新
Huang Jianzhong	黄健中
Huang tudi	黄土地
Huguang	弧光
hui dalu zuo shenmo	回大陆做什么
Huozhe	活着
Jia Leilei	贾磊磊
Jiang Jingguo	蒋经国
jianzheng	见证
Jiao Xiongping	焦雄屏
jiaoshu de	教书的
jiedao weiyuanhui	街道委员会
jing jianzheng	敬见证
jintong yunü	金童玉女
jiu sixiang, jiu wenhua, jiu fengsu, jiu xiguan	旧思想，旧文化，旧风俗，旧习惯
jiu wanmin	救万民
Judou	菊豆
Kongbu fenzi	恐怖份子
Lan fengzheng	蓝风筝
Li Jun	李俊
Li Shaohong	李少红
Liangjia funü	良家妇女
Lianlian fengchen	恋恋风尘
Liechang zasa	猎场扎撒
liuxia shan, liuxia shui, liuxia qingchun, liuxia mei	留下山，留下水，留下青春，留下美

Longxue shu	龙血树
Lu Xun	鲁迅
lun	伦
lushui fuqi	露水夫妻
Majiang	麻将
Mao Zedong	毛泽东
mianzi	面子
minquan zhuyi	民权主义
minsheng zhuyi	民生主义
minzhu renshi	民主人士
minzu zhuyi	民族主义
naer chuande chuqu ne	哪儿穿得出去呢
nan zhuwai, nü zhunei	男主外，女主内
nanzi han	男子汉
Nongnu	农奴
nuhua	奴化
nüren	女人
nüxing dianying	女性电影
Paoda shuangdeng	炮打双灯
piao	票
piaofang	票房
po sijiu	破四旧
Qin Zhiyu	秦志钰
qing	情
Qingchun ji	青春祭
Qingmei zhuma	青梅竹马
Qiqie chengqun	妻妾成群
quanmian xihua	全面西化
ren	人
rizi jiannan le jiu jixia le	日子艰难了，就记下了
sancong side	三从四德
sanmin zhuyi	三民主义
shandi zu	山地族
shange ye jiubuliao Cuiqiao wo	山歌也救不了翠巧我
sharen chengyin bei tuifan le	杀人成因被推翻了
Shennü	神女
shuangshu hao, jili	双数好，吉利
Shui Hua	水华
shuijia de nüzi buzou zhege lu	谁家的女子不走这个路
sihai	四害
sihe yuan	四合院
Su Tong	苏童
suanqu	酸曲
Sun Zhongshan	孙中山
Taiping tianguo	太平天国
teng'ai	疼爱
Teshu shoushushi	特殊手术室
Tian Zhuangzhuang	田壮壮

Tongnian wangshi	童年往事
waisheng ren	外省人
Wang Bin	王滨
wanling dan	万灵丹
wei yishu de yishu	为艺术的艺术
wen yi zaidao	文以载道
Wu Nianzhen	吴念真
Wu Yonggang	吴永刚
Wukui	五魁
wulun	五伦
xi	戏
Xiangnü Xiaoxiao	湘女萧萧
xiangtu wenxue	乡土文学
Xiao Mao	肖矛
xiao zichanjieji qingdiao	小资产阶级情调
xibu dianying	西部电影
Xie Fei	谢飞
Xie Jin	谢晋
Ximeng rensheng	戏梦人生
xin wenhua yundong	新文化运动
xing (family name)	姓
xing (sex)	性
xizi	戏子
xuanpiao	选票
Xuese qingchen	血色清晨
xuesheng bing	学生兵
Yan Fu	严复
Yang Dechang	杨德昌
Yaogun qingnian	摇滚青年
Yi wanran	艺宛然
Yige he bage	一个和八个
yiko qi	一口气
yizhi youxi	益智游戏
Youhua haohao shuo	有话好好说
zai jiaoyu	再教育
zalan kongjiadian	砸烂孔家店
zan gongjiaren jiukao zhe guiju da tianxia de	咱公家人就靠这规距打天下的
Zhang Junzhao	张军钊
Zhang Nuanxin	张暖忻
Zhang Yimou	张艺谋
zhengyi gan	正义感
zhishi qingnian	知识青年
Zhongguo	中国
zhugan mian	猪肝面
zigu hunjia you tianding, erjin fugui zai mingzhong	自古婚嫁由天定，而今富贵在命中

BIBLIOGRAPHY

Anderson, Benedict. *Imagined Communities*. London: Verso, 1983.

Appadurai, Arjun. *Modernity at Large: Cultural Dimensions of Globalization*. Minneapolis: University of Minnesota Press, 1996.

Arendt, Hannah. *On Violence*. San Diego: Harvest, 1970.

Baecque, Antoine de. "Le Temps suspendu." *Cahiers du cinéma* no. 438 (December 1990): 24–8.

Balibar, Étienne, and Immanuel Wallerstein. *Race, Nation, Class: Ambiguous Identities*. Trans. Chris Turner. London: Verso, 1991.

Berry, Chris, ed. *Perspectives on Chinese Cinema*. Worcester: Trinity Press/London: BFI, 1991.

Blussé, Leonard. "Retribution and Remorse: The Interaction between the Administration and the Protestant Mission in Early Colonial Formosa." In Gyan Prakash, ed., *After Colonialism: Imperial Histories and Postcolonial Displacement*. Princeton: Princeton University Press, 1995, pp. 153–82.

Bratton, Jacky S., Jim Cook, and Christine Gledhill, eds. *Melodrama: Stage Picture Screen*. London: BFI, 1994.

Browne, Nick, Paul G. Pickowicz, Vivian Sobchack, and Esther Yau, eds. *New Chinese Cinemas: Forms, Identities, Politics*. Cambridge: Cambridge University Press, 1994.

Buell, Frederick. *National Culture and the New Global System*. Baltimore: Johns Hopkins University Press, 1994.

Chang, Kang-I Sun. *The Evolution of Chinese Tz'u Poetry: From Late T'ang to Northern Sung*. Princeton: Princeton University Press, 1980.

Chen Kaige. "Life Reflection: Self-Examination" ("Sikao rensheng: shenshi ziwo"). *Dianying yishu cankao ziliao* [*Film Art Reference Materials*] 183 (1987): 10–30.

Tree of Dragon Blood (*Longxue shu*). Hong Kong: Tiandi, 1992.

Chen Wanying. "Interview with Chen Kaige, Director of *King of the Children, Yellow Earth*" ("Fangwen Chen Kaige, *Haizi wang, Huang tudi* daoyan"). *Playboy* (Chinese ed.) 22 (May 1988): 41–5.

Chow, Rey. *Chinese Woman and Modernity*. Minneapolis: University of Minnesota Press, 1991.

Primitive Passions: Visuality, Sexuality, Ethnography, and Contemporary Chinese Cinema. New York: Columbia University Press, 1995.

Writing Diaspora: Tactics of Intervention in Contemporary Cultural Studies. Bloomington: Indiana University, 1993.

Chion, Michel. *Audio-vision: Sound on Screen.* Trans. Claudia Gorbman. New York: Columbia University Press, 1994.

Cohen, Paul. *Discovering History in China: American Historical Writing on the Recent Chinese Past.* New York: Columbia University Press, 1984.

Deleuze, Gilles. *Critique et clinique.* Paris: Minuit, 1993.

Derrida, Jacques. *Dissemination.* Trans. Barbara Johnson. Chicago: University of Chicago Press, 1983.

   Of Grammatology. Trans. Gayatri Chakravorty Spivak. Baltimore: Johns Hopkins University Press, 1976.

Dirlik, Arif. *Origins of Chinese Communism.* Oxford: Oxford University Press, 1989.

   The Postcolonial Aura: Third World Criticism in the Age of Global Capitalism. Boulder, Colo.: Westview, 1997.

Doane, Mary Ann. *Femme Fatale: Feminism, Film Theory, Psychology.* London: Routlege, 1991.

Dooling, Amy, and Kristina Torgeson, eds. *Writing Women in Modern China: An Anthology of Women's Literature from the Early Twentieth Century.* New York: Columbia University Press, 1998.

Duara, Prasenjit. *Rescuing History from the Nation: Questioning the Narratives of Modern China.* Chicago: University of Chicago Press, 1995.

Eagleton, Terry, Fredric Jameson, and Edward W. Said. *Nationalism, Colonialism, and Literature.* Introduction by Seamus Deane. Minneapolis: University of Minnesota Press, 1990.

Elsaesser, Thomas. "Tales of Sound and Fury: Observations on the Family Melodrama." *Monogram* 4 (1972): 2–15. Reprinted in Christine Gledhill, ed., *Home Is Where the Heart Is: Studies in Melodrama and the Woman's Film.* London: BFI, 1987, pp. 43–69.

Encyclopedia of Chinese Cinema: Feature and Stage Films from 1977–1994 (Zhongguo yingpian dadian: gushi pian xiju pian 1977–1994). Beijing: Zhongguo dianying chubanshe, 1995.

Fairbank, John K., Edwin O. Reischauer, and Albert M. Craig. *East Asia: Tradition and Transformation.* Boston: Houghton Mifflin, 1973.

Fanon, Frantz. *Black Skin, White Masks.* Trans. Charles Lam Markman. New York: Grove, 1967.

Ferguson, Russell, Martha Gever, Trinh T. Minh-ha, and Cornel West, eds. *Out There: Marginalization and Contemporary Culture.* Documentary Sources in Contemporary Art no. 4. New York: New Museum of Contemporary Art/Cambridge, Mass: MIT Press, 1990.

Feuerwerker, Yi-tsi Mei. *Ding Ling's Fiction: Ideology and Narrative in Modern Chinese Literature.* Cambridge, Mass.: Harvard University Press, 1982.

García Márquez, Gabriel. *Chronicle of a Death Foretold (Cronica de una muerte anunciada).* Trans. Gregory Rabassa. New York: Alfred Knopf, 1983.

Heath, Stephen. "On Suture." In *Questions of Cinema.* Bloomington: Indiana University Press, 1981, pp. 76–112.

Hoffmann, E. T. A. *Eight Tales of Hoffmann.* Trans. J. M. Cohen. London: Pan Books, 1952.

Hu Sheng. *From the Opium War to the May Fourth Movement (Cong yapian zhanzheng dao wusi yundong).* 2 vols. Beijing: Renmin wenxue chubanshe, 1981.

Hu Shi. *Hu Shi wencun.* 4 vols. Taipei: Yuandong chubanshe, 1953.

Hu Zhiqian, ed. *Republic of China toward the Twenty-First Century (Zhonghua minguo maixiang ershiyi shiji).* Taipei: Xingzheng yuan xinwen ju, 1992.

Huang Chunming. *I Love Mary (Wo ai mali).* Taipei: Yuanjing chubanshe, 1975.

Huang Jianye. *Pursuit of Humanistic Films (Renwen dianying de zhuiqiu).* Taipei: Yuanliu, 1990.

Studies of Edward Yang's Films (Yang Dechang dianying yanjiu). Taipei: Yuanliu, 1995.

Huashuo "Huang tudi" [On "Yellow Earth"]. Beijing: Zhongguo dianying chubanshe, 1986.

Huxley, Thomas (Huoxuli). *Evolution and Ethics (Tianyan lun).* Trans. (from English) Yan Fu. Beijing: Shangwu shudian Beijing faxingshe, 1981 (1st ed., 1898).

Irigaray, Luce. *An Ethics of Sexual Difference.* Trans. Carolyn Burke and Gillian Gill. Ithaca: Cornell University Press, 1993.

Speculum of the Other Women. Trans. Gillian Gill. Ithaca: Cornell University Press, 1985.

This Sex Which Is Not One. Trans. Catherine Porter. Ithaca: Cornell University Press, 1985

Jameson, Fredric. *The Geopolitical Aesthetic: Cinema and Space in the World System.* Bloomington: Indiana University Press, 1992.

"Nostalgia for the Present," *South Atlantic Quarterly* 88(2) (1989): 517–37.

"Postmodernism and Consumer Society." *Amerikastudien/American Studies* 29(1) (1984): 55–73. Reprinted in John Belton, ed., *Movies and Mass Culture.* New Brunswick: Rutgers University Press, 1996, pp. 185–202.

The Seeds of Time. New York: Columbia University Press, 1994.

Jameson, Fredric, and Masao Miyoshi, eds. *The Cultures of Globalization.* Durham, N.C.: Duke University Press, 1998.

JanMohamed, Abdul R., and David Lloyd, eds. *The Nature and Context of Minority Discourse.* Oxford: Oxford University Press, 1990.

Jia Leilei. "The Language Strategy and Ritual Pattern in Narrative Form: Interpretation of the Film *Bloody Dawn*" ("Xushi zhong de yuyan celüe yu yishi yuanxing: yingpian *Xuese qingchen* chanshu lun"). *Yingshi wenhua [Film and Television Culture]* 5 (September 1992).

Jian Yingying, ed. *Identity, Difference, and Subjectivity: From Feminism to Post-colonial Cultural Imagination (Rentong, chayi, zhuti xing: cong nüxing zhuyi dao hou zhimin wenhua de xianxiang).* Taipei: Furen [Fu-jen] University, 1997.

Jiao Xiongping. "*City of Sadness:* A Tentative Epic of Taiwan History" ("*Beiqing chengshi:* shifu Taiwan shishi"). In *Authors and Types in Taiwan and Hong Kong Cinemas (Tai gang dianying zhong de zuozhe yu leixing).* Taipei: Yuanliu, 1991, pp. 48–59.

Taiwan New Cinema (Taiwan xin dianying). Taipei: Shibao wenhua chubanshe, 1988.

"The Tie to the Mainland in Taiwanese Cinema" ("Taiwan dianying de dalu qingjie"). *Jintian* 17 (February 1992): 84–93.

ed. *Life on a String (Bianzou bianchang).* Taipei: Wanxiang, 1991.

Jiao Xiongping and Cai Mingliang, eds. *The Hole (Dong).* Taipei: Wanxiang, 1998.

Jousse, Thierry. "Plus de Lumière." *Cahiers du cinéma* no. 454 (April 1992): 25–9.

Jusdanis, Gregory. *Belated Modernity and Aesthetic Culture: Inventing National Literature.* Minneapolis: University of Minnesota Press, 1991.

Lacan, Jacques. *Écrits: A Selection.* Trans. Alan Sheridan. New York: W. W. Norton, 1977.

Lan Bozhou. *Sinking Bodies, Exile, February 28 Incident (Chenshi liuwang, ererba).* Taipei: Shibao wenhua chubanshe, 1992.

Larson, Wendy. *Women and Writing in Modern China.* Stanford: Stanford University Press, 1998.

Li Bo. *Selected Poems of Li Po.* Trans. David Hinton. New York: New Directions, 1996.

Li Suyuan and Hu Jubin. *History of Chinese Silent Films (Zhongguo wusheng dianying shi).* Beijing: Zhongguo dianying chubanshe, 1996.

Li Tianlu. *Life as Performance: Li Tianlu's Memoir* (*Ximeng rensheng: Li Tianlu huyilu*). Ed. Zeng Yuwu. Taipei: Yuanliu, 1991.

Li Tong. "Questions and Answers on *King of the Children* at Canne" ("*Haizi wang* gena dawen"). *Dangdai dianying* [*Contemporary Cinema*] 28 (June 1988): 57–9.

Li Zehou. *On Modern Chinese History of Thought* (*Zhongguo jindai sixiangshi*). Beijing: Renmin wenxue chubanshe, 1979.

Lin Qixu. *A Synthetic Study of the February 28 Incident in Taiwan* (*Taiwan ererba shijian zonghe yanjiu*). Long Island, N.Y.: Taiwan Tribune, 1984.

Lin Yü-sheng. *The Crisis of Chinese Consciousness: Radical Antitraditionalism in the May Fourth Era*. Madison: University of Wisconsin Press, 1979.

Liu Shusheng. "The Religious Mood in *Horse Thief*" (*Daoma zei* de zongjiao qingxu). *Yingshi wenhua* [*Film and Telvision Culture*] 6 (March 1993): 88–108.

Lu Hsiao-peng, ed. *Transnational Chinese Cinemas: Identity, Nationhood, Gender.* Honolulu: University of Hawaii Press, 1997.

Lu Tonglin. *Misogyny, Cultural Nihilism, and Oppositional Politics: Contemporary Chinese Experimental Fiction*. Stanford: Stanford University Press, 1995.

[as Tonglin Lu] ed. *Gender and Sexuality in Twentieth-Century Chinese Literature and Society*. Albany: SUNY Press, 1993.

Lu Xun. *Diary of a Madman and Other Stories*. Trans. William A. Lyell. Honolulu: University of Hawaii Press, 1990.

Lu Xun quanji. 16 vols. Beijing: Renmin wenxue chubanshe, 1981.

Wild Grass (*Ye cao*). Trans. Yang Xianyi. Beijing: Foreign Language Press, 1974.

Marchetti, Gina. "Two from China's Fifth Generation: Interviews with Chen Kaige and Tian Zhuangzhuang." *Continuum* 2(1) (1988–9): 128–34.

Marcus, Millicent. *Italian Film in the Light of Neorealism*. Princeton: Princeton University Press, 1986.

Marx, Karl. *Marx on China: 1853–1860*. London: Lawrence and Wishart: 1951.

Mengzi. *Mencius (Mengzi)*. In Guoxue zhengli she, ed., *Zhuzi jicheng*, vol. 1. Beijing: Zhonghua shuju, (1954) 1986, pp. 185–240.

Meng Yue and Dai Jinhua. *Emerging on the Surface of History* (*Fuchu lishi biaomian*). Zhengzhou: Henan renmin chubanshe, 1989.

Mi Zou and Liang Xinhua, eds. *The Death of the New Cinema: From "All for Tomorrow" to "City of Sadness"* (*Xin dianying zhi si: cong "Yiqie wei mingtian" dao "Beiqing chengshi"*). Taipei: Tangshan chubanshe, 1991.

Morley, David, and Kuan-hsing Chen, eds. *Stuart Hall: Critical Dialogues in Cultural Studies*. London: Routledge, 1996.

Morrison, Toni. "Introduction." In Toni Morrison, ed., *Race-ing Justice, En-gendering Power: Essays on Anita Hill, Clarence Thomas, and the Construction of Social Reality*. New York: Pantheon Books, 1992, pp. vii–xxx.

Mulvey, Laura. *Visual and Other Pleasures*. Bloomington: Indiana University Press, 1989.

Ni Zhen. *Memoirs from the Beijing Film Academy: The Early Days of China's Fifth Generation*. Trans. Chris Berry. Durham, N.C.: Duke University Press, forthcoming.

Papastergiandis, Nikos. *Dialogues in the Diasporas: Essays and Conversations on Cultural Identity*. London: River Oram Press, 1998.

Peng Ruijin. *Forty Year New Literature Movement in Taiwan* (*Taiwan xin wenxue yundong sishi nian*). Taipei: Zili wanbao, 1991.

Peng Xing'er. "Who Is Able to Observe the World Without Emotion? Using the Ideology of Educated Youth to Explain Chen Kaige's *King of the Children*" ("Shui neng lengyan kan shijie? Yong zhiqing yishi xingtai dujie Chen Kaige de yingpian *Haizi wang*"). *Dangdai dianying* [*Contemporary Cinema*] 29 (February 1989): 105–15.

Peuker, Brigitte. *Incorporating Images: Film and the Rival Arts.* Princeton: Princeton University Press, 1995.

Polachek, James M. *The Inner Opium War.* Cambridge, Mass.: Council on East Asian Studies/Harvard University Press, 1992.

Pusey, James Reeve. *China and Charles Darwin.* Cambridge, Mass.: Harvard East Asian Monographs, 1983.

Rauger, Jean-François. "Naissance d'une nation," *Cahiers du cinéma* no. 469 (July 1994): 18–19.

Rayns, Tony. "Lonesome Tonight." *Sight and Sound* n.s. 3(13) (March 1993):14–17.

Said, Edward. *Orientalism.* New York: Columbia University, 1979.

Schwartz, Benjamin. *In Search of Wealth and Power: Yen Fu and the West.* Cambridge, Mass.: Belknap Press, 1964.

Semsel, George S., ed. *Chinese Film: The State of the Art in the People's Republic.* New York: Praeger, 1987.

Shi Ming. *The Four-Hundred-Year History of the Taiwanese (Taiwan ren sibai nian shi).* San Jose, Calif.: Paradise Culture Associates, 1980 (Japanese edition, 1962).

Silverman, Kaja. *The Acoustic Mirror: The Female Voice in Psychoanalyis and Cinema.* Bloomington: Indiana University Press, 1988.

Male Subjectivity at the Margins. New York: Routledge, 1992.

The Threshold of the Visible World. New York: Routledge, 1996.

Simmel, Georg. *The Philosophy of Money (Philosophie des Geldes).* Trans. Tom Bottomore and David Frisby. London: Routledge, 1991. First German edition, 1900.

Sklar, Robert. "People and Politics, Simple and Direct: An Interview with Tian Zhuang-zhuang." *Cinéaste* 20 (April 1994): 36–8.

Spivak, Gayatri Chakravorty. "Can the Subaltern Speak?" In Cary Nelson and Lawrence Grossberg, eds., *Marxism and the Interpretation of Culture.* Urbana and Chicago: University of Illinois Press, 1988, pp. 271–313.

A Critique of Postcolonial Reason: Toward a History of the Vanishing Present. Cambridge, Mass.: Harvard University Press, 1999.

Stanbrook, Alan. "The Worlds of Hou Hsiao-hsien." *Sight and Sound* 59(2) (Spring 1990): 120–4.

Su Dongpo (Su Shi). *Selected Poems of Su Tung-p'o.* Trans. Burton Watson. Port Townsend, Wash.: Copper Canyon Press, 1994.

Su Tong. "A Man and His Wives" ("Qiqie chengqun"). In *Qiqie chengqun.* Taipei: Yuanliu, 1990, pp. 161–230.

Su Xin. *Angry Taiwan (Fennu de Taiwan).* Taipei: Shibao wenhua chubanshe, 1993.

Sun Zhongshan [Sun Yat-sen]. *Complete Works of the Father of the Nation (Guofu quanshu).* Taipei: Zhongguo xinwen chuban gongsi, 1960.

Tam, Kwok-kan, and Wimal Dissanayake, ed. *New Chinese Cinema: Images of Asia.* Oxford: Oxford University Press, 1998.

Tianxian bianji (Editorial Board under Heaven [Yin Yunfan et al.]). *Discovering Taiwan (Faxian Taiwan).* 2 vols. Taipei: Tianxia zazhi, 1992.

Wakeman, Frederic, Jr. *Strangers at the Gate: Social Disorder in South China, 1839–1861.* Berkeley: University of California Press, 1966.

Wang Lan, ed. *Interviews with VIPs (Fengyun renwu fangwen ji).* Nanjing: Jiangsu wenyi chubanshe, 1993.

Wang Zhenho. *Rose, Rose I Love You (Meigui meigui wo ai ni).* Taipei: Yuanjing chubanshe, 1984.

Wei Qing. "*Taipei Story:* Edward Yang's Cultural Reflection" ("*Qingmei zhuma:* Yang Dechang de wenhua fanxing"). *Dianying yishu* [Film Art] 2 (1992): 79–85.

Wu Nianzhen. *In Search of "Buddha Bless America"* (*Xunzhao "Taiping tianguo"*). Taipei: Maitian, 1996.

Xiao Ye. "Debate on *Horse Thief*"("*Daoma zei* bianlun"), *Dianying yishu* [*Film Art*] 186 (July 1986): 3–24.

Xiao Ye (Hsiao Yeh). *The Beginning of a Movement* (*Yige yundong de kaishi*). Taipei: Shibao wenhua chubanshe, 1986.

Xie Renchang. "Hou Xiaoxian on *Puppetmaster:* A Report in the Process of My Life" ("Hou Xiaoxian tan *Ximeng rensheng:* wo shengming guocheng de yige baogao"), *Dianying xinshang* 64 (July–August 1993): 46–62.

Yan Zhongping, ed. *History of Modern Chinese Economy: 1840–1894* (*Zhongguo jindai jingjishi: 1840–1894*). 2 vols. Beijing: Renmin wenxue chubanshe, 1989.

Yau, Esther. "Is China the End of Hermeneutics? Or, Political and Cultural Usage of Non-Han Women in Mainland Chinese Films." *Discourse* 11(2) (1989): 115–36. Reprinted in Diane Carson, Linda Dittmar, and Janice R. Welsch, eds., *Multiple Voices in Feminist Film Criticism.* Minneapolis: University of Minnesota Press, 1994, pp. 280–92.

"*Yellow Earth:* Western Analysis and a Non-Western Text," *Film Quarterly* 41(2) (1987–8): 22–33.

Zhang Chengzhi. *History of the Soul* (*Xinling shi*). Guangzhou: Huacheng chubanshe, 1991.

Zhang Wei. "Talking about Zhuangzhuang with Zhuangzhuang" ("Yu Zhuangzhuang tan Zhuangzhuang"). *Dangdai dianying* [*Contemporary Cinema*] 29 (January 1989): 37–44.

Zhang Wei and Ying Xiong. "Getting Out from the Fixed Model: Talking with Li Shaohong about Her Filmmaking" ("Zouchu dingshi, yu Li Shaohong tan Li Shaohong de dianying chuangzao"). *Dangdai dianying* [*Contemporary Cinema*] 35 (May 1995): 46–52.

Zhang Xudong. *Chinese Modernism in the Era of Reform.* Durham, N.C.: Duke University Press, 1997.

Zhang Yanxian. "New Spirit in the Research on Taiwan History" ("Taiwan shi yanjiu de xin jingshen"). *Taiwan shiliao yanjiu* 1 (February 1993): 76–86.

Zhang Yinjun, "From 'Minority Film' to 'Minority Discourse': Questions of Nationhood and Ethnicity in Chinese Film Studies," *Cinema Journal* 36(3) (Spring 1997): 73–90.

Zhang Yiwu. *From Modernity to Postmodernity* (*Cong xiandaixing dao hou xiandaixing*). Nanning: Guangxi jiaoyu chubanshe, 1997.

Zhongguo jindaishi bianxie zu (Editorial Board of Modern Chinese History). *Modern Chinese History* (*Zhongguo jindaishi*). Beijing: Zhonghua shuju, 1979.

Zhu Tianwen. "Thirteen Questions on *City of Sadness*" ("*Beiqing chengshi* shisan wen"). *Jintian* 17 (February 1992): 94–110.

Zito, Angela, and Tani E. Barlow, eds. *Body, Subject and Power in China.* Chicago: University of Chicago Press, 1994.

Žižek, Slavoj. *The Indivisible Remainder: An Essay on Schelling and Related Matters.* London: Verso, 1996.

The Metastases of Enjoyment: Six Essays on Woman and Causality. London: Verso, 1994.

The Sublime Object of Ideology. London: Verso, 1989.

FILMOGRAPHY

Cai Mingliang (Ts'ai Ming-liang)
Vive l'amour (Aiqing wansui, 1994), Central Motion Pictures Corp.

Chen Kaige
Yellow Earth (Huang tudi, 1984), Guangxi Film Studios
Big Parade (Da yuebing, 1986), Guangxi Film Studios
King of the Children (Haizi wang, 1987), Xi'an Film Studio
Farewell My Concubine (Bawang bieji, 1993), Beijing Film Studio/China Film Co-
    Production Corp.
Temptress Moon (Fengyue, 1996), Shanghai Film Studios/Tomson Films

Fan Yuan
Master Shangang, the Defendant (Beigao Shangang ye, 1994), Emei Film Studio

Gu Rong
Red Dust (Hongchen, 1994), Beijing Film Studio

He Ping
Red Firecracker, Green Firecracker (Paoda shuangdeng [lit. "Shooting Double
    Lantern"], 1993), Beijing Salon Films/Xi'an Film Studio/Yung & Assoc.

Hou Xiaoxian (Hou Hsiao-hsien)
All the Youthful Days (Fenggui laide ren [lit. "Boys from Fengkui"], 1983), Youth Film
    Production Ltd./Yi Shi Ye Ltd. Corp.
A Summer at Grandpa's (Dongdong de jiaqi [lit. "Dongdong's Vacations"], 1984),
    Central Motion Pictures Corp.
A Time to Live and a Time to Die (aka *The Time to Live and the Time to Die*) *(Tongnian
    wangshi* [lit. "Reminiscence of My Childhood"], 1985), Central Motion Pictures
    Corp.
Dust in the Wind (Lianlian fengchen, 1987), Central Motion Pictures Corp.
City of Sadness (Beiqing chengshi, 1989), Era [Niandai] International
The Puppetmaster (Ximeng rensheng [lit. "Life as Performance and Dream"], 1993), Era
    [Niandai] International

Huang Jianxin
Wukui (aka *The Wooden Man's Bride*) (1993), Long Shong [Longxiang] Pictures/Xi'an
    Film Studio

Huang Jianzhong
Woman from a Good Family (*Liangjia funü,* 1985), Beijing Film Studio

Li Jun
Serfs (*Nongnu,* 1963), August First Film Studio

Li Shaohong
Bloody Dawn (aka *Bloody Morning*) (*Xuese qingchen,* 1990), Beijing Film Studio
Blush (*Hongfen* [lit. "Red Powder"], 1994), Beijing Film Studio/Ocean Film Corp.

Qin Zhiyu
The Single Woman (*Dushen nüren,* 1991), Beijing Film Studio

Tian Zhuangzhuang
Red Elephant (*Hong xiang,* 1982), Children's Film Studio
On the Hunting Ground (*Liechang zasa,* 1985), Inner Mongolia Film Studio
Horse Thief (*Daoma zei,* 1986), Xi'an Film Studio
The Street Players (*Gushu yiren* [lit. "Storytellers with Drum"] 1987), Beijing Film Studio
Rock Kids (*Yaogun qingnian,* 1988), Beijing Film College Youth Film Studio
The Imperial Eunuch (*Da taijian Li Lianying,* 1990), Beijing Film Studio
Unforgettable Life (*Teshu shoushushi* [lit. "Special Operation Room"], 1992), Xiaoxiang
    Film Studio
Blue Kite (*Lan fengzheng,* 1993), Beijing Film Studio/Longwick Film

Wang Bin and Shui Hua
The White-Haired Girl (*Baimao nü,* 1950), Northeast Studio

Wu Nianzhen (Wu Nien-chen)
A Borrowed Life (*Duosang,* 1994), Chang Shu A & V Production/Long Shong
    [Longxiang] Pictures
Buddha Bless America (*Taiping tianguo* [lit. "Peaceful Heavenly Kingdom"], 1996),
    Taiwan Film Center

Wu Yonggang
The Goddess (*Shennü,* silent, 1935), Lianhua Studio

Xie Fei
A Girl from Hunan (aka *Married to a Child*) (*Xiangnü Xiaoxiao,* 1986), Beijing Film
    College Youth Film Studio

Xie Jin
Red Detachment of Women (*Hongse niangzi jun,* 1961), Tianma Studio

Edward Yang (Yang Dechang)
That Day, on the Beach (*Haitan de yitian,* 1983), Central Motion Pictures Corp./Shaw
    Brothers
Taipei Story (*Qingmei zhuma* [lit. "Green Plum and Bamboo Horse"], 1985),
    Wannianqing Film Corp.
The Terrorizers (aka *The Terrorist*) (*Kongbu fenzi,* 1986), Central Motion Pictures Corp.
A Brighter Summer Day (*Gulingjie shaonian sharen shijian* [lit. "Murder Case by a
    Youngster on Guling Street"], 1990), Central Motion Pictures Corp./AtomFilms
Confucius's Confusion (*Duli shidai* [lit. "Independence Era"], 1994), AtomFilms
Mahjong (*Majiang,* 1995), AtomFilms

Zhang Junzhao
One and Eight (Yige he bage, 1984), Guangxi Film Studio
Arc Light (Huguang, 1988), Guangxi Film Studio

Zhang Nuanxin
Sacrificed Youth (aka *Sacrifice of Youth*) *(Qingchun ji,* 1985), Beijing Film College
   Youth Film Studio

Zhang Yimou
Red Sorghum (Hong gaoliang, 1987), Xi'an Film Studio
Judou (1990), China Film Co-production Corp./China Film Importation
Raise the Red Lantern (Da hong denglong gaogao gua, 1991), Century
   Communications/Era [Niandai] International
To Live (aka *Living; Lifetimes*) *(Huozhe,* 1994), Era [Niandai] International/Shanghai
   Film Studio
Keep Cool (Youhua haohao shuo, 1997), Guangxi Film Studio

NON-CHINESE FILMS CITED

The Bicycle Thief (aka *Bicycle Thieves*) *(Ladri di biciclette),* dir. Vittorio De Sica
   (PDS–ENIC, Italy, 1948)
Bullets over Broadway (Miramax/Magnolia/Sweetland, USA, 1994), dir. Woody Allen
The Godfather, dir. Francis Ford Coppola (Paramount, USA, 1972)
The Last Emperor, dir. Bernardo Bertolucci (AAA/Hemdale/Recorded Pictures/
   Screenframe/Soprofilms/TAO/Yanco, Italy–Great Britain–China, 1987)
Metropolis, dir. Fritz Lang (UFA, Germany, 1926)
Modern Times, dir. Charles Chaplin (Chaplin / United Artists, 1936)
Open City (Roma, città aperta, aka *Rome, Open City),* dir. Roberto Rossellini (Minerva/
   Excelsa, Italy, 1945)
Ticket of No Return (aka *Portrait of a Female Drunkard*) *(Bildnis einer Trinkerin),* dir.
   Ulrike Ottinger (InterNations, West Germany, 1979)
Tokyo Story (Tokyo monogatari), dir. Yasujiro Ozu (Shochiku, Japan, 1953)

INDEX

DH

791.
430
951
LUT

500103235X

Printed in the United Kingdom
by Lightning Source UK Ltd.
120742UK00002BA/184-186